# RUSSIAN LITERATURE
# AND THOUGHT

Gary Saul Morson,
Series Editor

# RELATED TITLES

*1920 Diary*
Isaac Babel

*The Lower Depths and Other Plays*
Maxim Gorky

*Stalin's Letters to Molotov*
Josef Stalin

*A History of Russian Literature*
Victor Terras

*A Voice from the Chorus*
Abram Tertz (Andrei Sinyavsky)

*Strolls with Pushkin*
Abram Tertz (Andrei Sinyavsky)

# MAXIM GORKY

# UNTIMELY THOUGHTS

ESSAYS ON REVOLUTION,
CULTURE AND THE BOLSHEVIKS
1917–1918

*With a new introduction and chronology
by Mark D. Steinberg*

*Translated from the Russian and
with notes by Herman Ermolaev*

*Yale University Press
New Haven & London*

Originally published 1968 in the United States by Paul S. Eriksson, Inc.

Paperbound edition published 1995 by Yale University Press

Printed in the United States of America by BookCrafters, Inc.,
Chelsea, Michigan.

Library of Congress Card Catalogue Number: 94-61488

International standard book number: 0-300-06069-6 (pbk.)

A catalogue record for this book is available from the British Library.

The paper in this book meets the guidelines for permanence and durability of
the Committee on Production Guidelines for Book Longevity
of the Council on Library Resources.

10    9    8    7    6    5    4    3    2    1

# CONTENTS

# INTRODUCTION

*Mark D. Steinberg*

Socialism is possible only when there is a fundamental change
in people's psychology.
—Nadezhda Krupskaia, *Pravda,* March 23, 1918

A revolution is fruitful and able to renew life only when it
happens first spiritually, in the minds of people, and only then
physically on the streets and barricades. . . . [Otherwise,] it
cannot change our life but will only increase brutality and evil.
—Maxim Gorky, April 7, 1918

Among the many texts by Russian writers and intellectuals that were suppressed in the Soviet Union, Maxim
Gorky's essays of 1917–1918 stand out as exceptional historical and personal documents. Appearing during a time
of deep crisis and radical transformation in Russian life,
these essays on politics, culture, and morality offer among
the most searching reflections on the meaning of Russia's
revolution. This was a sharply critical view, but it was the
dissenting view of an insider. "Gorky is one us," Lenin
observed in 1918, as he gave the approval to shut down
the independent socialist newspaper *Novaia zhizn'* (New
Life), which Gorky edited and in which these essays originally appeared. "He is linked with the working class and
the workers' movement, and himself came from the 'lower
classes.'"[1] That Gorky should chastise both the common
people and the Bolsheviks was, therefore, especially painful. But he felt that this was his special right and respon-

sibility—as a socialist and as a "writer from the people."
More than any other contemporary voice, Gorky's was self-
consciously a voice of conscience—of sympathy, knowledge,
and principle—from *within* the socialist and even the Bolshevik camp. At the same time, Gorky's thoughts were also
self-consciously "untimely" (the heading he gave to many
of his columns)—addressing issues whose importance lay
beyond the momentary concerns of the revolution: the individual and society, national identity, cultural values, socialism, free will, and morality.

When these essays appeared, Gorky was one of the most
respected and influential public figures in Russia. His stories,
novels, plays, journalistic sketches and essays, and autobiography were widely read in Russia (and were translated
and read in many other countries as well). His esteem on
the political left was strengthened by his involvement in
the socialist underground since the 1890s, including a brief
spell in jail as a political prisoner. Gorky was stubbornly
independent in politics—he did not formally join any political parties and generally liked to see himself as "a heretic
everywhere" (April 25, 1917).[2] Nonetheless, he was most
often associated with the Bolsheviks, and he aided the party
financially.[3] In 1917, although most of his collaborators on
the newspaper *Novaia zhizn'* were Mensheviks (a rival fac-
tion within Russian social-democracy), they were "socialist-
internationalists," a group that stood closest to Bolshevism.
Generally, the newspaper uniquely and effectively occupied
the steadily shrinking terrain of independent, non-party
socialism.[4]

Gorky's status as "one of us" did not protect him from
criticism. On the contrary, he was subjected to especially
harsh words for becoming a "traitor" to the revolutionary
cause. A succession of letters, essays, and even poems in
the Bolshevik party's newspaper *Pravda* accused Gorky of
"slandering" and "betraying" the revolution and the work-

ing class.[5] Perhaps because of Gorky's reputation, the regime
hesitated to silence him. When other opposition papers were
closed during the early months of 1918, Gorky's *Novaia
zhizn'* received only warnings and brief temporary closures.
But patience ran out and on July 16, 1918, and with Lenin's
personal approval, the paper was shut permanently. Up to
the very moment of closure, harsh criticism and threats of
repression did not cause Gorky to moderate his statements.
On the contrary, as other critical voices were silenced, his
own grew sharper and more fervent. He increasingly saw
himself as the conscience of the revolution and the people.

In autumn 1918, Gorky published a selection of forty-
eight of his essays from *Novaia zhizn'*, thematically organized, as a separate book titled *Untimely Thoughts: Notes on
Revolution and Culture*).[6] Earlier in the year, Gorky's essays
of 1917 were published by a Russian press in Germany.[7] During the early 1920s, Gorky prepared a new and expanded
edition that was to have included almost all of his essays
of 1917–1918. But it did not appear in print until 1990.[8]
The present collection, compiled and translated by Herman
Ermolaev in the 1960s, is the most inclusive edition, bringing together all but a couple of Gorky's essays from *Novaia
zhizn'*.[9]

In Soviet memory, Gorky's role as conscience of the revolution was officially repressed. Because Gorky was canon-
ized as the "father of Soviet socialist literature," his reputation had to be recrafted and simplified (a process Gorky
himself helped to promote in the 1930s). In particular, the
troubling essays of 1917–1918 had to be pushed into the
shadows. Thus, they did not appear in any of the Soviet
editions of his works, including the thirty-volume *Collected
Works* (1949–1956). Only scholarly works even mentioned
Gorky's essays in *Novaia zhizn'*, but with relatively little
direct quotation or indication of the substance of Gorky's
critique. At best, scholars mentioned, as Gorky himself

later would, that Gorky made "mistakes" in thinking that
the October revolution was premature and the Bolsheviks
brutal.[10]

Gorky's criticisms of Bolshevism cut wide and deep. He
objected to almost every major Bolshevik action: the encouragement of armed demonstrations in July 1917; the
seizure of state power in October; the suppression of opposition newspapers (including socialist papers); the imprisonment of liberal ministers of the overthrown Provisional
Government; the "disgraceful and criminal" use of threats
of "violence and terror" to silence opponents; the provoking
of social hatred and "mob" violence; the disbanding of the
democratically elected Constituent Assembly in early January 1918 and the use of violence against its defenders; and
the "cynical" separate peace with Germany signed at Brest-
Litovsk in March. Above all, Gorky objected to the Bolsheviks' "shameful attitude toward freedom of speech, the
individual, and the sum total of those rights for the triumph
of which democracy struggled" (November 7, 1917).

Bolshevik policies and actions disturbed Gorky, but he
saw these as symptoms of deeper, essentially moral flaws.
Indeed, the pervasiveness of moral rhetoric in Gorky's dis-
cussions of the Bolsheviks is striking. Lenin was described as
"cold-blooded," "pitiless," and "lacking morality" (November 7 and 10, 1917). Local representatives of Soviet power
were as "coarse" and "crude" as tsarist officials, if not worse
(December 7 and 19, 1917). Most troubling, Bolshevik revolutionary tactics, rather than improving the people morally
—the historic responsibility and tradition of the intelligentsia, Gorky believed—instead aroused the "crude instincts"
and "animal anarchism" of the masses (December 6, 1917,
and March 22, 1918). And rather than teaching that the
socialist revolution was supposed to emancipate all people
from oppression, the Bolsheviks taught that the social revolution was only about "the bloody smashing of faces" ( January 13, 1918).

——— • ———

Filled with the immediacy of their time, these essays require us to recall the historical setting that was for Gorky's readers everyday life (for an overview of events see the Chronology).

The collapse of the tsarist autocracy in February 1917 resulted not only in the passing of power to more democratic hands but also in the disintegration and fracturing of power. The authority of the new Provisional Government, composed mainly of liberals from the Constitutional Democratic Party who were soon joined by moderate socialists, was limited by the competing authority of the Soviets (a national network of elected "Councils [Soviets] of Workers', Soldiers', and Peasants' Deputies," headed by a national executive committee in Petrograd, composed primarily of leaders of the Menshevik and Socialist Revolutionary parties). But power was fractured far beyond this familiar problem of "dual power."

Power was being challenged, subverted, and seized daily by people in the streets and especially in factories, workshops, barracks, and villages.[11] The struggles between political parties, at the center of most accounts of the revolution, was only a facet of this larger struggle for power. Crowds of workers and other townspeople, only loosely controlled by political organizations, seized city streets in demonstrations, especially in the capital, Petrograd. In factories and shops, workers and employees demanded control over work rules, wages, and even hiring and firing. Insubordination and assertion also took direct forms, especially against foremen, managers, and employers: these acts ranged from simple rudeness to rituals in which foremen and managers were carted out of the plant in wheelbarrows to beatings and even murder. In the army, soldiers disregarded orders, rudely mocked officers (or simply beat them up), organized committees to approve orders, and sometimes elected new officers. They also deserted in increasingly large numbers. In the countryside, peasants seized lands—from both the gentry and the richer peasants—without waiting for legal sanction, cut wood in private forests, and looted and burned landlords' houses. Alongside these acts of social defiance, and not entirely unrelated, was a good deal of drunkenness, hooliganism, robbery, criminal violence, and murder. Gorky had much to say about this spreading "anarchy."

The revolution was not only about power, of course. People acted as they did for a variety of reasons and motives. Even within the Bolshevik party—as Gorky, who had been closely associated with such unorthodox Bolsheviks as Alexander Bogdanov and Anatoly Lunacharsky, well knew—there were widely divergent views on the meaning of the revolution, the uses to which Soviet power should be put, and the larger philosophical and ethical questions to which these questions were connected.[12]

Even more varied and unstable was the meaning of the revolution among lower-class supporters, even among the "proletariat." That the majority of politically active urban workers sided with the Bolsheviks by autumn 1917 is hardly in doubt now; what is in doubt is what people meant by their support. Thus, though urban workers overwhelmingly came to support the Bolshevik demand for "all power to the Soviets" (never for "all power to the Bolsheviks," however), diverse concerns and values motivated them to reject the liberal-socialist Provisional Government: distrust and resentment of the privileged classes; deepening material suffering; ideas about the equal dignity of all human beings and thus the injustice of all inequality; even secularized ideals of apocalyptic salvation and final judgment. Popular aspirations and attitudes varied enormously in 1917–1918. Even among people ostensibly sympathetic to the revolution, perspectives and values often poorly fit with Bolshevik ideology and practice. This can be seen, for example, in the flood

of petitions and letters workers and peasants sent to figures in authority in 1917–1918. Amid, and often intertwined
with, the familiar expressions of lower-class support for
peace, bread, land, and Soviet power, one constantly heard
less orthodox themes: distrust of all authority; hatred of
intellectuals; bigotry against foreigners and Jews; Christian
ethics and faith; desires for a government of all "democratic"
parties; patriotism and non-Russian nationalism.[13] Gorky's
socialist dissent was not a lone voice.

In cultural life as well—an area that especially concerned
Gorky—supporters of the revolution clashed over fundamental issues of value and perception.[14] Some revolutionaries
called for a radical break with the culture of the old world:
"In the name of our Tomorrow / We will burn Raphael /
Destroy the museums, trample down the flowers of art."[15]
Others, including many Bolshevik officials, did all they
could to protect museums, organize lectures for workers on
the history of world art and literature, and generally preserve
and promote the established culture. Some revolutionaries
spoke of submerging the individual in an embracing col-
lectivism, while others demanded the emancipation of the
individual from all restraints. Some envisioned the socialist
society of the future as a "machine paradise"; others imagined a pastoral socialist idyll. The revolution about which
Gorky wrote was a time of diverse brutalities and diverse
imagination. And the outcome was far from certain.

———— • ————

Although Gorky has much to say about the immediate
passions of the revolution, his perspective was also deliberately "untimely." As mentioned, when he prepared a selection of his *Novaia zhizn'* editorials for republication toward
the end of 1918, he reorganized the essays thematically to
emphasize their intellectual significance beyond their time.

Indeed, many of the key themes in these essays—their essential values—echoed and refined themes in Gorky's earlier literary and publicistic writings.

Gorky's values were reflected in the people he admired. Christ, Prometheus, John of Damascus, Francis of Assisi, Giordano Bruno, Garibaldi, and Leo Tolstoy appear in these essays as "heroes of the spirit" (May 6, 1917), "half-gods, half-men, of whom mankind can be proud" ( July 19, 1917). They were also, of course, often martyrs. They were joined by the names of Radishchev, Pushkin, Herzen, Belinsky, Nekrasov, and Chernyshevsky—key figures of the nineteenth-century Russian intelligentsia who also fought, and suffered, for absolute truths and values. This "untimely" devotion to "universal values" was the hallmark of the intelligentsia's self-identity and of their views of the role of the writer. Gorky cast his own self-identity and public persona in this mold. It lay at the heart of his chosen role as moral witness to the revolution.[16]

Orthodox Marxists, Lenin in particular, normally insisted on the relativity of ethics. The definition of good and evil depended entirely on whether one's behavior benefited one's class and furthered historical progress. Gorky, in the tradition of the Russian intelligentsia, was repelled by this moral relativism. Instead, his analytical vocabulary was pervaded with lists of virtues (freedom, brotherhood, truth, kindness, humaneness, friendship, love, honesty, reason, conscience) and sins (enmity, vengeance, hatred, cowardice, greed, envy, egoism, ambition, pettiness, cynicism, hypocrisy, lies, vulgarity, cruelty, coercion, violence, murder).

Beyond this general and conventional ethics, specific values strongly shaped Gorky's judgments on the revolution. First among these was the individual. This echoed important traditions within the Russian intelligentsia. Notwithstanding the stereotype of Russian culture as alien to notions of individuality, educated Russians had been writing about the innate worth, freedom, and rights of the individual since the late eighteenth century. Among Russia's prerevolutionary intelligentsia, from liberals to even many Marxists, it was an article of faith that social change ought above all to promote the dignity of the person by removing the social, cultural, and political constraints that hindered the full development of the individual personality (*lichnost'*, which may be translated variously as individual, personality, and selfhood, was a commonly used term). And the acceptance of this value was spreading. By the early twentieth century, many of the most widely read newspapers and magazines, including those appealing mainly to lower-class and lower-middle-class readers, featured articles and works of fiction chastizing conditions that degraded and humiliated individuals and promoting models of autonomous moral choice and individual achievement.[17] Nietzsche's expanding influence in Russia starting in the early 1890s—including on Gorky, who enthusiastically read a translation of *Thus Spoke Zarathustra* while writing his first stories—reflected and reinforced this growing valuation of individual worth and will.[18]

Gorky's short stories and novels, as well as his autobiography, often featured strong, vital, restless, individuals—plebeian supermen—living and wandering on the fringes of society, challenging oppressive moralities and authorities, and condemning the slavish submissiveness and fatalism of the masses. The positive heroes in Gorky's works—such as Makar Chudra in the short story of that name (1892), Artem in "Kain and Artem" (1899), Satin in the play "The Lower Depths" (1902), and Gorky himself in his autobiography (1913, 1916)—often illustrate and voice his contempt for weakness and fatalism and his admiration for strength and will.

But this was a complex and even ambivalent individualism, as it was for earlier Russian *intelligenty*. Among socialists, ethics of individual worth and rights were inter-woven—not always neatly, to be sure, but persistently—with notions of society and humanity. In the most coherent expression of this socialized individualism, Russian *intelligenty* like Alexander Herzen and Nikolai Chernyshevsky maintained that individuals could realize their full dignity and potential only in serving others. In the early 1900s, Anatoly Lunacharsky—one of the Bolshevik party's leading intellectuals and Soviet Russia's first Commissar of Enlightenment—made the same argument when he insisted that the vital and autonomous revolutionary must strive not for wolfish personal gain but for the progress of all humanity.[19]

Gorky's sympathy in his stories and novels was similarly focused on strong and vital heroes who use their strength and will to serve others, and not out of pity but as an intrinsic expression of their heroic selves.[20] Most of all, Gorky abhorred materialistic egoism. This is especially visible in his stories and novels set in commercial and business milieus, which Gorky knew from his youth. Although Gorky admired the hard work and entrepreneurial vitality of many business owners, he despised their selfish money-grubbing, pervasive vulgarity, and authoritarian cruelty to others. The hero of his novel *Foma Gordeev* (1899) rebels precisely against the crass, egoistic individualism of the emerging Russian bourgeoisie: "You bastards, what have you created? Not a new life, not a new order. You have shackled human beings in chains. . . . You murder men's souls."[21]

Gorky refined and spelled out these ideas about the individual in society in two essays, "Notes on the Petty Bourgeois Spirit" (*Zametki o meshchanstve,* 1905) and "The Destruction of Personality" (*Razrushenie lichnosti,* 1909). More sharply than in earlier stories, Gorky here expressed his scorn for philistine individualism, which in effect degraded the individual with its obsession with private material gain, its disregard for the human dignity of others, and its security-minded fear of risk and struggle. In opposition to this degraded individualism of the petty bourgeoisie, Gorky idealized the "epic personality" (*epicheskaia lichnost'*) created by the people in struggle.[22]

At the same time, however, Gorky continued to honor vital individualists. Thus, in 1916 he wrote an essay (not included in the Soviet collections of his works) in praise of the wealthy print capitalist Ivan Sytin, owner of one of Russia's largest printing and publishing businesses. Gorky admired Sytin as one of those "special, strong" people who occasionally emerge in Russia against the prevailing current. Figures like Sytin were the exceptions that proved the rule in Russia, which was "a weak development of initiative, a passive and involuntary relationship to work, dishonesty in all public matters, and the absence in people of the consciousness that they are personally responsible for the chaos, ugliness, and filth in our life."[23]

In Gorky's essays of 1917–1918, the worth and rights of the individual remained a pervading theme. The autocracy was overthrown, Gorky observed, because of its degrading "treatment of man" (May 2, 1917). In the intervening months, the greatest threat to the revolution, he warned, lay in "crimes against the individual" (April 23, 1917). After October, Gorky similarly attributed much of what was wrong with Bolshevism to the absence—in the streets as well as in the new government—of any "conception of the freedom of the individual or of the rights of man" (November 7, 1917). "Man," he stated bluntly barely two months after the Bolsheviks came to power, "is valued just as cheaply as before" (December 19, 1917).

Gorky's defense of individual dignity and rights owed much to liberal tradition. But he was also a socialist in his understanding and use of such notions as the "freedom of the individual" and "the rights of man." When Gorky appealed to people, as he often did, to have greater self-respect and faith in themselves and to cultivate their "selfhood" (*lichnost'*) and "will" (*volia,* implying also inner freedom), he blended these notions of individual assertion with ideas about social solidarity and community. In part, Gorky continued to insist that a truly heroic individualist realizes himself only in serving others. Thus, a true revolutionary embodies the "Promethean revolutionary principle" ( June 6, 1918). Like Prometheus, the titan who challenged the Gods to bring humanity the fire needed for civilization, the true revolutionary represented free, heroic will dedicated to the cause of human progress.

Equally important for Gorky was that respect for the dignity and rights of man should infuse the collectivist spirit of socialism. Gorky shared, in his own way, the Marxist view that the working class was destined by history to bring to the world a new moral and social order. Indeed, as he often wrote in 1917–1918 (and repeated in later years), it was his fear that the Bolsheviks were squandering this social force in a hasty and dangerous experiment that helped to provoke his opposition. But for the working class to play its destined role and bring about the reign of socialism—"the idea of universal brotherhood" (April 20, 1917)—the proletariat had to nurture in itself a more developed spiritual culture. This meant more knowledge and reason but also certain values, first of which was "respect for man." Without this value, Gorky feared, the revolution would betray its mission—its destiny according to the traditional teleology of Marxism—to liberate humanity and would instead become merely an occasion for grabbing power and material goods.

Closely connected to these concerns was Gorky's constant reference in these essays to the "spiritual" (*dukhovnost'*)—a term meaning, roughly, a mixture of intellectual culture, ethics, and emotional attitude. This was a continuous preoccupation in his work. Many of the positive heroes in his earlier fiction were inspired by a type of religious spirit—a spirit of ethical certainty, faith, and an exalted sense of mission, though not formal religious belief or ritual. Even in Gorky's novel *Mother* (1906), which Soviet tradition treated as the forerunner of socialist realism, the revolutionary transformation of the heroine involves less a journey from a religious to a rationalist outlook than movement from conventional religion to a new faith in the possibility of establishing a kingdom of heaven on earth.

Gorky's efforts to bring a religious enthusiasm to Marxism became most elaborate—and most worrisome to orthodox Marxists like Lenin—during the years 1907–1909, when, together with Lunacharsky, Bogdanov, and other Bolsheviks, he advocated ideas that became known as "God-building" (*bogostroitel'stvo*). Reacting against the cold rationalism and determinism of Marxism, these Marxist God-builders believed that the socialist movement, if it was to inspire collective heroism, must appeal to the subconscious and the emotions in order to harness the inspiring force of myth and faith.[24] Gorky invented the term "God-building" in his novel *Confession* (Ispoved', 1908). At the center of this novel is a figure much like Gorky who seeks a way to spiritually counter the "grief and fear, malice and despair, greed and shamelessness" that is everywhere "devouring life." He looks to the church but finds among priests and monks too much hypocrisy, greed, authoritarianism, and debauchery. He eventually finds his answer in the miraculous power of the people—symbolized by a crowd healing a dying girl through its faith.

Viewing the revolutionary people in 1917–1918, Gorky saw neither sufficiently developed knowledge and reason nor sufficient spiritual culture and strength to heal Russia—to create a just and vital society—and saw the people's leaders only degrading their spirit further. The revolution, Gorky believed, should have been a time of "spiritual rebirth," when people would have the power and will to clear

away the "thick fogs of detestable vulgarity [*poshlost'*]" that
surrounded them and the "filth of life which has accumulated for centuries" (December 24, 1917). The revolution
should have inspired the people with "emotions of beauty
and goodness" (March 28, 1918). Instead, it unleashed the
people's most degraded "instincts": the people acted, and
the Bolsheviks encouraged them to act, like "a wild beast . . .
[that] has opened wide its vengeful jaws and in triumph
roars out its rancor and malice" (December 24, 1917).

In these essays, as in earlier writings, Gorky constantly returned to the spiritual—intellectual, moral, and emotional
—poverty and deformity of the Russian people, especially
the common people; he cites their "seed-chewing" aversion
to work, "Oriental" passivity before fate, "dreamy spine-
lessness," disdain for human dignity, hatred of individual
strength and will, cruelty toward others, bigoted intolerance
of people who are different and especially better than themselves (in particular Jews), tendency to look for "enemies"
and "saviors" everywhere except within themselves, and
general lack of initiative and self-reliance. Gorky blamed
these traits on oppressive and demoralizing social and political conditions: the Russian people had been "beaten senseless by cruel reality" (April 22, 1917), their "will" suppressed
by "slavery" (April 23, 1917), and their spirit "enraged by
long captivity" (December 24, 1917). But Gorky was more
concerned with the effects, for they tended to outlast the
causes. Though free at last, Russians continued to "live
dominated internally by the feelings of slaves" (April 23,
1917).

Gorky claimed to have a special right, due to his back-
ground and experiences, to speak the "bitter truth" (March
21, 1918) about the Russian people. Although his social origins were petty-bourgeois rather than proletarian, the death
of his father when he was three and of his mother when he
was eleven, the impoverishment of his grandparents (who
largely raised him), and especially his years of wandering

and work (in a shoestore, bakery, and icon workshop and on a building project and river boats) established Gorky's reputation as a "writer from the people." Gorky cultivated this public image in semi-autobiographical stories and sketches and especially in the first volumes of his autobiography—*Childhood* (*Detstvo*, 1913) and *Among People* (*V liudakh*, 1916; often translated *Apprenticeship*)—which appeared in installments in popular periodicals and then as separate volumes. Even his choice of a literary pseudonym (he was born Aleksei Maksimovich Peshkov) reminded readers that he was one who knew the "bitter" (*gor'kii*) life of the people and would speak the "bitter" truth.

Gorky used this image to make a living as an author—as a writer about the people who came from the people—but also to strengthen and legitimize his civic voice. Thus, in 1917, he would taunt Lenin with the fact that "he does not know the popular masses, he has not lived with them" (November 10). Gorky, everyone understood, had lived with the people. And what Gorky "knew"—though his values shaped this knowledge at least as much as his observations—was that the people needed not flattery but culture. Ironically, and to Gorky's satisfaction, Lenin would increasingly agree. During the final years before Lenin's death in 1924, Lenin would repeatedly write of the need for "cultural revolution," for teaching the people greater discipline, reason, and knowledge.[25] Meanwhile, Gorky repeatedly warned all who would listen that Russian backwardness was smothering the promises of the revolution: "The fire was kindled; it burns poorly, it stinks of Russia, filthy, drunk, and cruel" (March 16, 1918).

———•———

The coming of civil war intensified Bolshevik intolerance of dissent, including Gorky's. On July 16, 1918, the Petrograd censorship office shut down *Novaia zhizn'*. Gorky personally appealed to Lenin, but in vain. Lenin is reported to have told the censor, "Of course, *Novaia zhizn'* must be closed. In current conditions, when we need to raise the whole country in defense of the revolution, any sort of intelligentsia pessimism is extremely harmful."[26] Gorky, it seems, was also troubled by his "intelligentsia pessimism." In June 1918 he had written to Ekaterina Peshkova, his first wife and still a close friend, "I am planning to work with the Bolsheviks on an autonomous basis. I am sick of the fruitless, academic opposition of *N[ovaia] zh[izn']*."[27] Gorky always despised "wordmongers"—so plentiful in Russia, he felt—and admired practical people who did things. It seemed that he had become a wordmonger.

For the next three years, Gorky devoted himself to practical activity in the field that most concerned him—protecting and promoting culture and those who were its caretakers and creators. A comment he made in a letter to Ekaterina Peshkova a year earlier could easily have applied then: "I am living in emotional contradiction with my own self [*zhivu v dushevnom protivorechii s samym soboiu*] and see no other way out besides cultural work."[28] He secured government financing for a new publishing house, "World Literature," which he ran. World Literature served a double function: to promote popular enlightenment by publishing the classics of Western European literature and to give employment to needy Russian authors (whose material lives during the civil war were often desperate) as translators, editors, and proofreaders. Gorky also helped to establish a "House of Scholars" in Petrograd to give material aid to intellectuals, and he was chairman of the Commission to Improve Scholars' Living Conditions. He also helped many intellectuals, artists, and writers by providing them with food, lodging, and money. Finally—and least pleasing to those in power— he frequently interceded with the authorities on behalf of writers who found themselves in political trouble. As Viktor

Shklovsky described all this a couple of years later, "Gorky was the Noah of the Russian intelligentsia."[29]

Gorky's relations with the Bolshevik regime remained difficult. When he decided to work with the government, many opponents of the regime (including some of the writers he helped) reviled him for having "sold his conscience"; many Communists likewise applauded him for "returning to the cause." But his reconciliation remained troubled. As he recalled in his obituary for Lenin in 1924, "During 1917–1921 my relations with Lenin were far from what I would have liked them to be, but they could not be otherwise." Among the causes of continuing friction, he acknowledged, were Lenin's continuing intolerance of criticism, toleration of brutality, and disdain for the intelligentsia.[30] Gorky gave up his "academic opposition"—in any case, it was no longer tolerated—but remained, as he had said, in "emotional contradiction" with himself.

In October 1921, Gorky left Russia, ostensibly for his health. He revisited the Soviet Union for the first time in 1928, after years of efforts by emissaries from Moscow to persuade him to return and after a good deal of flattering praise. He returned permanently—preceded by a number of extended visits—only in 1933, three years before his death. This second return and reconciliation has long baffled and dismayed Western observers and many Russians as well. This is not the place to fully examine Gorky's motives, though one may mention his declining health, homesickness, vanity, and a desire to do something useful for his country. But the essays in this volume suggest deeper reasons.

Much in Stalin's Soviet Union was likely to appeal to Gorky. Although the years 1928–1936 were a time of brutality and repression—forced labor, collectivization, famine, cultural rigidity, and growing terror—these were also years of enthusiastic construction, a celebration of heroism (both individual and collective), and a pervading official optimism. Like Gorky, Stalin and his supporters imagined revolutionaries as Promethean heros inspired by exceptional faith and will—terms that pervaded Stalinist public rhetoric as it had pervaded Gorky's essays of 1917–1918. Here in Stalin's revolution was the daring, the challenge to "petty-bourgeois" complacency, that Gorky had admired all his life.

The campaign of rapid industrialization, which began in 1928, almost certainly impressed Gorky. In his essays of 1917–1918, as in his earlier fiction, Gorky often insisted on the importance of industry, on the "redemptive power" of work (March 28, 1918), and on the heroism of economic construction (he even mentioned as an example the digging of canals [April 22, 1917], foreshadowing his notorious praise in the 1930s of the digging of the White Sea Canal with convict labor). What he wrote in 1918, he (or Stalin) could have written in the 1930s: in the "struggle of man against nature, and only in this struggle will man develop the forces of his spirit to perfection, only here will he acquire the uplifting awareness of his own significance" (April 30, 1918).

Forced collectivization also likely appealed to Gorky's long-held values, for it promised to subject the dark ignorance of the village to the civilization of the city. Before, during, and after the revolution, Gorky repeatedly warned that the Russian peasantry had a different "soul" than urban workers (December 10, 1917) and that the peasant spirit was alien and dangerous to urban culture and a moral threat to the revolution. What the revolution had to do, he wrote even more bluntly in 1925, foreshadowing actual Stalinist policies, was to "master the anarchy of the countryside, cultivate the will of the peasant, teach him to work rationally, and transform his economy, and thereby move the country forward rapidly. All this can be achieved only by subjecting the instincts of the countryside to the organizing reason of the city."[31] Last, the Stalin regime was committed, as Gorky was, to promoting popular education and even shared Gorky's traditionalist cultural tastes (Gorky's own works, of course, had become part of the Soviet literary canon).

We still know little about what lay behind the calm and uniform face of Gorky's public reconciliation with the Soviet order. The evidence that Gorky was discontented in Stalinist Russia is fragmentary,[32] though we know that there were others within the ruling elite who tried to limit Stalin's power and moderate his policies. The suggestion, still often heard, that Gorky was poisoned on Stalin's instructions rather than dying of natural causes in 1936 remains only a supposition. Such a conclusion might provide a tidy conclusion to the story of Gorky's life and might offer the satisfaction that Gorky ultimately remained true to his conscience, that he had not forgotten the values that informed his critique of Bolshevism—the freedom of the personality, the corrupting effects of power over people, the harm of seeing enemies everywhere. But it may also be that in his old age and ill health, and enjoying his prestige, his moral courage of 1917–1918 failed him. Or perhaps, more complexly, he tried to be useful, and in so trying "stood on the throat of [his] own song," as the poet Vladimir Mayakovsky, who also tried, said of himself.

———— • ————

Seventy years passed before Gorky's *Untimely Thoughts* could again be published in Russia. Once permitted, in 1988, several large editions appeared in succession and immediately sold out.[33] As historical documents, these essays were for many a revelation. Among the many "white spots"— silences as well as half-truths—in the Soviet Union's historical record that the coming of *glasnost'* promised to fill, the details (and for many the mere fact) of Gorky's opposi-

tion to Bolshevism and the Bolshevik revolution represented
an important recovery of the past. The essays helped decon-
struct the mythicized official image of Gorky, which, as Iosif
Vainberg wrote in 1988, had become "iconographic" and
"canonical," and thus purged of "complexities and contradictions."[34] But these essays speak to Russian readers not
only about the past. With Russia again facing a deep crisis of
civic and moral order and national identity, Russians under-
standably often look to their history not merely for new facts
about the past but for meanings and lessons for the present.

*Untimely Thoughts* reappeared in the Soviet Union during the height of Mikhail Gorbachev's efforts to "renew"
socialist society. Gorky's message was suddenly appropriate again and welcome. As the author of the first major
article devoted to *Untimely Thoughts* since its original publication observed, referring to Gorky's frequent mention of
values and ideals common to all humanity: "One cannot
but notice the relevance of this Gorkian idea for our own
times, when the Communist Party, in decisions made at the
Twenty-Seventh Congress and at plenums, has shown the
priority of the universal human values of peace and the preservation of peace on Earth, democratism, *glasnost'*, legality,
conscience, and honesty!"[35] Gorbachev himself constantly
appealed to a model of socialism that had much in common
with Gorky's. Like Gorky, he chastized Russians (to use
phrases most commonly found in his speeches) for their passivity, unwillingness to work, moral nihilism, materialism,
spiritual emptiness (*bezdukhovnost'*) and philistine vulgarity
(*poshlost'*).[36] Convinced that socialism presupposed cultural
and spiritual changes in people, Gorbachev began speaking of "psychological perestroika" and "perestroika of the
mind" even before he used the term *perestroika* to mean economic and political reconstruction.[37] Echoing ideals that had
become increasingly widespread among educated Soviets,
Gorbachev appealed specifically for greater efforts to pro-

mote the dignity of the individual person (*lichnost'*) and other "universal human values."[38]

The collapse of Communist rule in Russia has not made Gorky's words any less current. Gorky's descriptions of Russia's "spiritual crisis" of 1917–1918 contain much that is strikingly familiar today: "hooliganism" among the youth, public drunkenness, homeless children, declining public health, crude struggles for power among the "politickers" (*politikany,* a term that is again current), and economic collapse. More important, many Russians now feel, as Gorky did in 1917, that people's lives are "morally off-balance" (April 27, 1917). Russian intellectuals now often write, as Gorky did, about the pervasiveness of vulgar tastes, aversion to work, irresponsibility for themselves and their country, petty envy and greed, intolerance, and hypocrisy. They write, as Gorky did, of Russians' obsession with finding "enemies" and "traitors" to blame and looking for "saviors" to believe in. Some point, as Gorky did, to the upsurge of antisemitism not only as "a shameful, bloody, and filthy stain" on the Russian conscience ( June 18, 1917) but also as a symptom of Russians' lack of self-respect.[39] Even Gorky's explanation of the historical causes of moral failure in Russia remains applicable: "Reproaching our people . . . for all their savagery and ignorance, I keep in mind: they cannot be different. The conditions in which they lived could foster in them neither respect for the individual, nor awareness of the citizen's rights, nor a feeling of justice—those were conditions of absolute lawlessness, of the oppression of the individual, of the most shameless lies, and bestial cruelty" (May 18, 1917).

Gorky saw one source of hope: "What will cure us, what will revive our strength, what can renew us from within? Only faith in ourselves, and nothing else" (May 16, 1918). "Let us believe in ourselves, let us work stubbornly. All is within our will" (December 24, 1917). One hears in Russia today appeals similar to Gorky's, but also similar doubts.

Gorky admired optimism and faith, but he found them elusive. More constant was his foreboding of tragedy. Still, "contemplating a tragedy," Gorky wrote on June 4, 1918, "cannot but lift a sensitive observer above the chaos of the humdrum, the everyday. . . . Tragedy humanizes." Gorky hoped that his contemplations on the tragic in Russia in 1917–1918 might inspire others and, thus, make them more human.

## NOTES TO THE INTRODUCTION

*Note to epigraph:* M. Gor'kii, "Revoliutsiia i kul'tura," speech prepared for the first public meeting of the cultural-enlightenment society, "Culture and Freedom," which Gorky helped to organize. RTsKhIDNI [former Central Party Archive], fond 75 (A. M. Gor'kii), opis' 1, delo 67, list 1.

1. *Letopis' zhizni i tvorchestva A. M. Gor'kogo,* vol. 3 (Moscow, 1959), 83.

2. Dates in parentheses refer to essays in this volume. I use the first listed date in the original—that is, old style for 1917 (the Julian calendar, which was thirteen days behind the Gregorian) and new style after February 1918, when Russia adopted the Western calendar.

3. For details, see Alexander Kaun, *Maxim Gorky and His Russia* (New York, 1931); Richard Hare, *Maxim Gorky: Romantic Realist and Conservative Revolutionary* (Oxford, 1962); and Bertram D. Wolfe, *The Bridge and the Abyss: The Troubled Friendship of Maxim Gorky and V. I. Lenin* (New York, 1967).

4. As such, the paper attracted contributions from Bolshevik and nonparty authors as well as from Mensheviks. Precisely

because of this independent socialist reputation, when Lev Kamenev, a member of the Bolshevik Central Committee, decided in October 1917 to publicize and warn against Bolshevik secret plans for an insurrection, he told *Novaia zhizn'*.

5. These are itemized in *Letopis' zhizni i tvorchestva A. M. Gor'kogo*, vol. 3. See, especially, T. Tkachenko's letter in *Pravda*, November 23 (10), 1917; V. Polianskii [P. I. Lebedev-Polianskii, a powerful Bolshevik cultural critic, soon to become Soviet Russia's leading government press official], "V putakh starogo mira (Po povodu 'Nesvoevremmenykh myslei' M. Gor'kogo v 'Novoi zhizni')," *Pravda*, December 23 (10), 1917; and "Sotsial'naia revoliutsiia i M. Gor'kii," signed "Intelligent iz naroda," *Pravda*, January 20 (7), 1918.

6. M. Gorkii, *Nesvoevremennye mysli: zametki o revoliutsii i kul'tura* (Petrograd, 1918). The publisher was an organization Gorky helped to establish, "The Enlightenment Society 'Culture and Freedom' in Memory of 27 February 1917."

7. M. Gor'kii, *Revoliutsiia i kul'tura: stat'i 1917 g.* (Berlin, 1918).

8. The manuscript is in the Gorky archive in Moscow. See the commentary by I. Vainberg in M. Gorkii, *Nesvoevremennye mysli: zametki o revoliutsii i kul'ture* (Moscow, 1990), 263, and the notes in M. Gorkii, *Nesvoevremennye mysli: zametki o revoliutsii i kul'ture. Rasskazy* (Moscow, 1991), 121.

9. A Russian edition, which included two essays not in the English edition, was published in France in 1971. Maksim Gor'kii, *Nesvoevremennye mysli: Stat'i 1917–1918 gg.*, sostavlenie, vvedenie i primechaniia G. Ermolaeva (Paris, 1971).

10. Devoting by far the most serious attention to Gorky's 1917–1918 writings is A. Ovcharenko, *Publitsistika M. Gor'kogo,* 2d ed. (Moscow, 1965), 366–387.

11. Although no adequate history of Russian society during the revolution yet exists, good partial accounts can be found in Marc Ferro, *The Russian Revolution of 1917* (London, 1972), and *The Bolshevik Revolution* (London, 1980); Diane Koenker, *Moscow Workers and the 1917 Revolution* (Princeton, 1981); Diane Koenker and William G. Rosenberg, *Strikes and Revolution in Russia, 1917* (Princeton, 1989); Tim McDaniel, *Autocracy, Capitalism, and Revolution in Russia* (Berkeley, 1988); S. A. Smith, *Red Petrograd: Revolution in the Factories, 1917–1918* (Cambridge, Eng., 1983); and Allan K. Wildman, *The End of the Russian Imperial Army,* 2 vols. (Princeton, 1980, 1987).

12. For a discussion of divergent Bolshevisms before World War I, see Robert C. Williams, *The Other Bolsheviks: Lenin and His Critics, 1904–1914* (Bloomington, 1986). On intraparty dissent in 1917 and after, the classic work, which focuses mainly on political issues, is Robert V. Daniels, *The Conscience of the Revolution: Communist Opposition in Soviet Russia* (Cambridge, 1960). For a rich portrait of the varieties of revolutionary idealism, see Richard Stites, *Revolutionary Dreams: Utopian Vision and Experimental Life in the Russian Revolution* (New York, 1989).

13. I base these comments mainly on my reading of hundreds of petitions, letters, and other unpublished archival documents (in the State Archive of the Russian Federation) sent by lower-class Russians to various political authorities (especially to the Provisional Government, the Soviet Central Executive Committee, and the Constituent Assembly) from February 1917 to June 1918.

14. Cultural and intellectual life during the revolution is least well studied. The best accounts are Jane Burbank, *Intelligentsia and Revolution: Russian Views of Bolshevism* (New York, 1986); Abbott Gleason, Peter Kenez, and Richard Stites, eds., *Bolshevik Culture: Experiment and Order in the Russian Revolution* (Bloomington, 1985); Lynn Mally, *Culture of the Future: The Proletkult Movement in Revolutionary Russia* (Berkeley, 1990); and Richard Stites, *Revolutionary Dreams*.

15. Vladimir Kirillov (a Bolshevik worker-poet), "My" (We), written in December 1917 and first published in the Proletkult journal *Griadushchee,* no. 2 (May 1918): 4.

16. A recent Soviet critic described Gorky's stance in 1917–1918 accurately, though somewhat contemptuously, as "ahistorical, abstract-humanistic, and naive-utopian." Leonid Reznikov, "O knige M. Gor'kogo 'Nesvoevremennye mysli,' " *Neva,* 1988, no. 1: 158.

17. George L. Kline, "Changing Attitudes Toward the Individual," in *The Transformation of Russian Society,* ed. Cyril E. Black (Cambridge, 1960), 606–625; Jeffrey Brooks, *When Russia Learned to Read: Literacy and Popular Literature, 1861–1917* (Princeton, 1985), and "Competing Modes of Popular Discourse: Individualism and Class Consciousness in the Russian Print Media," in *Culture et révolution,* eds. M. Ferro and S. Fitzpatrick (Paris, 1989), 71–81; and Mark D. Steinberg, "Worker-Authors and the Cult of the Person," in *Cultures in Flux: Lower-Class Values, Practices and Resistance in Late Imperial Russia,* ed. Stephen P. Frank and Mark D. Steinberg (Princeton, 1994), 168–184.

18. Bernice Glatzer Rosenthal, ed., *Nietzsche in Russia* (Princeton, 1986). On Nietzsche and Gorky, see Mary Louise

Loe, "Gorky and Nietzsche: The Quest for the Russian Superman," ibid., 251–273, and Edith W. Clowes, "Gorky, Nietzsche and God-Building," in *Fifty Years On: Gorky and His Time,* ed. Nicholas Luker (Nottingham, 1987), 127–144.

19. A. V. Lunacharskii, "Voprosy morali i M. Meterlink" (1904), quoted in Kline, "Changing Attitudes Toward the Individual," 619. See also A. V. Lunacharskii, "Meshchanstvo i individualizm" [1909], in *Meshchanstvo i individualizm: sbornik statei* (Moscow and Petrograd, 1923), 5–136.

20. For a discussion of Gorky's literary works that highlights this theme, see F. M. Borras, *Maxim Gorky the Writer: An Interpretation* (Oxford, 1967). On Nietzschean elements in Gorky's attitudes toward the individual, see Loe, "Gorky and Nietzsche," 251–273.

21. M. Gor'kii, *Polnoe sobranie sochinenii,* vol. 4 (Moscow, 1969), 446.

22. *Zametki o meshchanstve* first appeared serially in the Bolshevik newspaper *Novaia zhizn'* (October 27, 30, November 13, 20, 1905). *Razrushenie lichnosti* was first published, accompanied by essays by Lunacharsky and others, in *Ocherki filosofii kollektivizma,* vol. 1 (St. Petersburg, 1909), 351–403.

23. *Polveka dlia knigi* (Moscow, 1916), 29–32.

24. George L. Kline, *Religious and Anti-Religious Thought in Russia* (Chicago, 1968), chap. 4; Robert C. Williams, *Artists in Revolution* (Bloomington, 1977), chap. 2; Jutta Scherrer, "L'intelligentsia russe: sa quête de la 'vérité religieuse du socialisme,'" *Le temps de la réflexion* 2 (1981): 134–151.

25. See especially Lenin's 1923 essays "On Cooperation" and "Better Fewer, But Better." This was also a strong theme in the writings of Nadezhda Krupskaia, Lenin's wife and close intellectual companion and a key figure in Soviet cultural and educational policy. See, for example, her essay "Kakim dol'zhen byt' kommunist" (1922), in N. K. Krupskaia, *Pedagogicheskie sochineniia,* vol. 2 (Moscow, 1958), 121–126. Parts of this essay are translated in William G. Rosenberg, *Bolshevik Visions,* pt. 1 (Ann Arbor, 1990), 26–29.

26. V. Malkin, "V. I. Lenin i M. Gor'kii," *Pravda,* March 29, 1928, in *V. I. Lenin o literature i iskusstkve* (Moscow, 1957), 599.

27. *Letopis' zhizni i tvorchestva A. M. Gor'kogo,* 3: 83.

28. Ibid., 41.

29. Viktor Shklovsky, *A Sentimental Journey: Memoirs, 1917–1922,* trans. Richard Sheldon (Ithaca, 1970), 189.

30. M. Gorky, "V. I. Lenin," *Russkii sovremennik,* no. 1 (1924): 229–244. A 1930 version of this essay, from which Gorky removed some of his more critical comments about Lenin, appears in volume 17 of his *Sobranie sochinenii* and in *V. I. Lenin i A. M. Gor'kii: pis'ma, vospominaniia, dokumenty,* 3d ed. (Moscow, 1969), 290–335. A summary of the fuller first version, with extensive quotations, may be found in translation in Kaun, *Maxim Gorky and His Russia,* 503–510.

31. M. Gorky, "V. I. Lenin," *Sobranie sochinenii,* vol. 19: *Vospominaniia, rasskazy, zametki* (Berlin, 1925): 13. The quoted words were added when Gorky revised the original 1924 draft of this essay.

32. For a rare indication of Gorky's discontent in a Soviet source, see I. Shkapa, *Sem' let s Gor'kim: vospominaniia* (Moscow, 1964), 379.

33. The first to appear was a republication of the 1918 edition of collected and thematically reorganized essays, in the journal *Literaturnoe obozrenie,* 1988, nos. 9, 10, 11, 12 (prepared by I. Vainberg). Separate editions followed: M. Gorkii, *Nesvoevremennye mysli: zametki o revoliutsii i kul'ture* (Moscow, 1990) (also prepared by I. Vainberg, this edition included the unpublished expanded collection of essays Gorky prepared in the 1920s, supplemented by essays from *Novaia zhizn'* not included in that text and accompanied by excellent annotations); M. Gorkii, *Nesvoevremennye mysli i rassuzhdeniia o revoliutsii i kul'tura (1917–1918 gg.)* (Moscow, 1990) (a large edition of 200,000 copies presenting Gorky's essays from *Novaia zhizn'* in chronological order, identical to Ermolaev's Paris edition of 1971); and M. Gorkii, *Nesvoevremennye mysli: zametki o revoliutsii i kul'ture. Rasskazy* (Moscow, 1991) (includes the text of the original 1918 edition).

34. I. Vainberg, "Gor'kii, znakomyi i neznakomyi," introduction to M. Gor'kii, *Nesvoevremennye mysli: zametki o revoliutsii i kul'ture* (Moscow, 1990), 10. This essay is a revised version of Vainberg's article "Vo imia revoliutsiia i kul'tury: publitsistika M. Gor'kogo 1917–1918 godov," *Literaturnoe obozrenie,* 1988, no. 9: 91–98, and 1988, no. 10: 93–99.

35. Leonid Reznikov, "O knige M. Gor'kogo 'Nesvoevremennye mysli,'" *Neva,* 1988, no. 1: 157 (the article is dated 1987 by the author). For similar comments, see the essays by I. Vainberg cited in note 34.

36. *Materialy plenuma Tsentral'nogo Komiteta KPSS (27–28 ianvaria 1987 g.)* (Moscow, 1987), 11–12. *XIX vsesoiuznaia konferentsiia: stenograficheskii otchet,* vol. 1 (Moscow, 1988), 52. For earlier examples, see M. S. Gorbachev, *Izbrannye rechi i stat'i,* 3 vols. (Moscow, 1987), 2: 16, 96–98, 105–106.

37. Gorbachev, *Izbrannye rechi i stat'i,* 1: 159, 315; 2: 218; *Materialy XXVII s"ezda KPSS* (Moscow, 1986), 38; *Materialy plenuma Tsentral'nogo Komiteta KPSS (27–28 ianvaria 1987 g.),* 11.

38. For example, *XIX vsesoiuznaia konferentsiia,* 1: 41; *Pravda* (November 26, 1989): 2; Mikhail Gorbachev, *Perestroika* (New York, 1987), 28–35.

39. For a compendium of Gorky's writings on the subject, see Maksim Gor'kii, *Iz literaturnogo naslediia: Gor'kii i evreiskii vopros,* ed. Mikhail Agurskii and Margarita Shklovskaia (Jerusalem, 1986).

# CHRONOLOGY OF THE REVOLUTION
## February 1917–July 1918
*Mark D. Steinberg*

### 1917

FEBRUARY 23 (MARCH 8): International Women's Day. Strikes and demonstrations in Petrograd, the capital, growing over the next few days.

FEBRUARY 26 (MARCH 11): Tsar Nicholas II orders commander of Petrograd garrison to suppress disorders.

FEBRUARY 27 (MARCH 12): FEBRUARY REVOLUTION: Garrison mutinies. Formation of Provisional Committee of the Duma by liberals from Constitutional Democratic Party (Kadets), and Petrograd Soviet of Workers' Deputies, headed by Mensheviks and Socialist Revolutionaries (SRs).

FEBRUARY 28–MARCH 2 (MARCH 13–15): Political strikes and demonstrations spread to Moscow and provincial capitals. Soviets— councils of elected workers' and soldiers' deputies, usually led by activists from socialist parties—form in most Russian cities.

MARCH 2 (15): Nicholas II abdicates. Provisional Government composed mainly of Kadet party ministers established after agreement with Petrograd Soviet.

MARCH: Provisional Government declares amnesty to political prisoners and exiles; enacts freedom of speech, press, assembly, association, and strikes; ends death penalty; abolishes flogging and exile to Siberia; removes all legal restrictions of rights based on nationality or religion; begins preparations for elections to Constituent Assembly on the basis of universal, secret, direct, and equal suffrage; and promises land reform.

APRIL 3–4 (16–17): Lenin returns to Petrograd from his exile in Switzerland and issues "April Theses," which call for revolution against "bourgeois" Provisional Government, political power to the Soviets, an end to the war, nationalization of land and its distribution to peasants, and industry under the control of workers' councils.

APRIL 20–21 (MAY 3–4): APRIL DAYS: armed demonstrations by workers and soldiers in the streets of Petrograd and Moscow after leak to the public of a diplomatic note to the Allies from Foreign Minister Pavel Miliukov apparently expressing annexationist war aims.

MAY 5 (18): First coalition government: six socialist ministers (Mensheviks and SRs) join Provisional Government.

SPRING AND SUMMER: Continuing labor strikes amid inflation and fuel and food shortages; agrarian unrest, including such direct violations of gentry property rights as illegal wood cutting, theft of seed and tools, and land seizures; strengthening of national independence movements; and growing Bolshevik success in elections to factory committees, soldiers' and sailors' committees, and neighborhood Soviets.

JUNE 3–24 (JUNE 16–JULY 7): First All-Russian Congress of Workers' and Soldiers' Deputies elects Central Executive Committee, headed by Mensheviks and SRs.

JUNE 16 (29): Russian offensive on Austrian front begins; within days, it becomes a rout.

JUNE 18 (31): Street march in Petrograd, organized by Congress of Soviets, is unexpectedly dominated by Bolshevik slogans: "Down with the Ten Capitalist Ministers," "Down with the Offensive," "All Power to the Soviets."

JULY 3–5 (16–18): JULY DAYS: mass armed demonstrations in Petrograd, encouraged by the Bolsheviks, demanding "All Power to the Soviets." Bolshevik leaders arrested or go into hiding.

JULY 11 (24): Socialist Alexander Kerensky becomes prime minister. Other ministerial changes follow, bringing other moderate socialists into the government.

AUGUST 12–15 (25–28): State Conference in Moscow, bringing together representatives from a wide range of civic organizations and parties (Bolsheviks refuse to participate). Fails to unite society in support of Provisional Government, but reveals widely held sentiments for firm authority and order.

AUGUST 26–30 (SEPTEMBER 8–12): Commander-in-Chief of the Russian Army Gen. Lavr Kornilov attempts military putsch.

AUGUST 31 (SEPTEMBER 13): Bolsheviks win majority in Petrograd Soviet.

SEPTEMBER 5 (18): Bolsheviks win majority in Moscow Soviet.

SEPTEMBER 14–22 (SEPTEMBER 27–OCTOBER 5): Democratic State Conference in Petrograd—composed of representatives of urban and rural Soviets, city Dumas, soldiers' committees, trade unions, and other organizations—refuses to support Bolshevik appeals to form a Soviet government.

OCTOBER 24–25 (NOVEMBER 6–7): OCTOBER REVOLUTION: Bolshevik Military Revolutionary Committee overthrows Provisional Government.

OCTOBER 25–26: In protest against Bolshevik seizure of power, Mensheviks and SRs walk out of Second Congress of Soviets, which endorses seizure of power.

OCTOBER 26 (NOVEMBER 8): Congress passes Decree on Peace, appealing to belligerents to conclude an immediate peace without annexations or indemnities and promising to publish all secret treaties.

OCTOBER 26 (NOVEMBER 8): Congress passes Decree on Land, abolishing private ownership of land and use of hired agricultural labor. In conformity with peasant tradition, land is to be distributed among households according to need or available family labor.

OCTOBER 26 (NOVEMBER 8): Congress approves formation of an all-Bolshevik government, the Council of People's Commissars (*Sovnarkom*), headed by Lenin.

OCTOBER 27 (NOVEMBER 9): Decree on the Press—first legislative act of Sovnarkom—gives Sovnarkom the power to suspend or shut any publication "inciting to open resistance or disobedience" against the government. Causes dissent among Bolshevik leadership and Left SRs.

OCTOBER 31–NOVEMBER 2 (NOVEMBER 13–15): Fighting in Moscow ends in Bolshevik victory.

NOVEMBER 2 (15): Bolshevik party rejects demands—made by

Union of Railroad Employees and supported by several leading Bolsheviks, including Kamenev and Zinov'ev—for a multi-party socialist government.

NOVEMBER 2 (15): Declaration of the Rights of the Peoples of Russia promises all nationalities the right to "free self-determination."

NOVEMBER 12 (25): Elections to Constituent Assembly begin, as scheduled by Provisional Government. Bolsheviks, who win most cities and garrisons, gain 24 percent of the vote, but are outnumbered by Socialist Revolutionaries with 40 percent.

NOVEMBER 14 (27): Decree on Workers' Control gives workers extensive supervisory power in industrial enterprises.

NOVEMBER 28 (DECEMBER 11): Constitutional Democratic Party banned and leaders arrested as "enemies of the people."

DECEMBER 7 (20): Cheka established to fight "counterrevolution and sabotage."

DECEMBER 9–10 (22–23): Agreement on cooperation with Left SRs, who enter Sovnarkom and Cheka collegium.

DECEMBER 12 (25): Lenin's Theses on the Constituent Assembly justifies disbanding Assembly.

DECEMBER 16 (29): Decree abolishes all ranks and titles in the army, recognizes authority of soldiers' committees and councils, and requires democratic election of officers.

LATE DECEMBER: Tsarist generals Mikhail Alekseev and Kornilov establish Volunteer Army to fight against Soviet government.

## 1918

JANUARY 1 (14): Attempt to assassinate Lenin.

JANUARY 5 (18): Constituent Assembly meets in Petrograd. Fifty thousand demonstrate in support, despite ban on demonstrations. Dispersed with force, killing between eight and twenty-one people.

JANUARY 6 (19): Constituent Assembly disbanded. Some protests.

JANUARY 19 (FEBRUARY 1): Patriarch Tikhon anathematizes the Bolsheviks for bringing harm to the church and for "sowing the seeds of hatred, enmity, and fratricidal strife." He calls on believers to defend the church.

JANUARY 24 (FEBRUARY 6): Adoption of new calendar, to begin

January 31 (Old Style), in order that Russia "calculate time" in same way as "almost all cultured nations."

FEBRUARY 18 (New Style): After unsuccessful peace negotiations, German and Austrian troops resume offensive against Russia. Following rapid success, Germans add new territorial demands to peace terms.

MARCH 3: At Brest-Litovsk, Russians agree to peace terms, which Lenin admits are "obscene." Provokes widespread dissent in party and society.

EARLY MARCH: Capital moved to Moscow.

MARCH: Meetings of factory deputies in Petrograd—organized by Menshevik-led Assembly of Factory Plenipotentiaries—protest worsening economic conditions and Bolshevik rule.

MARCH 8: Russian Social Democratic Workers' Party (Bolshevik) renamed Russian Communist Party (Bolshevik).

MARCH 9: Allied forces land at Murmansk.

MARCH 14: Left SRs quit government in protest against Brest-Litovsk. During April–June, SRs increasingly critical of Bolshevik policies.

APRIL 4: "Left Communists"—based in Moscow party organization and including Nikolai Bukharin—issue manifesto criticizing Soviet foreign and economic policies as insufficiently revolutionary and democratic.

MAY 13: To end food shortages, declaration of struggle against "greedy kulaks and wealthy peasants," who are accused of hoarding and speculating in grain.

MAY 20: Decree creates armed "food supply detachments" to collect grain from peasants.

MAY 22: Rebellion of Czechoslovak Legion (army of former Czech and Slovak war prisoners trying to return to the front via Vladivostok) begins after government attempts to disarm them.

MAY–JUNE: Meetings of workers' representatives in Petrograd and Moscow protest economic breakdown and Bolshevik authoritarianism toward workers and peasants and demand reconvening of Constituent Assembly and new elections to Soviets.

EARLY JUNE: British troops land at Archangel.

JUNE 7–8: Czech Legion takes Samara, after which deputies to Constituent Assembly form an anti-Bolshevik socialist government (Committee of Members of the Constituent Assembly, or Komuch).

JUNE 11: Committees of the Village Poor established to intensify class struggle in villages.

JUNE 14: After new elections bring large numbers of Mensheviks and right SRs into local Soviets, Central Executive Committee expels these parties from its ranks and advises local Soviets to do the same.

JUNE 16: Capital punishment reintroduced.

JUNE 28: Nationalization of industry ordered.

JULY 2: Assembly of Factory Plenipotentiaries calls unsuccessful political strike in Petrograd.

JULY 5–6: Left SR uprisings in a few provincial cities.

JULY 6: Assassination of German ambassador von Mirbach by Left SR, followed by Left SR insurrection in Moscow (suppressed July 7).

JULY 16: Gorky's *Novaia zhizn'* permanently closed.

NIGHT OF JULY 16–17: Execution of Nicholas II and imperial family in Ekaterinburg.

# ACKNOWLEDGMENTS

The search for materials for this book required visits to a number of American and European libraries. I should like to express my deep gratitude to the very helpful librarians of the Hoover Institute, the University of California, the Library of Congress, the New York Public Library, Columbia University, Princeton University, Helsinki University Library, the British Museum, and the Institute for the Study of the USSR in Munich. I am equally grateful to the Princeton University Committee on Research in the Humanities and Social Sciences for its generous financial support of the project in all its stages.

For their cooperation in revising the English text I extend special thanks to my undergraduate assistants Alan C. Lopez and Stephen T. Kerr who worked on the first draft of the manuscript, to the graduate student James G. Kelso Russell who helped edit the final version, and to my colleagues Clarence F. Brown and Richard T. Burgi, and my friend Alexander Beck who read parts of the translation and made valuable improvements and suggestions. To Mrs. H. Elizabeth Skaar goes my appreciation of her efficient typing, her patience and understanding.

For all shortcomings in the translation and notes the responsibility is, of course, mine.

H. E.

# CONCERNING DATES
# AND TRANSLATION

To facilitate the work of those who may wish to check on historical events mentioned in the text or notes, the dates of both the Julian calendar and the Gregorian calendar were retained exactly as they appeared in various publications. In some cases a missing date was added. Until February 1918 Russia used the Julian calendar which in the twentieth century ran thirteen days behind the Gregorian calendar adopted in the West. In my comments I followed the Gregorian calendar or gave both dates.

Notes are to be found at the end of the book, numbered consecutively. Titles of some books and articles appearing in the notes were translated into English when it was felt that this might help the reader who is unfamiliar with Russian. Obvious misprints in the original were corrected in translation.

H. E.

# ESSAYS

*from Novaya Zhizn*

# REVOLUTION AND CULTURE

*Novaya Zhizn, No. 1,*
*April 18 (May 1), 1917*

If we try to take in, at a single glance, all the apparently diverse activities of the monarchist regime in the realm of "internal policy," the meaning of these activities will appear before us as an all-out effort by the bureaucracy to check the quantitative and qualitative development of our thinking material.

The old rulers were shiftless and giftless, but their instinct of self-preservation correctly showed them that their most dangerous enemy was the human brain, and, consequently, by all means available to them, they tried to hamper or distort the growth of the country's intellectual forces. In this criminal activity they were successfully aided by a church enslaved by the bureaucracy and, no less successfully, by a society psychologically unbalanced as well as, in the last years, completely submissive to force.

The war revealed with terrifying clarity the results of this prolonged dampening of spirit. Before an educated and superbly organized enemy, Russia stood feeble and unarmed. People who had shouted so boastfully and disgustingly that Russia had risen "to liberate Europe from the fetters of a false civilization through the spirit of the true culture"—these people, probably sincere and therefore all the more unfortunate, buttoned their overly eloquent lips in haste and embarrassment. "The spirit of the true culture" turned out to be the stench of every kind of ignorance, detestable egotism, rotten laziness and slovenliness.

In a country lavishly endowed with natural wealth and

talent, complete anarchy in all spheres of culture has sur-
faced as a result of the country's spiritual destitution. Industry and technology are in the embryonic stage and
without a firm link to science; science itself is somewhere
in the backyard, in darkness, and under the hostile surveillance of civil servants; art, restricted and distorted by censorship, has broken away from society and is absorbed in
the search for new forms, having lost its vital, exciting,
and ennobling content.

Everywhere, within man and without, there is devastation, instability, chaos, and evidence of some kind of prolonged rout of Mamay.[1] The legacy left to the revolution
by the monarchy is terrible.

And no matter how ardently one might wish to say a
word of well-meaning consolation, the truth of stark reality does not allow consolation, and one must say in all
sincerity that in its striving to decapitate Russia spiritually, the monarchist regime achieved almost complete
success.

The revolution has overthrown the monarchy, true! But
perhaps this means that the revolution simply has driven
the skin disease inside the organism. By no means should
we think that the revolution has spiritually cured or enriched Russia. And old and not unwise proverb says: "Illness comes in pounds but leaves in pinches"; the process
of intellectual enrichment of a country is an extremely
slow one. Even so, we need it; and the revolution, represented by its leading forces, should right now, without
delay, assume the responsibility of creating such conditions, institutions, and organizations as will engage, ur-
gently and persistently, in the development of the country's intellectual forces.

Intellectual force is qualitatively the first and foremost
productive force, and concern for its rapid growth should
be the ardent concern of all classes.

Together we must undertake the work of developing all aspects of culture; the revolution has demolished the barriers standing in the way of free creativity, and now it is up to us to show, to ourselves and to the world, our gifts, talents, and our genius. Our salvation is in work, but let us also take delight in that work.

"The world was created not by word but by deed";[2] this is excellently put and is the indisputable truth.

## UNTIMELY THOUGHTS

*Novaya Zhizn, No. 2,*
*April 20 (May 3), 1917*

The new structure of political life demands from us a new structure of the soul.

Of course, one cannot be reformed in two months; however, the sooner we take the trouble to cleanse ourselves of the grime and filth of the past the stronger our spiritual health will be and the more productive the work of creating new forms of social existence.

We live in a turmoil of political emotions, in the chaos of a struggle for power; this struggle arouses, along with good feelings, some very dark instincts. This is natural, yet it cannot but threaten us with a certain distortion of the psyche, with its artificial development in one direction. Politics is the soil in which the nettle of poisonous enmity, evil suspicions, shameless lies, slander, morbid ambitions, and disrespect for the individual grows rapidly and luxuriantly. Name anything bad in man and it is precisely in the soil of political struggle that it grows with particular liveliness and abundance.

In order not to be suffocated by emotions of one kind, one should not neglect emotions of another kind.

Enmity between people is not a normal phenomenon; the finest of our emotions and the greatest of our ideas are directed precisely toward the elimination of social enmity in the world. I would call the finest of these emotions and thoughts "socal idealism"—it is its strength that enables us to overcome the vileness of life and to strive untiringly and stubbornly for justice, for the beauty of life, and for freedom. On this path we have created heroes, martyrs for the sake of freedom, the finest people on earth; and all that is wonderful in us has been fostered by this striving. The good qualities in our soul are most successfully and forcefully awakened by the power of art. Just as science is the intellect of the world, art is its soul. Politics and religion divide people into separate groups; art, revealing in man that which is common to all humanity, unites us. Nothing corrects the soul of man as gently and swiftly as the influence of art and science.

———•———

The right of the proletariat to be hostile to other classes is fully justified. But at the same time it is precisely the proletariat that is bringing into our life the great and beneficent idea of a new culture, the idea of a universal brotherhood.

Therefore, it is precisely the proletariat that must be the first to discard as unfit the old ways of treating man; it is precisely the proletariat that must most persistently strive for the broadening and deepening of the soul, repository of the impressions of our existence. For the proletarian the gifts of art and science should have the highest value; for him they are not an idle pastime but the means of fathoming the mysteries of life.

It is strange for me to see that the proletariat, represented by its thinking and functioning organ, "The Council of Workers' and Soldiers' Deputies," takes such an indifferent and uncaring attitude toward the dispatch—to the front, to the slaughter—of soldiers who are musicians, artists, actors, and other people indispensable to the proletariat's soul. Clearly, in sending her talents to the slaughter, the country is exhausting her heart, and the people are tearing out the best pieces of their flesh. And what for?

Perhaps only so that a talented Russian should kill a talented German artist.

Just think, what an absurdity this is, what a terrible mockery of the people! Think also what a great amount of energy is spent by the people to create a talented person who expresses their feelings, the thoughts of their soul.

Can it be that this accursed slaughter must turn even artists, who are dear to us, into murderers and corpses?

## UNTIMELY THOUGHTS

*Novaya Zhizn, No. 3,*
*April 21 (May 4), 1917*

We strove for freedom of speech in order to be able to speak and write the truth.

But to speak the truth is the most difficult of all arts, for in its "pure" form, not connected with the interests of individuals, groups, classes, or nations, truth is almost completely unsuitable for use by the Philistine and is unacceptable to him. Such is the accursed peculiarity of "pure" truth, but at the same time it is the best and most vital truth for us.

Let us set ourselves the task of telling the truth about the German atrocities. I hope that we can quite accurately establish the facts concerning the brutal treatment by the German soldiers of the soldiers of Russia, France, and

England, as well as of the peaceful populations of Belgium, Serbia, Rumania, and Poland. I have the right to hope that these facts are beyond doubt and as indisputable as the facts of Russian atrocities in Smorgon, in the towns of Galicia, etc. I do not deny that the revolting methods of exterminating people, which are being applied by the Germans, have been allowed for the first time in the business of murder. I cannot deny that the treatment of Russian prisoners of war by the Germans is abominable, for I know that the treatment of German prisoners of war by the old Russian regime was also abominable.

This is the truth; this truth has been created by the war. In war it is necessary to kill as many people as possible— such is the cynical logic of war. Brutality in a fight is unavoidable; have you seen how cruelly children fight in the streets?

"Pure" truth tells us that, in general, brutality is something peculiar to man, a quality which is not alien to him even in peaceful times—if such a thing exists on earth. Let us recall how, in Kiev, Kishinev, and other cities, the good-natured Russian people drove nails into the skulls of Jews; how, in 1906, the workers of Ivanovo-Voznesensk boiled their comrades in cauldrons of scalding water, throwing them in alive; how sadistically gaolers tortured prisoners; how the Black Hundreds[3] tore apart the young female revolutionaries, driving stakes into their sexual organs; let us recall, for a moment, all the bloody shameless deeds of 1906, 1907, 1908.

I am not comparing German atrocities with those common to all mankind or with Russian atrocities in particular. Making use of my freedom of speech, I am simply discussing the truth of the present day, the truth created by war, and the "pure" truth which is of universal significance for all time and which, indeed, is "brighter than the sun," although it often saddens and hurts us.

When condemning a man—German or Russian, it is all the same—we should not forget about "pure" truth, for it is our most precious possession, the brightest flame of our conscious being; the existence of this truth is indicative of the high level of moral demands which man makes on himself.

———— • ————

Fraternization between German and Russian soldiers is taking place at the front; I think this is caused not only by physical fatigue but also by an awakening in the people of a feeling of repugnance for senseless slaughter. I shall not speak about the fact that the glow from the flame of the Russian revolution could not help but kindle bright hopes in the breast of the German soldier.

Perhaps the examples of fraternization between enemies are quantitatively insignificant; this by no means detracts from their moral and cultural significance. Yes, it is apparent that the accursed war, begun by the greed of the classes in command, will be ended by the power of the common sense of the soldiers, i.e., by democracy.

If this happens, it will be something unprecedented, great, almost miraculous, and will give man the right to be proud of himself—his will shall have conquered the most abominable and bloody monster, the monster of war.

General Brusilov,[4] pointing out the "excessive credulity of the Russian soldier," does not believe in the sincerity of the German soldier, who extends the hand of reconciliation to us. The general says in his order:

*"All enemy attempts to make personal contacts with our troops, must always be met with only one answer— the bayonet and bullets."*

And, apparently, this order is being carried out. Yesterday a soldier who returned from the front told me that when our troops meet with the Germans between the trenches to discuss current events, the Russian artillery begins to shoot at them, and the German artillery does the same.

There was an incident when Germans who came up to our barbed wire encountered Russian bullets, and when they started to run back to their side, their own troops began to machine-gun them. I am trying to speak calmly. I know that generals also serve a certain professional "truth" of their own and that even recently this "truth" of theirs was the only one that had freedom of speech.

But now the other truth can also speak as freely, the truth free from crimes, born of man's aspirations for unity, and incapable of serving the ignoble business of stirring up hate and enmity, the business of exterminating people.

Just think, reader, what will happen to you if the truth of a mad beast overpowers the sane truth of man?

## UNTIMELY THOUGHTS

*Novaya Zhizn, No. 4,*
*April 22 (May 5), 1917*

Some tens of millions of the sturdiest and healthiest people have been torn away from the great business of life—from the development of the productive forces of the earth—and have been sent to kill one another.

Having dug themselves into the ground, they live in rain and snow, in filth, in cramped conditions; they are being worn out by disease and eaten by vermin; they live like beasts, lying in wait for one another in order to kill.

They kill on land and sea, destroying daily hundreds and hundreds of the best and most cultured people of our planet, people who have created what is most precious on earth, European culture.

Thousands of villages and scores of towns are being destroyed, the centuries-old labor of a great many generations has been undone, forests have been burnt out and cut down, roads have been ruined, bridges have been blown up, and the treasures of the earth, created by the persistent and painful labor of man, lie in ashes and dust. The fertile topsoil has been destroyed by the explosions of mines, mortars, and shells and has been gouged with trenches; barren subsoil has been exposed, all the land is churned up and is polluted by the rotting flesh of the guiltless dead. Women are raped and children are killed—there is no infamy that is not permitted by war, there is no crime that is not justified by it.

This is the third year we have been living in a bloody nightmare and we have been brutalized and have lost our senses; art arouses a thirst for blood, murder, and destruction; science, violated by militarism, obediently serves the business of the mass annihilation of people.

This war is the suicide of Europe!

Just think how many healthy, splendidly endowed brains have been spilled out on the filthy ground during this war, how many sensitive hearts have stopped beating!

This senseless extermination of man by man and the destruction of the fruits of great human labors are not limited to material damage alone—no!

Tens of thousands of maimed soldiers will not forget about their enemies for a long time, until their very death. Through their tales about the war they will pass on their hatred to children, who for three years have been fed on impressions of the daily horror. A great deal of enmity has been sown on earth during these years; this sowing will produce an abundant growth!

And yet for such a long time and so eloquently we have been told about the brotherhood of men, about the unity of mankind's interests. Who, then, is guilty of this diabolical deceit, of creating this bloody chaos?

Let us not search for the guilty ones only among others, let us speak the bitter truth: we are all guilty of this crime, each and every one of us.

Imagine for a moment that there are sensible people in the world who are sincerely concerned with the building of a normal life and who are confident of their creative powers; imagine, for example, that in the interests of the development of our industry it is necessary for us Russians to dig a Riga-Kherson canal in order to link the Baltic Sea with the Black Sea—a project about which even Peter the Great dreamed. And so instead of sending millions to be slaughtered, we send a portion of them to this work which is vital to the country and to all of its people. I am confident that those killed during three years of war would have been able in this time to drain the thousands of versts of swamps in our country, to irrigate the Hungry Steppe and other deserts, to connect the rivers of the Trans-Urals with the river Kama, to lay a road through the Caucaus mountain ridge, and to accomplish still other great feats of labor for the good of our native land.

But we are expending millions of lives and enormous reserves of working energy on murder and destruction. Great quantities of terribly expensive explosives are being produced; wiping out hundreds of thousands of lives, these explosives vanish into thin air. From exploded shells nonetheless remain pieces of metal out of which we shall at least forge nails some day; but all these melinites, lyddites, and dinitrotoluenes are literally "scattering to the winds" the country's wealth. The question is not of billions of rubles, but of millions of lives that are being senselessly destroyed by the monster of Greed and Stupidity.

When I think about this, a cold despair grips my heart and I feel like yelling madly to the people:

Wretched ones, have pity on yourselves!

## ON MURDER

*Novaya Zhizn, No. 5,*
*April 23 (May 6), 1917*

The bright wings of our young freedom are bespattered with innocent blood.

I don't know who shot at the people the day before yesterday on the Nevsky, but whoever these men may be they are evil and stupid, men poisoned by the venoms of the old, rotten regime.[5]

It is criminal and vile to kill one another now that we all have the wonderful right to argue honestly and to disagree with one another honestly. Those who think otherwise are incapable of feeling and realizing that they are free people. Murder and violence are the arguments of despotism; they are base arguments and they are powerless, for to violate somebody else's will or to kill a man does not mean and never can mean killing an idea, proving a thought wrong, or an opinion erroneous.

The great happiness of freedom must not be darkened by crimes against the individual; otherwise we will kill freedom with our own hands.

We must understand, it is time for us to understand, that the most dreadful enemy of freedom and justice is within us; it is our stupidity, our cruelty, and all that chaos of dark, anarchistic feelings, that chaos which has been cultivated in our souls by the monarchy's shameless oppression, by its cynical cruelty.

Are we capable of understanding this?

If we are incapable, if we cannot refrain from the most flagrant use of force on man, then we have no freedom. It is simply a word which we do not have the strength to invest with the proper content. I say that our inherent enemies are stupidity and cruelty.

Are we able, are we trying to combat them?

This is not a rhetorical question, but a question of how profoundly and sincerely we understand the new conditions of political life, the new evalution of man's significance and of his role in the world.

It is time to cultivate in ourselves a feeling of aversion to murder, a feeling of revulsion towards it.

Of course, I am not forgetting that we may possibly— more than once—have to defend our freedom and our rights with weapons, indeed we may!

But on April 21, revolvers in threateningly outstretched hands were ridiculous things, and there was something childish in this gesture, which, unfortunately, ended in a crime.

Yes, a crime against free man.

Is it possible that the memory of our vile past, the memory of how hundreds and thousands of us were shot in the streets, has implanted in us, too, the calm attitude of the executioner toward the violent death of a man?

I cannot find harsh enough words to reproach those who try to prove something with bullets, bayonets, or a fist in the face.

Were not these the arguments against which we protested, were not these the means of repressing our will, the means by which we were kept in shameful slavery?

And now, having freed ourselves from slavery externally, we continue to live dominated internally by the feelings of slaves.

I repeat—our most merciless enemy is our past.

Citizens! Is it possible that we are unable to find within

ourselves the strength to get rid of its infection, to throw off is filth, to forget its bloody outrages? A greater maturity, a greater thoughtfulness and wariness with respect to ourselves—this is what we need!

The struggle is not over. We must conserve our strength, unite our energies in one, and not separate them, succumbing to the mood of the moment.

## ON POLEMICS

*Novaya Zhizn, No. 6,*
*April 25 (May 8), 1917*

Following the tradition established in the epoch of Tsarist politics, certain journalists continue to use old methods in their polemics and try to "belt" a person they dislike "up the throat," "in the bread basket" and "in the kidneys."

Of course, the newspapers are not the place for calm academic debates, but nonetheless I think that a free press ought to develop a feeling of respect for the individual, and if it becomes necessary to hurt one's neighbor, he should be hurt only when he has given sufficient reason for pinches, kicks, slaps, and other methods of social pedagogy.

In the struggle of ideas it is not at all necessary to strike a person, even though he may be the bearer and embodiment of this or that idea. I resolutely protest in every possible way against personal attacks in polemics, without forgetting that I myself have been guilty of such attacks.

——— • ———

The newspaper *Rech* (Speech) expresses—I would say —bewilderment concerning my alleged leap from the newspaper *Luch* (Ray) to *Novaya Zhizn.* I deem it necessary to explain.

Yes, I tried to organize *Luch* with M. V. Bernatsky, P. G. Vinogradov, and other persons whom I had long ago come to respect.

*Luch* was meant to serve as the organ of the Radical-Democratic party. I also took some part in the work of the party's organizing committee, confident that this party was necessary in Russia and that it would draw in—insofar as possible—all the unorganized mass of people between the Cadets on the right and the socialists on the left. As early as 1910 I began to think about organizing such a party; later I spoke about this with G. V. Plekhanov and, as I remember, he reacted favorably to this idea, recognizing the need for the organization of such a party.

Organizing *Luch,* I deliberately imposed on myself certain restraints;[6] I suppressed myself to some extent, it may be said. I do not consider such suppression criminal, for only one person suffers from it—the one who does the suppressing.

Some of my honorable colleagues from *Luch* also acknowledged restraints as compulsory for themselves.

Because of some complex and obscure obstacles the newspaper *Luch* never came out. At the present time, when even our constitutionalists—"His Majesty's Opposition"[7]—have turned republican and the broad democratic masses follow the working class, I regard the Radical-Democratic party as, perhaps, already superfluous.

———— • ————

It is very likely that there will appear righteous ones who will not fail to rebuke me for such "flexibility." They, of course, will name it differently. Not being a stingy person by nature, I shall give the righteous ones even more

material for burning me on a pyre of fiery words. In my
opinion, a man should do all the good and necessary
things he can, even though the "deed" may not completely
harmonize with his fundamental beliefs. For a long time I
have felt that I have been living in a country where a vast
majority of the population are windbags and idlers, and all
the work of my life amounts, in essence, to stimulating in
people the ability to act.

It is already seventeen years that I have considered myself a Social-Democrat and I have served the great aims of
this party insofar as I was able, without refusing assistance
to other parties and without disdaining any meaningful
activity. People who have become like wood and stone
under the pressure of a faith professed by them have never
won my sympathies. I can admire theoretically their strict
consistency, but I cannot like them.

I shall say more: I consider myself a heretic everywhere. In my political views one can probably find no
small number of contradictions which I cannot and do not
wish to reconcile, because I feel that for the harmony of
my soul, for my spiritual tranquility and comfort, I should
have to kill precisely that part of my soul which most
passionately and painfully loves the living, sinning, and—
forgive me—pitiful Russian man. I think I have said quite
enough to enable the righteous ones "to cut me to rib-
bons" by tongue-lashing.

———— • ————

Mr. Ivanov-Razumnik of *Delo Naroda* (The People's
Cause) reproaches me for signing the appeal to the German scientists.[8] I do not remember the text of this appeal
and I am not even sure I read it. My signature on it is one
of those accidents in which Russian life abounds and
which are explained by a careless attitude toward man.

But I am not trying to justify myself and I am not accusing anyone. I am prepared to sign yet another appeal if it condemns the participation of men of science in the fratricidal and senseless slaughter. When science invades or is forcibly drawn into the bloody filth of politics, it is not only the purity and freedom of science that suffers but also the finest ideals and hopes of mankind, and the reasoning power of the entire world is destroyed.

I shall conclude all this by expressing my respect and admiration for the people who never make mistakes, who do not get carried away by anything, and who, in general, conduct themselves in exemplary fashion.

Hallowed be their names!


# UNTIMELY THOUGHTS

*Novaya Zhizn, No. 8,*
*April 27 (May 10), 1917*

In the very first days of the revolution some shameless creatures threw into the streets heaps of filthy pamphlets, disgusting stories on the subject of "court life." These pamphlets deal with "the autocratic Alix,"[9] "the Licentious Grishka,"[10] with Vyrubova[11] and other figures of the gloomy past.

I shall not set forth the contents of these pamphlets—they are unbelievably filthy, stupid, and lewd. But the young people feed on this poisonous filth; the pamphlets have a ready sale both on the Nevsky and in the outlying areas of the city. We must combat this poison—I don't know how, exactly—but we must combat it, especially since along with this foul "literature" of morbid and sadistic fabrications, there are on the book market too few of those publications which are really needed at this moment.

Obscene "literature" is especially dangerous, especially contagious precisely now when all the dark instincts are aroused in people, and feelings of indignation and insult are still persistent—feelings which give rise to vengefulness. We should keep in mind that we are experiencing not only economic dislocation but also that social decomposition which always and inevitably arises out of economic collapse.

It is unquestionable that we have the right to place part of the blame for our being impotent and untalented on those forces which have always sought to keep us far removed from the active work of social construction. It is unquestionable that Russia was and is still educated by teachers even less gifted politically than the average man in the street. It is indisputable that our every attempt toward independent action met ugly resistance from the regime, morbidly vain and occupied solely with the protection of its position in the country. All this is unquestionable; we should say, however, facing up to the truth, that there is no reason why we should be praised. Where, when, and in what, during the recent years of furious abuse of Russian society in its entirety—of its reason, will, and conscience—in what and how did society manifest its resistance to the dark and evil forces of life? How was its civic consciousness manifested, the consciousness denied in hooligan fashion by all those to whom the right of this denial was given? And in what, beside eloquence and epigrams, was our insulted feeling of self-esteem expressed?

No, the truth must be known: we ourselves are morally off balance no less than are the forces hostile to us.

We are living in days of awesome events, the extent of which, apparently, cannot be rightly understood by us, and the tragedy of these days is not sensed. Least of all at this time should we pay attention to adventures of a criminal nature, no matter how entertaining they may be on the surface. It is very likely that we should be prepared to accept more than one such adventure, but we should not forget that the fact of the crime in itself is not as important as its educational, socio-pedagogical impact.

History educates the spiritually healthy and destroys the unhealthy, but a scandal can corrupt the former and does distort to an even greater extent the world view of the latter. There are too many spiritually unhealthy people among us, and events threaten to increase their number further. The knife, revolver, and all other things of this kind are only the props of the melodrama; not by these is a normal life created, and it is time to understand that history and scandal—no matter how loud the latter might be—have nothing in common.

The most frightening people are those who do not know what they want; we, therefore, must devote all our energy to the business of making our wishes completely clear. We are faced with the necessity of performing some kind of historical exploit, and any exploit requires a concentration of the will.

How can we be carried away by filthy cheap novels when around us all over the world an awesome tragedy is taking place! All the mighty forces of world history have been set in motion, all the man-beasts have broken loose from the chains of culture; they have torn its thin vestments to pieces and revoltingly stripped themselves naked. This phenomenon, equivalent to a catastrophe, is shaking the buttresses of social relations to their foundation. And we must summon to real life all the finest reasoning, all our will, in order to correct the consequences of our tragic neglect of ourselves, a neglect which has produced a terrible blunder.

Mankind has not labored for centuries over the creation of tolerable conditions of existence so that what has been created shall be destroyed in the twentieth century, A.D.

We must learn sensible lessons from senseless events,

bearing in mind that all that is called Destiny or Fate is none other than the result of our thoughtlessness and our mistrust of ourselves; we should know that all that is created on earth is created by its sole Master and Laborer— Man.

## UNTIMELY THOUGHTS

*Novaya Zhizn, No. 12,*
*May 2 (15), 1917*

Without waiting for the decision of the Council of Soldiers' Deputies on the question of sending actors, painters, and musicians to the front, the Battalion Committee of the Izmaylovsky Regiment is sending forty-three artists into the trenches, among whom are extraordinarily talented and culturally valuable people.

All these people have no idea of military service, they have had no combat training. They don't know how to shoot. Today, for the first time, they are being taken to the firing range and by Wednesday they will have to go off to the front. Thus these valuable people will go to the slaughter without knowing how to defend themselves.

I don't know who makes up the Battalion Committee of the Izmaylovsky Regiment but I am sure that these people "know not what they do."

For to send talented artists to war is as wasteful and stupid as to put gold horseshoes on a dray horse. And to send them without having taught them the science of war is a death sentence on innocent people. It was for such treatment of man that we cursed the Tsarist regime. Precisely because of this we overthrew it.

The demagogues and lackeys of the crowd will probably cry out to me:

"But what about equality?"

Of course, I keep this in mind. I, too, spent no small amount of energy to prove the necessity of political and economic equality for the people; I know that only when he possesses equality, will man receive an opportunity to be more honest, kinder, more humane. The revolution was made so that man might live better and so that he himself might become better.

But I must say that for me the writer Leo Tolstoy, or the musician Sergey Rakhmaninov, or any talented man, are not equal to the Battalion Committee of the Izmaylovsky soldiers.

If Tolstoy himself had felt the desire to send a bullet through somebody's head or to stick him in the belly with a bayonet, then certainly the devil would laugh and idiots would rejoice together with the devil, but people for whom talent is a most wonderful gift of nature, the basis of culture, and the pride of the country—these people would once again weep bloody tears.

No, I protest with all my soul against making poor soldiers out of talented people.

Addressing myself to the Council of Soldiers' Deputies, I ask them: Do they consider the resolution of the Battalion Committee of the Izmaylovsky Regiment right? Do they think that Russia must throw the best pieces of her heart—her artists, her talented people—into the insatiable jaws of war?

And, having wasted our best brains, with what shall we live?

## A NIGHTMARE
(From a Diary)

*Novaya Zhizn, No. 13,
May 3 (16), 1917*

Small, slender, and elegantly dressed, she came to me in
the morning when the sun was looking into the window of
my room; she came and sat so that the rays of the sun
embraced her neck and shoulders and made her fair hair
seem golden. Very youthful she was, and, judging by her
manners, well-bred.

Her hazel eyes smiled with the nervous smile of a child
who is embarrassed by something and somewhat angry
because it cannot overcome its embarrassment.

Pulling a glove off her thin hand and looking at me
from under her eyebrows, she began in a soft voice:

"I know my intrusion is rude; you are so busy, indeed,
you are very busy."

"Yes."

"Of course," she said, nodding her head and knitting
her pretty eyebrows. "Now everyone acts as if he's going
to move to a new apartment. . . ."

She sighed and, looking at her foot in its expensive
shoe, continued:

"I shall not detain you, I only need five minutes. I want
you to save me."

Smiling, I said:

"If a person thinks he can be saved in five minutes, he,
in my opinion, is far from perishing. . . ."

But this woman, looking right into my face with clear
eyes, said in a businesslike manner:

"You see, I was an agent of the Secret Police. . . . Oh,
how you . . . what eyes you have. . . ."

I was silent, smiling stupidly and not believing her, and

I tried to overcome some dark, convulsive desire. I was
sure she had brought a poem or a story.

"It is nasty, isn't it?" she asked quietly.

"You are joking."

"No, I am not joking. Is it very nasty?"

Overwhelmed, I muttered:

"You've just said it."

"Yes, of course, I know," she said sighing, and sat
down in one of the more comfortable armchairs. A
grimace of disappointment appeared on her face. The
small fingers of her graceful hand slowly played with the
chain of her medallion. The rays of the sun tinted her ear
the color of coral. All of her was so spring-like, festive. In
a hasty, confused, and offhand manner, as if telling about
a prank, she began:

"This happened three years ago . . . not quite. I had an
affair; I was in love with an officer, he later became an
adjutant with the gendarmerie, and well, then . . . I had
just graduated from the institute[12] and enrolled in the
women's college. Various serious people involved in politics gathered at my house. . . . I don't like politics, I don't
understand it. He kept asking me about them. For the
sake of love anything is possible—do you agree? You
have to permit everything if you are in love. I loved him
very much. And those people were so unpleasant, they
criticized everything. Also I did not like my classmates at
the college. Except one."

Her childlike babble convinced me more and more that
she did not understand her guilt, that crime was for her
only a prank unpleasant to recall.

I asked:

"Were you paid?"

"Oh, no. However. . . ."

She thought for a few seconds, looking at the ring on
her hand. "He gave me various things—this ring and

medallion, and other things. . . . Perhaps that was pay-
ment, wasn't it?"

Tears appeared in her eyes.

"He is a dishonorable man, I know. Listen," she softly
cried out, "if my name appears in print, what shall I do?
You must save me, I am young, I love life, people, and
books so much. . . ."

I looked at this woman and the sun, on this spring day,
seemed wrong for her and for me. A gloomy day, fog
outside the windows, slush and mud in the streets, silent
and dejected people—that would have been more in
harmony with her story than the springtime brightness of
the sky and kind human voices.

What can one say to such a person? I could find nothing
that would reach the heart and mind of the woman in the
light blouse cut very low in front. The gold ring with a
blood-red ruby fit her finger tightly; she admired the play
of the sun on the facets of the stone and carelessly strung
word after word on the capricious thread of her sensations.

"Bad things are often done out of love," sounded her
sweet little voice as if repeating banal lines from the
cinema screen. Then she leaned toward me with a strange
look in her eyes.

"I cannot help you in any way."

"You can't?" she asked quietly.

"I am absolutely sure that I cannot."

"But, perhaps."

Tenderly, she spoke words about the goodness of man,
about his sensitive heart, about how Christ and somebody
else taught us to forgive sinful people—all these words
astonishingly irrelevant and repellent.

In the opening of her blouse I saw her breasts and I
involuntarily closed my eyes. A scoundrel who has corrupted this creature, a trader in honest people, has

caressed these breasts, experiencing the same delight as an honest man caressing his beloved. It is stupid but I feel like asking somebody: is this really fair?

"Just look how young I am, but lately I have felt an old woman. Everybody is happy, everybody is rejoicing, but I cannot. Why?"

Her question sounded sincere. She cringed, pressing her hands against her knees and biting her lips; her face paled and the gleam faded from her eyes. She was like a flower crushed by someone's heavy heel.

"Did you betray many?"

"I didn't count them, naturally. But I told him only about those whom I especially disliked."

"Did you know what the gendarmes did to them?"

"No, that didn't interest me. Of course, I heard that some were put in prison or exiled somewhere, but I was not concerned with politics. . . ."

She spoke about this indifferently, as about the distant, uninteresting past. She was calm; not a single hysterical shriek, no cry of a tormented conscience—nothing that would indicate suffering. Probably after a slight tiff with her sweetheart, she felt much worse, more upset.

After talking for two or three more minutes, she stood up, nodded graciously to me and, with the light step of a woman who loves to dance, started toward the door, flinging at me as she went:

"How cruel people are, if you think about it."

I felt like saying to her:

"You are a little late thinking about that."

But I kept silent, with an enormous effort of will concealing my anguished wrath.

Stopping in the doorway and elegantly turning her head toward me, she said over her shoulder:

"But what will happen to my relatives and friends when my name appears in print? Just think!"

"Why didn't you think about that yourself?"

"But who could have thought a revolution would come along?" she exclaimed. "So, you cannot offer anything to me?"

I said quietly:

"To you—nothing."

She left.

I knew Gurovich, Azef, Serebryakova, and a great number of other traitors.[13] From lists of them which were recently published, I learned that more than a dozen were my acquaintances; they called me "comrade" and, of course, I trusted them. When their names were exposed one after another, I felt that someone ruthlessly evil spat with irony in my heart. This is one of the vilest mockeries of my faith in man.

But the terrible crime is the crime of a child.

When this woman left, I thought with the dull calm of despair:

"Isn't it time for me to shoot myself?"

Two or three days later she again appeared, dressed in black and even more elegant. In mourning she seemed more adult, and her pretty, fresh face seemed more earnest, more severe. She apparently liked colored stones; her blouse was pinned with an almandine brooch, and on her neck a large imitation ruby hung from a gold chain.

"I realize that you are disgusted," she said, "but I have no one to ask for advice, except you. I had grown to believe you, it seemed to me that you loved people, even sinners, but you are so cold, so callous . . . it's strange!"

"Yes, it's strange," I repeated and I laughed thinking how shamelessly life abuses people. And I felt guilty of having wronged this woman in some way. In what way? I did not comprehend.

She told me there was a man who was ready to marry her.

"He is middle-aged, perhaps even an old man, but what can I do? You see, if I change my name, I shall no longer exist."

And, smiling, she repeated almost gaily:

"I won't be what I am now, will I?"

I felt like saying: "Madam. Even if the earth begins to break up, flying off into space as dust, and all the people go mad with fear, I daresay you will nonetheless remain the same as you are. And if peace, love, and as yet unexperienced happiness descend on earth by the miracle of our will, I think you will still remain your own self."

But it was useless talking to her; she believed too strongly that all is forgiven a beautiful woman.

I said: "If you think that it will help you. . . ."

"Oh, I don't know what to think. I'm simply scared."

She spoke in the already familiar tone of a spoiled child who has been naughty and wants its mischief forgotten.

I kept silent.

Then she said: "Would you give me away at my wedding? I have no father, that is, he is divorced from my mummy. I don't love him and don't see him. Please do it!"

I shook my head. Then she got down on her knees and said:

"But listen, listen."

There was something theatrical in her gestures, and she obviously tried to remind me that she was a woman, she wanted me to feel my maleness. Throwing her head back in a beautiful gesture and thrusting out her breast, she looked like a poisonous flower; her pretty little head resembled a pistil in the black petals of the lace of her blouse.

"Do you want me to be your mistress, your *fille de joie?*" she asked in French for some reason.

I moved away from her. Lithely getting up on her feet, she said:

"Your talk about love and about compassion is a lie. It's all a lie. All! You have written about women so . . . in what you say they are always right—that is also a lie! Good-bye!"

Then, leaving, she said confidently and angrily:

"You have ruined me."

She disappeared, having left a black shadow sticking to my soul. Perhaps these are inappropriate and showy words, but she had thrown me into a thorny brier patch of tormenting thoughts about her and about myself. I don't know how to say what I felt in any other way. An oppressive black shadow stuck to my soul. Very likely, these are stupid words. Like all words.

Am I not the one who is responsible for all that vileness of life which is seething all around me, am I not responsible for that life which was basely besmirched at its dawn by the filth of betrayal?

The torrent of a liberated people roared in the street; the bee-like buzzing of hundreds of voices was heard through the window panes. The city was like a hive in the spring when the bees awaken; it seemed to me that I smelled the fresh, sharp odor of new words and that I felt how the honey and wax of new ideas was being created everywhere.

This made me glad, it really did.

But I felt myself nailed to some rotten wall, crucified on it with the sharp thoughts about the ravished woman whom I could not help, could not help in any way, at any time. . . .

## UNTIMELY THOUGHTS

*Novaya Zhizn, No. 16,*
*May 6 (19), 1917*

Not long ago, a novelist lamented the fact that there is no
romanticism in the Russian revolution, that it has not created a Théroigne de Méricourt and has not produced
heroes, illustrious people.[14]

Well, perhaps Théroigne did not appear because we did
not besiege the Bastille; but if we had done that, I think
that out of fifty-thousand Petrograd *"filles de joie"* some
heroines would probably have turned up. But, generally
speaking, heroes in our country have always been scarce,
if we except those whom we ourselves clumsily invented:
Susanin, the merchant Igolkin, the soldier who rescued
Peter the Great, Kuzma Kryuchkov,[15] and other heroes
of physical action, so to speak.

While engaged in polemics one can, of course, forget
about heroes of the spirit, about people who, by turning
their lives into a great and difficult exploit, have finally led
Russia out of a spellbound reign of lawlessness and violence.

But I think that romanticism, nevertheless, has not
dried up and romanticists are alive, if by calling someone
a romanticist we can honor—or insult?—a person passionately in love with his idea, his dream.

A few days ago just such a romanticist—a peasant of
the Perm province—sent me a letter, the following lines of
which deeply moved me:

> Yes, not everyone can bear the truth; at times the truth is
> so grim that it is frightful to remain eye to eye with it.
> Doesn't one become frighened when one sees how dirty
> hands and pocket interests are seizing the great and sacred

banner of socialism . . . ? The peasantry, greedy for property, will receive land and turn away, having torn up for
leggings the banner of Zhelyabov and Breshkovskaya.[16]

A party worker, a student and Social-Democrat, frankly
states that at the present he cannot work for the party
because in his regular job he gets 350 rubles, while the
party won't even pay him 250. Perhaps he would agree to
take a hundred rubles less as a tribute to his "former"
idealism. . . .

Soldiers willingly take up the banner of "peace for the
whole world"; however, they strive for peace not in the
name of the idea of international democracy, but in the
name of their own selfish interests: preservation of life and
hoped-for personal prosperity.

I remember very well my mood when, as a seventeen-
year-old youth, I walked behind a wooden plough under
the hot sun; if I saw a clerk, a priest, or a teacher walking
by, I always asked myself the question: "Why am I working while those people are blissfully idle?" For I recognized
as labor only physical labor, and all my aspirations were
directed toward freeing myself from this labor. I see the
very same thing now in many people who are willingly
joining socialist parties. When I see these "socialists," I feel
like crying, for I want to be a socialist not in words, but in
deeds.

We need leaders who are not afraid to speak the truth to
one's face. And if the socialist press would expose not only
the bourgeoisie, but also those led by the bourgeoisie, it
would stand to gain from this in the future. We have to be
stern and merciless not only with enemies, but also with
friends. The Bible says: "Rebuke a wise man, and he will
love thee."

Here is the voice of an indubitable romanticist, the
voice of a man who feels the organizing force of truth and
loves its soul-purifying fire.

I respectfully bow to this man.[17] Life is hard for people
of his kind, but their lives leave a beautiful imprint.

## UNTIMELY THOUGHTS

*Novaya Zhizn, No. 18,*
*May 9 (22), 1917*

Yes, we are living in anxious, dangerous times—this is borne out with gloomy conviction by the outrages in Samara, Minsk, and Yuriev, by the savage acts of soldiers at railroad stations, and by a whole series of other instances of disorderly behavior, stupidity, and loutishness.

Of course, one should not forget that the cry "the Fatherland is in danger" can be evoked not only by a feeling of sincere anxiety but also out of considerations of party tactics.

It would, however, be a mistake to think that political freedom creates anarchy; no, as I see it, freedom has merely transformed an existing internal disease—the disease of the spirit—into a skin disease. Anarchy has been injected into us by the monarchist regime, and it is from this regime that we have inherited the infection.

And we should bear in mind that the outrages in Yuriev, Minsk, and Samara, for all their ugliness, were not accompanied by murder, whereas the pogroms of Tsarist times, including the "German" pogrom in Moscow[18] were bestially bloody. Recall Kishinev, Odessa, Kiev, Belostok, Baku, Tiflis,[19] and a countless number of abominable murders in dozens of small towns.

I am not consoling anyone, least of all myself, but nonetheless I cannot fail to call the reader's attention to that which, even to a small degree, mitigates the vile and filthy crimes committed by people.

Let us also bear in mind that the very people who now shout louder than anyone "the Fatherland is in danger"

had every reason to shout these words of alarm as far
back as three years ago—in July 1914.[20]

Out of considerations of party and egotistical class
tactics they didn't do it, and for three years the Russian
people were witness to a most foul anarchy generated
from above.

Delving even deeper into the past, we encounter at the
helm of the Russian state Stolypin,[21] an undisputed
anarchist, who was supported by the cheers of precisely
those well-intentioned republicans who now wail loudly
about anarchy and the need to combat it.

Of course, "he who does nothing, does nothing wrong,"
but we have an appalling number of people who, no matter what they do—they do wrong.

Yes, yes—it is always necessary to fight anarchy, but
sometimes one must also know how to conquer his own
fear of the people.

The fatherland would feel itself less in danger if there
were more culture in the fatherland.

Unfortunately, regarding the need for culture and the
form in which we need it, we have, it seems not yet come
to definite decisions; at least these decisions were not clear
to us at the beginning of the war when the Moscow phi-
losophers ingeniously and quite sincerely compared Kant
and Krupp.

One might think that the preaching of an "indigenous"
culture appears among us invariably during periods of
harsh reaction, precisely because we are a people who,
from ancient times, have been conditioned to think and
act "along the line of least resistance."

But however it was, we concerned ourselves least of all
with the development of European culture—experimental
science, free art, and an industry strong in technology.
And it is only natural that the significance of these three
foundations of culture is not understood by the masses.

One of the first tasks of the moment should be the stimulation in the people of ethical and aesthetic emotions, in addition to their already stimulated political emotions. Our artists should at once invade the chaos of the moods of the street with all the power of their talents, and I am sure that the triumphant invasion by beauty of the soul of a somewhat crazed Russian would allay his anxieties, subdue the turbulence of certain not-very-laudable feelings—as, perhaps, greed—and would generally help him become more humane.

But he was given a lot of—excuse me!—bad newspapers at a very high price and nothing else, for the time being.

Both the humanities and sciences can play a great part in the ennobling of instincts, but participation of scientists in the life of the times is even less noticeable than before.

I don't know a single sensibly and convincingly written book in popular literature which tells how great the positive role of industry is in the process of cultural development. And the Russian people have long been in need of such a book.

It is possible to say much more on the subject of the need for persistent cultural work to be immediately undertaken in our country.

It seems to me that the cry "the Fatherland is in danger!" is not as frightening as the cry:

"Citizens! Culture is in danger!"[22]

# UNTIMELY THOUGHTS

*Novaya Zhizn, No. 21,*
*May 12 (25), 1917*

A few days ago I received a letter the contents of which
are as follows:*

Yesterday I read your "Nightmare," and my soul, the
soul of a man who also served in the Secret Police, weeps
from the realization of the hopelessness of my situation, to
which this story awakened me. I won't tell you how I fell
into this filthy pit: that is uninteresting. I will only say that
hunger and the advice of a man who was then close to me
and on trial and who thought that I might be able to
mitigate his fate pushed me to that horrible step.

I will say that I despised myself all the time I served
there and I still despise myself. But—do you know what
hurts? It is that even a sensitive person, such as you, did
not understand, apparently, that each of us secret agents
probably had to burn much of what he felt in his soul. It is
not that we suffered the time we served, but that we
suffered earlier, when there was no way out, that society,
which now throws dirt at us, did not support us, did not
extend a helping hand to us at that time. You know, not
everyone is so strong that he can give everything away,
receiving nothing in return! *If there hadn't been faith in
socialism, in the party—but, you know, I reasoned this
way in my own vile head: the harm I can do to the
movement is too small, I believe too much in the idea not
to be able to work so that there will be more good than
harm.* I am not making excuses, but I would like the psychology of even such a pitiful creature as an informer to
be understood by you. You know—there are many of us!
—all of us the best party workers. *This is not an isolated*

* The grammatical and stylistic peculiarities of the following letter are
retained.

*abnormal phenomenon, but it is obvious that some kind of
deeper general reason drove us into that impasse.* I ask of
you: overcome your aversion, draw nearer to the soul of a
traitor and tell us all: what precisely were the motives that
guided us when we, believing with all our soul in the party,
in socialism, in all that is sacred and pure, could "honestly" serve in the Secret Police and, despising ourselves,
still found it possible to go on living?

It is difficult to live in holy Russia!
It is difficult.
They sin here disgustingly, they repent their sins even
more disgustingly. The logic of the emphasized words
about faith in socialism is amazing. Can a person, reasoning so strangely and frightfully, bite off an ear or finger of
a beloved woman arguing that he loves all of her, all her
body and soul, and that the finger or ear is very small
compared to her as a whole? Probably, he cannot. But,
believing in the cause of socialism, loving the party, he
tears off one after another its living parts and thinks—
sincerely?—that this will do more good than harm to the
cause. I repeat the question: does he sincerely think so?
And I am afraid that he does, that this reasoning appeared
not after, but was born simultaneously with, the fact of
treason. A truly unique trait of the Russian is that at any
given moment he is sincere. Precisely this uniqueness is, I
think, the source of the moral confusion in which we have
become accustomed to live. Take a look: nowhere are
people involved so extensively and intensively in problems
and arguments, in anxieties about their personal "self-
perfection" as they are involved in this, apparently fruitless, pursuit in our country.
It has always seemed to me that precisely this kind of
pursuit creates an especially dense and stifling atmosphere
of hypocrisy, lies, and bigotry. This atmosphere was espe-

cially heavy and oppressive in the circles of the "Tol-stoyans," people who practiced "self-chastisement" with extraordinary fury.

Morality, as a feeling of inherent disgust for all that is filthy and bad, as an instinctive propensity for purity of the soul and fine actions, this morality is not to be found in our way of life. Its place has long since been taken by cold, "cerebral," reasoning about rules of behavior; and this reasoning, not to mention its repulsive scholasticism, creates an icy atmosphere of endless, tedious, and utterly shameless mutual recriminations, of scheming against each other, of peering into one's soul with the scowling and vigilant glance of an enemy. And—the nasty enemy who doesn't compel you to put out all your strength, to strain wit and will to the utmost in the struggle with him.

He is a wordmonger. The only thing he is after is to prove to you that he is more intelligent, more honest, more sincere, and, in general, better than you in every possible way. Allow him to prove this and he will rejoice for a minute, but then he'll become empty, played out, soft, and bored. But, unfortunately, people do not allow this to happen to him; entering into an argument with him, they themselves become corrupted and squander their feel-ings on trifles. And thus the wordmonger begets word-mongers, thus our not-very-rich store of feelings is squan-dered on the jingling copper of empty words.

Look how insignificant the amount of sympathy is in and around each of you, how weakly developed the feeling of friendship is, how heated our words are, and how mon-strously cold our attitude toward man is. Our feelings toward him become white-hot only when he, having vio-lated the standards of behavior established by us, affords us the delightful opportunity of judging him with "unfair judgment." Peasant children, on winter evenings when they are bored and not yet sleepy, catch cockroaches and tear off their legs one by one. This pleasant pastime reminds one very much of the general significance of our attitude toward our neighbor and of the character of our judgments of him.

The author of the letter, the comrade and informer, speaks about the mysterious "general reason" which drives many and drove him "into an impasse."

I think that such a "general reason" exists and that it is a very complex one. Probably, one of its components is the fact that we treat each other with utter indifference, that is, provided we are in good spirits. . . . We do not know how to love, we do not respect one another, our consideration for man is not developed; it has long been said of us and with absolute truth that we:

"To good and evil are shamefully indifferent."[23]

The comrade and informer wrote his letter very sincerely, but I think the reason for his misfortune is precisely this indifference to good and evil.


## UNTIMELY THOUGHTS

*Novaya Zhizn, No. 26,*
*May 18 (31), 1917*

"Anarchy, anarchy!" the "sensible" people shout,[24] intensifying and spreading panic at a time when all people, even the least fit, must take up the routine workaday job of building a new life, when it is obligatory for everyone to rise to the defense of the great values of the old culture.

"Anarchy!" And again, as after 1905, the floods of inky wrath and cowardly malice are streaming over our Russian democracy, over all the Russian people; the geysers of filthy accusations are spouting.

It is awkward to talk about oneself, and I don't feel like doing it, but when, about a year and a half ago, I published "Two Souls," an article in which I said that the Russians are organically inclined to anarchism, that they are passive but cruel when power falls into their hands, that the famed goodness of their soul is Karamazovian sentimentalism, that they are appallingly unreceptive to the influences of humanism and culture—because of these thoughts—not new, not my own, but only sharply expressed by me—because of these thoughts I was accused of every transgression against the people.[25]

Even recently, in fact, just the other day, someone in *Rech* (Speech)—a newspaper which is, above all, literate —stated that my "defeatism" can best be explained by my attitude toward the people.[26]

Incidentally, I am completely innocent of "defeatism," and I have never sympathized with it. To condemn the law of the fist, duelling, and war, as abominations which shame everyone utterly, as acts which cannot settle arguments and which only intensify hostility—to condemn all this still doesn't mean being a "defeatist" and "non-resister." This is especially alien to me as one who preaches a positive attitude toward life. I may not, in some cases, defend myself, but for the defense of that which is dear to me I have enough strength.

I am now recalling the attitude toward the thoughts set forth by me in the article "Two Souls," not for the purpose of self-defense or self-justification. I understand that in a vicious verbal battle which, for the sake of propriety, we call a "polemic," the combatants are not concerned with the truth; they all seek out each other's verbal mistakes, slips of the tongue, and weak spots, and hit at each other not so much to prove the truth of their own beliefs, as to demonstrate publicly their skill.

No, I recall "Two Souls" in order to ask my paper

enemies: when were they more sincere—when they cursed me for my uncomplimentary opinion of the Russian people, or now, when they curse the Russian people with my very words?

I have never been a demagogue and will not be one. Reproaching our people for their tendency toward anarchism, for their dislike of work, for all their savagery and ignorance, I keep in mind: they cannot be different. The conditions in which they lived could foster in them neither respect for the individual, nor awareness of the citizen's rights, nor a feeling of justice—those were conditions of absolute lawlessness, of the oppression of the individual, of the most shameless lies, and bestial cruelty. And one must be amazed that, with all these conditions, the people nevertheless retained in themselves quite a few human feelings and some degree of common sense.

You complain: the people are destroying industry!

But who tried to instill in them—and when—that industry is the basis of culture, the foundation of social and national well-being?

In their eyes industry is a cunning mechanism, skillfully designed to fleece the consumer. And are they not right?

But, indeed, some three or five months ago you yourselves from day to day in all the newspapers and magazines exposed before them the shameless and fantastic growth of profits in Russian industry, and the people's view is your view.

Of course, you had to "expose," such is the duty of every herald of truth, the courageous defender of justice. But—polemics demands one-sidedness; therefore, when one spoke of this robbery, he forgot the cultural, the creative role of industry, its national significance.

The source of profit for some, industry is for others only the source of physical and spiritual oppression—this is the view accepted in our country without reservation by the vast majority even of educated people. This view took solid shape long ago—recall how G. V. Plekhanov's book *Our Disagreements* was received in Russia, and what a storm P. B. Struve, the "John the Baptist of all our renaissances," raised with his *Critical Notes.*[27]

To shout about anarchy is just as useless as it is useless and shameful to shout "Fire!"—seeing the fire destroying a house but taking no part, other than verbal, in fighting the fire.

Polemics is the dearest occupation of those who like scholastic exercises in wordmongering and of those who consider it their duty, always and in all they say and do, to show that they are right, that their thoughts are precise, and that they are the indisputable possessors of other superb qualities.

But it will be considerably more useful if we—leaving it to history to judge us—at once begin cultural work in the broadest sense of the word, if we give our talents, minds, and hearts to the Russian people in order to inspire them to intelligently create new forms of life.


## THE FREE ASSOCIATION OF POSITIVE SCIENCES[28]

*Novaya Zhizn, No. 35,*
*May 30 (June 12), 1917*

Citizens!

"The Free Association for the Development and Dissemination of the Positive Sciences" has been organized in Petrograd.

The Association is made up of the most talented and distinguished representatives of Russian science. These honorable persons intend to establish in Russia "The Scientific Institute in Commemoration of the 27th of February," in commemoration of the birthday of our political freedom.

The aim of the Institute is to broaden and deepen the work of scientists along all the lines of the interests of man, society, nation, and humanity.

The foremost of these interests is the struggle for life against those sources of disease which undermine our health.

Biology studies the phenomenon of life; bacteriology explores the sources of contageous diseases; medicine strives to exterminate them; hygiene studies and points out those conditions in which man's resistance to disease increases.

The biologist, the physician, and the hygienist must know chemistry and make use of physics to the same extent as the botanist who studies the life of plants and the agronomist who, relying on the work of the botanist and the geologist-soil specialist, works to increase the fertility of the soil and to raise its productivity.

All the sciences are closely connected with each other, and they all represent the striving of human intellect and will to conquer the grief, unhappiness, and suffering of our life.

Citizens!

Our peasantry lives in horrible conditions, lacking properly organized medical care. Half of all peasant children die of various diseases before the age of five. Almost all the women in the village suffer from women's diseases. The villages are rotting with syphilis; the villages have sunk into destitution, ignorance, and savagery. The Russian peasant is unable to cultivate his land so that it will yield the greatest possible amount of food. Ten years ago

Russian science showed that our peasant harvests twenty
poods of grain and potatoes from an area of three-quarters
of a dessiatine, while the same area yielded eighty-two
poods in Japan, eighty-four in England, and eighty-eight
in Belgium. In ten years these figures have not changed for
the better for us.

Agricultural technology is wholly undeveloped in Russia; the illiteracy of the peasantry, and its cultural helplessness, is the major reason for our backwardness as a
state and one of the sad conditions which explains our
foreign policy, a policy harmful to the interest of industry
and retarding its normal growth.

The urban population lives in conditions not much better than those in the village. There are no sewage systems
in the cities; there are no flues in factory chimneys; the
open ground in the cities has been poisoned by the miasm
of rotting refuse, the air—by smoke and dust.

All this is prematurely exhausting our strength, is killing
us. The city children are unhealthy, sickly, and suffer from
nervous tension to the point of being ill.

In this is hidden the reason for hooliganism; here is the
source of crime and spiritual ill-health.

Remember how long we poisoned ourselves with vodka;
drinking does not pass without leaving a trace, for, weak-
ening the organism, it makes it susceptible to all kinds of
bodily and mental disease.

For the purpose of improving our health we need an
"Institute of Biology" with auxiliary establishments for
bacteriological, medical, hygienic, and other areas of research.

———— • ————

Our country is large and abounds in natural resources,
but we live like beggars, in filth and unhappiness. Back-
breaking and senseless work exhausts our strength, killing

46

UNTIMELY THOUGHTS

us; we work senselessly and poorly because we are ignorant. We regard work as if it were the curse of our life,
because we do not understand the great meaning of work,
because we are unable to love it. To improve working
conditions, to reduce the quantity of work, and to make
work easy and pleasant is possible only with the help of
science, the sole force capable of decreasing the expenditure of man's physical energy by subjugating to his will
and interests the elemental energies of nature such as falling water, etc. We do not know how to awaken the slum-
bering forces of nature in the shape of peat-bogs and
deposits of oil shale and cheap coal. These forces, awakened by us, would give us an enormous amount of motive
power, heat, and light, and would serve as conductors of
culture throughout our dark, somnolent country.

Only through love of work shall we attain the great goal
of life, the fusion of all the nations of the world into a
single friendly family on the basis of aspirations directed
toward subjugating the forces of nature to the mind and
will of man.

Russia is large and rich, but its industry is in the embryonic stage. Notwithstanding the incalculable quantity
of nature's gifts in and on our soil, we are unable to live
on the products of our country, of our labor. The countries
with industrial culture look upon Russia as upon Africa, a
colony where they can dispose of any kind of goods at a
high price and from which they can cheaply export raw
materials that we are unable to process ourselves due to
our ignorance and laziness. That is why, in the eyes of
Europe, we are savages, foolish people, and robbing us
is, like robbing Negroes, not considered shameful.

A technologically developed industry is the basis for
social and national well-being.

This is especially important to remember now, when
our weak industry which was destroyed by the war continues to be destroyed by the elemental forces of the revo-

lution, by the tragic ignorance of the popular masses, and by the egotism of the industrialists themselves, who are often people completely lacking in awareness of their responsibility to the country.

Our beautiful dreams will never come true in the soil of destitution and ignorance, a new culture will not take root in this rotten soil, a Garden of Eden cannot be grown in a rotten swamp—it is necessary to drain the swamp and make it fertile.

Full realization of the ideals of socialist culture is possible only in the presence of a wide-based, technologically developed, and strictly organized industry.

To attain its necessary and proper development an industry requires technology, and technology can only be created by science. We do not know how to build machines, so we need in Russia an "Institute of Applied Mechanics" where our scientists could invent new types of more efficient textile machines, engines, agricultural implements, etc.

We do not know how to process raw materials, so we should establish an "Institute of Chemistry" where scientists would seek better and cheaper methods of processing raw material.

We need still more; all this we must create if only we are not dead people, if we want to live a healthy and intelligent life.

———— • ————

Science is the clearest and most enduring expression of the striving of the human intellect for creative freedom and for the happiness of the whole world and all of its people.

The more extensive and profound the objectives of science, the more abundant the practical fruits of research.

It is particularly necessary for us Russians to organize

our higher intellect—science; only its creative power will
enrich our country and put our filthy, wicked, and shameful life in order.

All classes of society should understand the ennobling
significance of science.

The struggle among people for bread and for power
over one another is a disgraceful and abnormal phenomenon, even though it is as natural as the diseases of our
body. People should struggle against nature in a common
effort to conquer its wealth for their own benefit, to
harness its forces to serve their interests.

While the social sciences—history, law, and political
economics—are not free from the influence of their time,
country, and class, and easily succumb to various prompt-
ings of political life, the positive sciences serve incor-
ruptibly and indivisibly the interests of all humanity.

The chemist and biologist can take a most active part in
the political struggle for their social ideas, but chemistry,
biology, and mechanics can be neither liberal nor conservative. Science is social in the broadest sense of the word;
science is indeed international and belongs to all people.

———— • ————

Believing deeply in the intelligence of the Russian
people, in the sincerity of their striving for the blessings of
culture, I appeal to workers, peasants, industrialists, and
intelligentsia—to all Russians—suggesting that they assist
the great cause of organizing the country's scientific
forces, her scientific creativity.

In order to crown this vital national cause with success,
we need enormous sums, and they will be found. They
can be easily created if all people able to understand the
greatness of the goal set by "The Free Association" of

scientists, all the literate people, give but a ruble for this cause.

This appeal provides a gauge of the true level of Russian culture; it is a test of our civic maturity, a trial of the sincerity of our striving for the good of our native country.

Citizens!

The opportunity is before you to accomplish the greatest national task; by accomplishing it you will have organized the best brains of the country, you will have placed an intelligent and talented head on its broad shoulders. A little effort is required of you, but with a little effort you will accomplish the unprecedented—you will create a scientific establishment which as yet does not exist anywhere on earth.

Citizens!

There is a feeling that is called love for one's country. This feeling demands imperatively that each person work toward the goal of making his people intelligent, kind, healthy, and just, so that their talents will not perish but develop and shine forth for the good of the whole world and all its people.

Everyone who sincerely loves his people, who suffers in anxious torment for them, will understand how great is the significance of organizing the country's scientific capabilities, how majestic are the goals which "The Free Association" of our scientists sets for itself.

We must proceed immediately with the creation of a new Russia. Let us begin this work all together and calmly, let us begin with the foundation, and let us develop and disseminate the saving power of knowledge.

To work, citizens.
> Member of the Council of "The Free Association"
> *M. Gorky*

## UNTIMELY THOUGHTS

*Novaya Zhizn, No. 36,*
*May 31 (June 13), 1917*

It is very likely that my thoughts are "naïve"; I have already said that I consider myself a poor journalist, but, nevertheless, with stubbornness worthy, perhaps, of a better cause, "I shall carry on my policy" undisturbed by the fact that my "voice" will remain "a voice in the wilderness" which—alas!—is not uninhabited.

The good, honest book, the best instrument of culture, has all but completely disappeared from the book market. Why it has disappeared—about that some other time. There is no intelligible, objectively instructive book, but a great number of newspapers have been hatched, which, day in, day out, teach people enmity and hatred for each other, engage in slander, wallow in disgusting filth, howl, and gnash their teeth, pretending to work on the answer to the question—who is to blame for the ruin of Russia?

Of course, each disputant is most sincerely convinced that all his adversaries are in the wrong and only he is right, that the wonderful bird called Truth has been caught by him and quivers in his hands.

Having come to grips with one another, the newspapers are rolling around the streets, a tangle of venomous snakes, poisoning and frightening the average citizen with their wicked hissing and teaching him "freedom of speech" or, to be more precise, freedom to distort the truth, freedom to slander.

The "free word" is gradually becoming an indecent
word. Of course, "in a fight everyone has the right to hit
wherever he can with whatever he has"; of course, "politics is a shameless business" and "the best politician is the
most unscrupulous man," but, though one accepts the
repulsive truth of this Zulu morality, nevertheless, what
anguish one feels and how tormenting is one's anxiety for
young Russia, which has just partaken of the sacrament of
freedom!

What poison flows and splashes from the pages of that
disgusting paper on which newspapers are printed!

For a long time the Russian prayed to his God: "Open
Thou my lips!" His lips were opened and words of hate,
lies, and hypocrisy, words of envy and greed spewed forth
unrestrainedly. If only passion had seethed in this, passion
and love, but neither passion nor love is felt. The only
thing felt is the persistent and—one must say—successful
striving of the privileged classes to isolate democracy, to
heap on democracy's head all the mistakes of the past, all
the sins, and to put democracy in a position that would
inevitably force it to increase even further the number of
mistakes and sins.

This is cleverly conceived and not badly executed. It is
already quite clear that when they write "Bolshevik," they
imply democrat; and it is no less clear that if today they
hound the Bolsheviks for their theoretical extremism,
tomorrow they will hound the Mensheviks because they
are socialists, and the day after they will begin to harass
*Edinstvo* (Unity)[29] because it does not behave with sufficient "loyalty" toward the sacred interests of the "right-
thinking people." A democracy is not an inviolable sanc-
tuary; the right to criticize, the right to disapprove should
also extend to democracy itself, this is unquestionable.
But, although criticism and calumny begin with the same
letter, there is an essential difference between these two

concepts—how strange that this difference is quite imperceptible to many educated people! Oh, of course, some leaders of democracy "ring the bell before looking at the calendar"; but let us not forget that the leaders of the privileged classes respond to these mistakes with an "Italian" strike of inaction,[30] which is ruinous to the country, and with intimidation of the man in the street, an intimidation that is already giving such results as, for instance, the following "Letter to the Provisional Government," which I received:

"The revolution has ruined Russia because all were given their freedom; anarchy is everywhere among us. The Jews received equality and they rejoice; they have ruined and are still ruining the Russian people. In order to save the country we must have autocracy."

This is not the first letter in this tone I have received, and it is to be expected that the number of people who have become panic-stricken will grow faster and faster—the press is diligently taking care of this.

But especially now, during these tragically confused days, the press ought to keep in mind how weak the feeling of personal responsibility is in the Russian people, and how we are accustomed to chastise our neighbors for our own sins.

The free word! It seemed that precisely this word would serve to develop in our Russia the feeling of respect for our neighbor, for his human rights. But living through an epidemic of political impressionism, succumbing to the influence of the "burning issues" of the day, we are using the "free word" only in a furious argument on the subject of who is to blame for the destruction of Russia. But here there is no argument, because we are all to blame.

And we all—more or less hypocritically—blame each other, and nobody does anything to oppose the storm of emotions with the force of reason, the force of good will.

## AMERICAN MILLIONS

*Novaya Zhizn, No. 43,*
*June 8 (21), 1917*

In the pages *Novoe Vremya* (New Times) there was
printed an announcement stating that an anonymous
American society has allocated twenty million dollars to
buy up in Russia artistic antiques made of gold and silver,
as well as pictures, bronzes, china, and objects of art in
general.[31]

Twenty million dollars—this, it appears, is more than
seventy-five million rubles; as you can see, the undertaking is organized in "American fashion," on a grand
scale. The organizers of this undertaking apparently
took into account the implications of such things as the
devastation by thieves of the palace of the Duke of
Leuchtenberg, the possibility of destruction by the peasantry of old manors, and all other actions of this nature.

They have also taken into account the general lack of
culture of all strata of our country's population, the general low esteem in which we all hold the meaning of art,
the cheapness of Russian money, and the full force of the
tragic conditions in which we live.

The avalanche of American money undoubtedly will
arouse great temptations not only in the shady people of
the Aleksandrovsky Market[32] but also in better educated,
more cultured people. It won't be at all surprising if various adventurers organize gangs of thieves specifically for
the devastation of private and state collections of art objects.

Still less should we be surprised and indignant if the
owners of art collections, frightened by "the panic" which
is actively spread by clever politicians out of "tactical"
considerations, themselves begin to sell to America the

national treasures of Russia, the beautiful flowers of her
artistic creativity.

For all our shouting about our love for the mother
country, this love seldom rises above selfish love, above
abject egotism.

The American undertaking—it, of course, will be conducted with American vigor—this undertaking threatens
our country with great devastation; it will sweep out of
Russia a great many beautiful things, the historical and
artistic value of which is greater than any millions.

It will bring to life the dark instinct of greed, and possibly we shall witness events before which the fantastic
theft of Leonardo da Vinci's immortal picture from the
Louvre will pale.[33]

It seems to me that to avoid the corruption which will
certainly be brought into Russian life by the flood of dollars, to avoid the plunder of the country's national treasures and their panic selling by their possessors, the government should immediately issue a decree temporarily
forbidding the export of objects of art from Russia and
forbidding the sale of private collections until persons,
authorized by the government, have evaluated the national
significance of such collections.

## UNTIMELY THOUGHTS

*Novaya Zhizn, No. 44,*
*June 9 (22), 1917*

"Sufficient unto the day is the evil thereof"—this is natural, this is right; however, the present day has two
"evils": the struggle of the parties for power and the development of culture. I know that the political struggle is a
necessary matter, but I accept this matter as an unavoidable evil. For I can't help seeing that (under the conditions

of the present moment and in view of some of the peculiarities of the Russian psychology) the political struggle renders the building of culture almost completely impossible.

The task of culture—to develop and strengthen a social conscience and a social morality in man, to develop and organize all personal abilities and talents—can this task be fulfilled in times of widespread brutality?

Just think what is happening around you: every newspaper, having its own sphere of influence, introduces daily the most disgraceful feelings into the souls of its readers, such as malice, falsehood, hypocrisy, cynicism, and others of this order.

In some people they arouse fear and hatred of man; in others, contempt and revenge; still others they wear out by the monotony of slander and infect them with the indifference of despair. Such things done by those whose dark instincts have been inflamed to the point of illness not only have nothing in common with the preaching of culture, but are sharply hostile to its aims.

But the revolution was made in the interests of culture, and it was precisely the growth of cultural forces and cultural demands that called the revolution into being.

———— • ————

The Russian, seeing his old way of life shaken to its foundations by war and revolution, is yelling out high and low for cultural aid; he is yelling out and it is "to the newspaper" that he is turning and demanding from it solutions to the most diverse problems.

Here, for example, a group of soldiers of the "Caucasus Army" writes:*

"Instances of soldiers brutally punishing wives who be-

* The grammatical and stylistic peculiarities of all the following letters are retained.

trayed them are becoming more frequent. Please intercede
so that intelligent people and the social press will take up
the fight against this epidemic phenomenon and will explain that the wives are not at fault. We who are writing
know who is at fault and we don't blame the women,
because every human being is subject to his own nature
and wants what is intended for him by his nature."

Here is another report on this subject:

"I am writing on the train, having heard the story of a
soldier who told with angry tears that he was a deserter
from the front and had run away to provide for two little
children who had been left by his vile wife. He swears he
is going to make short work of her. There are hundreds
and thousands of deserters because of women. What is to
be done?

"In Rostov-on-the Don soldiers led through the streets a
naked libertine with loose hair, yelling about her lewdness
and beating on a broken bucket. The organizers of the
outrage were her husband and lover, a sergeant-major.
Permit me to remark that fear of disgrace will not curb an
instinct, and, incidentally, these vile acts are witnessed by
children. Why does the press remain silent?"

And here is a letter which shifts the "woman question"
to another plane:

"I beg you to inform us, by a registered letter or in
detail in a newspaper, how we are to understand the proclaimed equality of woman with us and what she is going
to do now.

"The undersigned peasants are alarmed by this law
from which lawlessness may increase, and the village now
is supported by the woman. The family is abolished, and
because of this the destruction of farming will follow."

Further: "I declare to you, a friend of the people, that a
lot of nonsense is going on in the villages because soldiers'
wives are allotted land, which is bad and good for nothing,

and they are howling like mad. When their husbands come back from the war, you can be sure there will be a good fight because of this. It is necessary to explain this to the muzhiks so that they will act justly."

And again: "Send a booklet on women's rights."

Not all the letters on this subject have been used by me, but there is a subject repeated even more frequently in the letters—that is the demand for books on various questions.

They write about attitudes toward the priests; they ask whether the "migratory laws will be changed"; they ask to be told "about the American nation," about how syphilis should be treated, and if there isn't a law "about the relocation of all cripples in one place"; they send "petitions" requesting that onions be delivered to soldiers in the trenches—for they "are very good against scurvy."

All these "petitions," "reports," and "inquiries" cannot find space on the pages of newspapers which are engaged in bitter and malicious squabbles. The editors of the newspapers seem to forget that, outside the circle of their influence, there remain tens of millions of people in whom the instinct of the struggle for power is still dormant but in whom the striving to build new forms of life has already been awakened.

And seeing what purposes are being served by the "free word," these millions might easily be led to feel a deadly contempt for it, and this would be fatal and irreparable for a long time to come.

Can't we give a little less space to empty phrasemongering and a little more space to the vital interests of democracy? Aren't we all concerned that people come to know the objective value of culture and its compelling charm?

## HELP!

*Novaya Zhizn, No. 50,*
*June 16 (29), 1917*

Three years of bloody nightmare have annihilated the flower of Europe's population; for three years all Europe, in bloody intoxication, has been destroying its healthiest and strongest sons.

History has pushed forward and demands an immediate solution to the question of the future of the country. Total impoverishment and savage brutality threaten us if we do not begin immediately to work in the name of the future. If it will be difficult for all countries to recover from this grave, protracted, and devastating catastrophe, it will be especially difficult for Russia: the population—for centuries alcoholized by Tsarist pubs; the villages—poisoned by syphilis; a fifty percent death rate among children up to five years of age; and almost complete illiteracy and ignorance. If we don't immediately apply all our energy to save the future of Russia, i.e. her children—a great country will perish, a great people will perish.

*The Union of Workers of Tobacco and Cigarette-Wrapper Factories made the first feeble attempt in the field of social care of children: they sent more than one thousand children out into the fresh air, countryside, and sunshine. But despite appeals to educators, to the League of Social Education, and to the intelligentsia, there is no response, and no one wants to assume the cultural leadership of our workers' undertaking.*

Educators, Fröbelites, intelligentsia—respond, come to our aid!

To delay will be fatal.

Chairman of the Union<br>
A. Kaplan

Is it possible that this thoughtful and passionate appeal will meet with no sympathetic response from the intelligentsia, is it possible that the deep significance of this undertaking created by Kaplan's energy will not be understood by people whose hearts are not deafened by the noise of the political struggle?

The whole world, all of us, yearn for the honest, healthy man; we love him in our dreams—can this be only a literary yearning, a platonic, bloodless love?

It would seem that the experiment of the "Union of Workers of Tobacco and Cigarette-Wrapper Factories" should attract the active attention of the intelligentsia. There is opening up before the intelligentsia an excellent opportunity for productive work in the field of social education and an opportunity to become widely acquainted with the cultural demands and aspirations of the workers. I am sure that this acquaintance would change the pattern of feelings and opinions which has taken shape among the intelligentsia in the past few months. It would shake that scepticism, those oppressive doubts which have been called forth and are being stirred up by the newspaper baiting which is carried on by high-minded politicians guided solely by the tactics of the struggle.

But this is a matter of secondary importance; first of all, we all ought to concern ourselves—and I think this is possible—with removing the children from the city atmosphere which is corrupting them. There has been a great deal said about this, but now when the workers themselves have begun to do this very thing, they receive no assistance. Thus—once again:

> We are destined nobly to aspire,
> But are fated never to achieve.[34]

## UNTIMELY THOUGHTS

*Novaya Zhizn, No. 52,*
*June 18 (July 1), 1917*

Equality for the Jews is one of the wonderful achievements of our revolution. Having recognized the Jew to be equal to the Russian, we have removed a shameful, bloody, and filthy stain from our conscience.

There is nothing in this act that gives us the right to be proud. Simply because Jews fought for the political freedom of Russia much more honestly and vigorously than did many Russians, and simply because Jews produced far fewer renegades and informers—we ought not to be and cannot be regarded as "benefactors of the Jews," as some "good-natured" and "soft-hearted" Russians call themselves in their letters to me.

Incidentally: these good-natured and soft-hearted people squabble with amazing shamelessness!

Having freed the Jews from the "Jewish pale," from the "bondage of restrictions," which disgraced us, we have given our country an opportunity to use the energy of people who know better than we do how to work, and everybody knows that we badly need people who like to work.

There is nothing for us to be proud of, but we can be glad that we have finally thought of doing something that is good both morally and practically.

However, no joy is felt on account of this, probably because we have no time to rejoice—we are all terribly busy with "higher politics," the sense of which is best of all set forth in some sort of cannibal chant:

> Tigers love to eat fruit jam
> Man devours fellow man

> Oh! What rare and joyful bliss
> Gnawing neighbor's bones sure is!

No joy is felt, but anti-Semitism is alive and, little by little, cautiously, it again raises its vile head, hissing, slandering and splattering its poisonous drivel of hatred.

What is the matter? You see, it is that two anarchy-minded Bolsheviks happened to be Jews. Perhaps, even three. Some people count seven and are convinced that these seven Samsons will smash to bits the Russian edifice of 170 millions.

That would be very funny and rather silly if it weren't base.

The awesome Jewish God saved a whole city of sinners because there was one righteous man among them; those who believe in the gentle Christ think that all the Jewish people should suffer for the sins of two or seven Bolsheviks.

Reasoning in this manner, one would say that all the natives of the Simbirsk province, and also of adjacent provinces, should answer for Lenin, a pure-blooded Russian sinner.

There are considerably more Jews among the Mensheviks, but my correspondents, pretending to be ignorant, insist that all Jews are anarchists.

This is a rotten generalization. I am convinced, I know, that most of the Jews, to my surprise, manifest more intelligent love for Russia than do many Russians.

This goes unnoticed, even though it is strikingly evident if one reads the articles of Jewish journalists.

Quite a few Jews work for *Rech* (Speech), a newspaper which may not be liked but which, nonetheless, is very respectable. *Novoe Vremya* (New Times), among whose contributors there are also some Jews, not long ago called *Rech* a "Jewish newspaper."

The contributors to *Rech* are completely devoid of even a shadow of sympathy for Bolsheviks.

There are thousands of additional proofs to show that equating Jews and Bolsheviks is stupid and is a product of the animal instincts of enraged Russians.

I certainly shall not cite these proofs. For honorable people they are unnecessary; for dishonorable people they are unconvincing.

Idiocy is an illness that cannot be cured by suggestion. For the person stricken with this incurable illness it is clear that since seven and a half Bolsheviks happen to be Jews, the Jewish people are to blame for everything. And therefore. . . .

And therefore the honest and healthy Russian again begins to feel anxiety and a tormenting shame for Russia, for the stupid Russian bungler who, in a difficult time of his life, invariably looks for his enemy somewhere outside himself, and not in the abyss of his own stupidity.

I hope that my numerous correspondents are satisfied with this answer to the "Jewish question."

And I shall add that for me there is no longer such a question.

I do not believe in the success of the slanderous anti-Semitic propaganda. And I believe in the intelligence of the Russian people, in their conscience, in the sincerity of their striving for freedom, a freedom which excludes any coercion of man. I believe that "all shall pass, only truth shall remain."

## UNTIMELY THOUGHTS

*Novaya Zhizn, No. 59,*
*June 27 (July 10), 1917*

A certain respectable citizen writes to me:

"Terror seizes your soul when you see how soldiers at street meetings, zealously defending the extreme Leninist slogans, easily succumb to the pogrom propaganda of those who whisper in their ear about the dominance of Jews in the 'Council of Workers' and Soldiers' Deputies.' I once asked a soldier how he could reconcile in his mind 'the social revolution' with the hostile attitude toward the nationalities? He answered:

'We are uneducated people, it is not the soldier's business to look into such complicated questions.' "

Another correspondent, a woman, reports:

"When I told a streetcar conductor that the socialists are fighting for the equality of all peoples, he retorted:

'We don't give a damn about the socialists; socialism is a rich man's invention, but we workers are Bolsheviks.' "

Outside the "Modern" circus, a group of soldiers and workers are carrying on a discussion with a very young, nervous student.

"If we are only going to argue with each other in a hostile manner, like you argue, and if we quit learning . . . ," shouts the student, hoarsely.

"What is there to learn?" asks an elderly soldier sternly. "What can you teach me? We know you—students have always rebelled. Now we are on top, and it is time to do away with all you bourgeois."

Some of the crowd laughs, but some sort of dandy, who looks like a barber, says excitedly:

"That's right, comrades! The intelligentsia has ordered us about long enough. Now, when there is freedom of rights, we'll manage without them."

Great and terrible dangers are hidden in this aroused
ignorance!

More than once, at night meetings on the Petrograd
Side,[35] it has been my lot to hear Bolshevism opposed to
socialism, attacks on the intelligentsia, and many
other equally absurd and harmful opinions. And this goes
on at the very center of the revolution, where ideas are
expressed in the most extreme terms and from where they
flow out over all the dark, uneducated country.

Is there under way in the country a process of uniting
intelligent revolutionary forces? Is the energy, vital for the
building of culture, really growing?

There are signs which seem to suggest a negative answer.

One of these signs is the increasingly noticeable tendency on the part of the intelligentsia to avoid work
among the masses and its sporadic attempts to create its
own independent organizations. It is obvious that there are
reasons which alienate the intelligentsia from the masses,
and it is very likely that one of these reasons is that skep-
tical, and frequently even hostile, attitude of ignorant
people toward the intelligentsia, an attitude which day in,
day out is being instilled in the masses by various demagogues.

This split may be very useful to the working intelligentsia—they will unite in a very impressive organization,
capable of accomplishing much cultural work.

But gradually moving away from the masses and being
carried away by their own interests, tasks, and moods, the
intelligentsia will deepen and widen the gap between instinct and intellect. This gap is our misfortune, it is the
source of our inability to work and of our failures in the
creating of the new conditions of life.

Left without leaders, in an atmosphere of wild demagoguery, the masses will begin, even more absurdly, to
look for differences between workers and socialism and

similarities between the "bourgeoisie" and the working intelligentsia.

But among the latter, one hears the appeals which undoubtedly are dictated by noble intentions and aspirations, but which divert intellectual energy away from the interests of the masses and from present-day demands. In *Izvestiya Yuga* (News of the South), the organ of the Kharkov and Regional Committees of the Councils of Workers' and Soldiers' Deputies, one Ivan Stankov writes:*

> There is an enormously important task for all of socialism: it is the raising of the level of culture, the development of self-awareness in people, the elevation of the personality, and the raising of the level of national intellectuality. There is a slogan: right here and now let us open wide the doors of the Sun, of Beauty, and of Knowledge to the whole nation so that there will be no uncultured people, so that our division into cultured and uncultured will become, as soon as possible, a fantastic vestige of the old order, of the old schools and systems.
>
> The propagation and the earliest possible realization of the idea of raising the level of 'national intellectuality' is precisely, to my way of thinking, one of those binding, urgent, and extremely important tasks of socialism which an honest and united intelligentsia, regarding it as their duty to the people, must make the point of departure for all their strenuous efforts. These tasks must also be included in the new construction, together and along with the general platform of socialist demands of all parties. Only intellectuality cleansed of the evils of the bourgeois order will become the sunlit truth of the people. It will become the sun of Wisdom and Beauty.

These are fine words. The proclamation of the Executive Committee of the Kharkov Council of the Deputies of the Working Intelligentsia is written even better:

* The grammatical and stylistic peculiarities of the two following items are retained.

To you, the working intelligentsia of the Kharkov province, this appeal is directed.

By the evil irony of fate the Russian intelligentsia, which strewed the bones of martyrs all along the Via Dolorosa of the liberation of the people and which performed great educational and organizational work during its entire history, is unorganized at the present moment when everything else is organized. Organizing others, the intelligentsia, as a class, forgot to or found no time to organize itself. With the direct participation of the intelligentsia, the workers, soldiers, and peasantry were organized; on the right, the bourgeoisie is vigorously organizing; and only the working intelligentsia, rich in knowledge, experience, and social skills, remains disunited and scattered to the winds.

The class best equipped for social work and struggle, a class of active traditions and bright social ideals, has to drag along slowly at the tail end of events, powerless to direct them.

This is not the place to search for the reasons, but it is an undeniable fact that the class of the working intelligentsia, as a whole, is not at this moment a member of, and cannot join, any existing social grouping.

Hence the necessity for its own independent organization.

But all the requisites for such an organization are at hand. The great economic fact, the fact of hired labor, the fact of the alienation to Capital, in return for wages, of its skilled work—this is that base on which the class of the working intelligentsia rests in its huge majority, this is that iron chain which is destined to forge it into one indivisible whole. In this sense the working intelligentsia is one of the sections of the great class of the contemporary proletariat, one of the members of the great workers' family.

But having defined the working intelligentsia as a section of the working class, we have, in this way, also defined their social essence.

The class of the working intelligentsia, which has become conscious of itself, can only be socialist.

The great Russian revolution has not come to an end, it is continuing. Enormous social tasks—the ending of the war, the formation of an orderly state system, the solution of the land problem, and the organization of the national economy, which is experiencing a very grave crisis—stand before the country in all their dreadful majesty and authoritatively demand solution.

Comrades, working intelligentsia of the city and province of Kharkov! Following the example of the heart of Russia, Moscow, where the intelligentsia of the proletariat organized into a powerful Council of the Deputies of the Working Intelligentsia, and, following the pattern of other democratic councils of workers', peasants', and soldiers' deputies, unite into your own Kharkov Council of the Deputies of the Working Intelligentsia.

Only in unity is there strength, only in solidarity is there power.

The urge on the part of the working intelligentsia to create independent organizations is arising not only in Moscow and Kharkov. Perhaps this urge is necessary and justified in every way, but won't the masses be left without a head?

But all the same, an alarming question arises: What do we have here—a process of unification of forces or of their disintegration?

## UNTIMELY THOUGHTS

*Novaya Zhizn, No. 61,*
*June 29 (July 12), 1917*

Whenever they talk about it, everybody agrees that the Russian state is splitting all along its seams and falling apart like an old barge in a flood.

No one, it seems, is arguing against the necessity to build culture. And, probably, no one will deny that all of us must be extremely cautious in treating man, and very attentive to facts. We have never been so cruelly in need of exact and courageously truthful evaluations of the facts of life, which is troubled to its very depths, facts that threaten all of us in our country with an endless economic dislocation.

But never have our evaluations, conclusions, and projects been marked by such unfortunate haste as in these tragic days.

Of course, I fully agree with the ironic words of Vl. Karenin, the author of a magnificent book about George Sand:[36]

"Politicians—conservatives or liberals—are people convinced of their knowledge of the truth and of their right to persecute other people for being in error. . . ." To the liberals and conservatives I would only add, in the interest of justice, the radical revolutionaries and proselytes of socialism.

"The struggle for power" is inevitable; however, over what will the victors "rule" when only rotten stumps and charred logs are left around them?

Passion for politics seems to exclude completely a sound interest in cultural matters; this is hardly beneficial for a sick country and its inhabitants, most of whose heads have been "stirred with the devil's stick." I shall permit myself to point out this fact: "The Free Association for the Development and Dissemination of Positive Sciences" arouses in democratic masses an extraordinary attention toward its tasks.

Here, for example, "the soldiers of the transport unit of the Nizhegorodsky Dragoon Regiment, sending their contribution to the fund of the 'Scientific Institute,'" write that the "Association is a great national concern." The

Union of the Office Workers of Poltava calls the Institute a "nation-wide affair," etc. One can cite dozens of responses by soldiers, workers, and peasants, and all these responses testify to a craving for enlightenment, to a profound understanding of the urgent need for cultural construction.

The press of the capital views this matter differently: when the "Association" sent its appeals regarding its aims and needs to the most important Petrograd newspapers, not one of these papers printed them, *Novaya Zhizn* excepted. The "House and Museum in Memory of the Fighters for Freedom," which is similar to an institute of social sciences and civic education, is being organized; only *Rech* (Speech) devoted a few sympathetic lines to this undertaking.

The "League of Social Education" is being formed. Its tasks include the pre-school education of children of the street—and this is the best means of fighting hooliganism, this will make it possible to plant the seed of civic-mindedness in the soul of the child.

The "free word" of the capital press is silent about this. It is also silent about the "Non-party Union of Youth," which is already embracing thousands of young people from thirteen to twenty years of age. Cultural construction is going on in the "provinces." Without exaggerating, one can say that, in scores of villages and district towns, "People's Houses"[37] are being organized and the most ardent striving for science and knowledge can be observed.

The press of the capital is silent about this salutary phenomenon; it is busy instilling fear of anarchy in the average citizen and does it with some kind of strange, dispassionate fury, which only increases anarchy.

The Petrograd newspapers convey the impression of a senseless "Day of Judgment" where all the participants

are judges and, at the same time, they are all being un-
mercifully accused.

If we are to believe our influential newspapers, then we
must acknowledge that there are no honest and intelligent
people whatsoever in "Holy Russia." If we agree with the
testimony of the journalists, then the revolution is our
greatest misfortune, it has corrupted us all and driven us
mad. This would be frightening if this weren't stupid,
weren't caused by "quick temper and irritability." It is
said that a disgustingly coarse attitude toward man has
established itself in the streets. No, it's not true!

The most acute questions of the moment are discussed
fervently in night street meetings, but personal insults, cutting words, and cursing are almost never heard.

It is worse in the newspapers.

"Scum," writes *Birzhevka*,[38] referring to some people
who disagree with it. The words thief, swindler, and fool
have become perfectly printable. The word "traitor" is
heard just as often as the call "Waiter!" was heard in the
taverns of the old days.

This lack of restraint, this wordmongering, raises sad
and alarming doubts regarding the sincerity of the newspapers' howlings about the demise of culture, about the
need to save it. These are not the cries from the heart, but
calculated exclamations. Nevertheless, culture is certainly
in danger, and we must be sincerely aware of this danger.
We must courageously fight it.

Are we capable of doing this?

——— • ———

By the way, here is an illustration of the attitude of the
press toward the facts. On one and the same day two
newspapers gave the following accounts:

One:

Sunday evening in the Bogoslovskoe cemetery, on the
grave of the anarchist Asnin, Cossack Lieutenant Fedorov,
using a saber, hacked up a case containing a wreath and
several flags. Policemen of the third Vyborg sub-district,
who were at the cemetery, arrested the lieutenant and took
him to the commissariat where a report was drawn up
concerning Fedorov's breach of order in a public place. An
hour later, a group of anarchists numbering about fifteen
men appeared at the commissariat and presented a demand
that the person being held be turned over to them. The
commissar rejected the anarchists' demand and took Fedorov
to the military commandant of the Polyustrovo sub-district,
from where the lieutenant, under the protection of a Cossack
mounted patrol, was taken home.

The other:

As has been reported, an incident, which nearly ended in
a bloody fight, occurred at the funeral of the "anarchist"
Asnin who had been killed at the Durnovo's country
house.

For some reason, the anarchists chose the Orthodox
Bogoslovskoe cemetery as the place to bury Asnin and they
erected a cross on the grave.

The Cossacks, who happened to be in the cemetery,
protested against the burial of Asnin in the Bogoslovskoe
cemetery and then removed the cross from the grave.

The anarchists were about to defend the grave, but the
Cossacks, having drawn their sabers, stopped them.[39]

Are these different facts?

No, they are merely varying interpretations of one
and the same fact.

If a person who is accustomed to thinking reads the
second account, he, of course, will question certain things
—for example, the erection of the cross by the anarchists.
The fact that the cross was removed from the grave will

offend the believer. The man in the street will again
shudder reading about the "drawn sabers."

And comparing the accounts, he will naturally ask:
"Where is the truth here?"

And it will be even more natural to doubt the educational significance of the "free word," the "miracle among
God's miracles."[40]

Will we not choke in the mud which we so diligently
produce?

## UNTIMELY THOUGHTS

*Novaya Zhizn, No. 74,*
*July 14 (27), 1917*

The disgusting scenes of the madness which seized
Petrograd the day of July 4 will remain in my memory for
the rest of my life.[41]

There, bristling with rifles and machine guns, a truck
flashes by like a mad hog; it is tightly packed with motley
members of the "revolutionary army," among them stands
a disheveled youth who shouts hysterically:

"The social revolution, comrades!"

Some people who have not yet lost their reason, unarmed but calm, hold the rumbling monster and disarm it,
plucking the bristles of rifles. The disarmed soldiers and
sailors mix with the crowd and disappear into it; the absurd wagon, now empty, heavily bounces along the
chewed-up, filthy pavement and also disappears—like a
nightmare.

And it is clear that this frightening sortie into the "social revolution" was undertaken by somebody hastily, un-
thinkingly, and that stupidity is the name of the force
which pushed people, armed to the teeth, into the streets.

Suddenly a shot cracks out somewhere, and hundreds of

people fly convulsively in all directions driven by fear, like dry leaves before a whirlwind. They fall to the ground, tripping over one another, screaming and shouting:

"The bourgeois are shooting!"

It was not the "bourgeois," of course, who were shooting, i.e., not the fear of the revolution, but the fear that something might happen to it. We have too much of this fear. It was felt everywhere—in the soldiers' hands lying on the bipods of machine guns, and in the trembling hands of workers holding loaded rifles and revolvers with safety catches forward, and in the strained look of wildly staring eyes. It was clear that these people did not believe in their strength and it is very unlikely that they understood why they had gone out into the street with weapons.

Especially characteristic was the scene of panic on the corner of Nevsky and Liteyny at about four o'clock in the afternoon. Some two companies of soldiers and several hundred civilians were meekly standing near the Palkin restaurant and beyond in the direction of Znamenskaya Square, when suddenly, as if by the force of some evil, ironic sorcerer, all these armed and unarmed people turned into a frantic flock of sheep.

I was not able to catch what exactly caused the panic and made the soldiers shoot at a house on the Nevsky, the fifth from the corner of Liteyny; they began to fire at the windows and columns of the house without taking aim, with the feverish haste of people who fear that any minute their guns will be taken from them. About ten men were shooting, no more; and the rest, having thrown their rifles and flags into the street, began, together with the public, forcing the doors and windows, knocking out glass, breaking doors, and forming, on the sidewalk, piles of flesh turned mad from fear.

A young girl ran along the pavement among the scattered rifles and shouted:

"It is our people who are shooting, our own people!"

I put her behind a trolley pole; she said indignantly:
"Shout that our people...."

But all had already disappeared, having escaped to
Liteyny or Vladimirsky and hidden in any crack they
could make for themselves; but rifles, hats, and caps were
lying about the pavement, and the filthy wood-block
roadway was covered with the red cloth of flags.

That is not the first time I have seen a crowd panic; it is
always disgusting, but I have never had such a dispiriting,
murderous impression.

And is this the same "free" Russian people who, an
hour before they became frightened of themselves, had
"denied the old world" and shaken "its dust" from their
feet?[42] Are these the soldiers of the revolutionary army
who ran away from their own bullets, throwing down their
rifles and hugging the sidewalk?

This nation must work a great deal in order to acquire
an awareness of its identity, of its human dignity; this
nation must be tempered and cleansed of its inbred slavery
by the slow flame of culture.

Again culture? Yes, once again culture. I know of nothing else that can save our country from ruin. And I am
sure that if the part of the intelligentsia which, fearing
responsibility and avoiding danger, has hidden somewhere and is idle while taking delight in criticizing what is
going on; if this intelligentsia, from the first days of freedom, had tried to introduce other guiding principles into
the chaos of aroused instincts, if it had attempted to arouse
feelings of a different order—none of us would have experienced the multitude of those abominations which we are
now experiencing. If the revolution is incapable of immediately undertaking the strenuous building of culture in the
country, then, from my point of view, the revolution has
been in vain, it makes no sense, and we are a nation
incapable of living.

Having read what is set forth above, various shameless people will, of course, not fail to shout joyfully:

"But not a word is said about the role of the Leninists in the events of July 4, aha! This is where the hypocrisy is!"

I am not a detective, I do not know who is more to blame for this loathsome drama. I do not intend to justify adventurers, I detest and abhor people who arouse the dark instincts of the masses, no matter what names these people bear and no matter how considerable their service to Russia may have been in the past. I think that foreign provocation of the events of July 4 is possible, but I must say that the evil joy displayed by some people after the events of the 4th is also extremely suspicious. There are people who talk so much about freedom, about the revolution, and about their love for these things that their talk often reminds one of the sweet talk of merchants who wish to sell their wares as profitably as possible.

However, in my opinion, the principal stimulus for this drama was provided not by the "Leninists," the Germans, the informers, or the sinister counterrevolutionaries, but a more evil and stronger enemy—the oppressive Russian stupidity.

It is precisely our stupidity which is more to blame for the drama of July 4 than all the other forces which contributed to the drama; call it stupidity, lack of culture, absence of a sense of history—whatever you please.

## THE THREE YEARS

*Novaya Zhizn, No. 78,*
*July 19 (August 1), 1917*

Three years of merciless, senseless carnage; for three years
the blood of the finest peoples of the earth has flowed day
after day, and the most precious brains of the cultured
nations of Europe are being destroyed.

France, "the leader of humanity," has been bled white;
Italy, "God's best gift to our sad earth," is being exhausted; England, which "has calmly taught the world the
miracles of labor," is expending all its strength; and "the
industrious peoples of Germany" are somberly suffocating
in the iron vise of war.

Belgium, Serbia, Rumania, and Poland have been destroyed; dreamy, spineless Russia, a country which has
not yet lived and not yet shown its hidden forces to the
world, has been ruined economically and corrupted spiritually by the war.

In the twentieth century, after Europe had, for nineteen
centuries, preached humaneness in churches (which she is
now destroying with cannons), and in books (which soldiers are burning like firewood)—in the twentieth century,
humanism is forgotten and ridiculed, and all that has been
created by the unselfish work of science is being seized
and directed toward the extermination of people by the
will of shameless murderers.

What are the thirty-year and hundred-year wars of the
past in comparison with this nightmarish three-year
carnage? Where can we find a justification for this unprecedented crime against world culture?

There is no justification for this hideous self-extermina-
tion. No matter how much the hypocrites lie about the
"great" aims of the war, their lies will not hide the terri-

ble, shameful truth: this war is born of Profit, the only god in whom the "realistic politicians," the murderers who trade in the lives of the people, believe and to whom they pray.

Scoundrels of all countries have declared that those who believe in the triumph of the ideal of universal brotherhood are dangerous lunatics and dreamers without hearts who have no love for their native land.

It is forgotten that among these dreamers were Christ, John of Damascus, St. Francis of Assisi, Leo Tolstoy—scores of half-gods, half-men, of whom mankind can be proud. For those who destroy millions of lives in order to take into their hands a few hundred versts of foreign soil—for them there is neither God nor devil. For them people are cheaper than stone, and love for their native country is only a set of habits. They like to live the way they live, and the dust of the whole world can be scattered about in the universe—they do not want to live otherwise than they are accustomed to live.

Here they have already lived for three years up to their necks in blood which by their will is being shed by tens of millions.

But when the strength of the masses is exhausted, or when their urge for a "pure, human life" flares up all at once and puts an end to this bloody nightmare, then those who are exterminating the people of Europe will shout:

"We are not to blame! It is not we who have mutilated the world, not we who have destroyed and sacked Europe!"

But we hope that by that time the "voice of the people" will indeed be the stern and just "Voice of God," and will drown out the howling of lies.

Those who believe in victory over shamelessness and madness should strive for the unification of their forces.

In the end—reason triumphs.[43]

# UNTIMELY THOUGHTS

*Novaya Zhizn, No. 79,*
*July 20 (August 2), 1917*

An attorney at law—one of those who, under the old
regime, calmly risking their personal freedom and not
thinking about their careers, courageously appeared as
defenders in political trials and dealt not a small number
of blows to the autocracy—a man who knows very well
the depths of the injustice and cynicism of the monarchy,
told me recently:

"Just as I did under Nicholas Romanov, I am appearing
as a defender in a hastily arranged political trial; just as
before, mothers, wives, and sisters of the prisoners come
to me to weep and complain; as before, arrests are made
'by a wave of the wand,' those arrested kept in abominable
conditions; and officials of the 'new order' treat a person
under investigation in the same bureaucratic and heartless
manner as they did before. It seems to me that in my field
there has been no change for the better."

Moreover, I think that in this field one ought to expect
all possible changes for the worse. Under the monarchy,
the obedient servants of Romanov did not deny themselves at times the pleasure of talking like liberals, of criticizing the regime, of moaning on the theme of humanism,
and, generally, of showing off their magnanimity; of
demonstrating to an unwilling listener that, in the heart of
a diehard official, not all good qualities have been destroyed by the zealous work of guarding rot and rubbish.

The more intelligent ones understood that the "politician" was a man not really dangerous to them; working
for the liberation of Russia he also worked for the libera-

tion of the official from the somewhat boorish "supreme authority."

Now there is no autocracy and one can show all the "beauty of the soul" freed from the bondage of strict regulations.

Now the official of the old regime, whether a Cadet or an Octobrist,[44] faces an arrested democrat as his natural enemy; no one needs liberal Manilovism[45] and it is inappropriate.

From the viewpoint of the interests of parties and the political struggle, all this is perfectly normal, but "in terms of humanity" it is abominable and will become even more abominable as the inevitable aggravation of relations between democracy and its enemies increases.

———— • ————

Somebody has published his impressions of a trip to Tsarskoe Selo in one of the filthy street newspapers.[46] In a practically illiterate article, which is intended for the amusement of the street and which relates how Nicholas Romanov saws wood and how his daughters work in the kitchen garden, there is this passage:

A sailor brings in Aleksandra Fedorovna[47] in a wheelchair. She is thin, with sunken cheeks, and all in black. Slowly, with the help of her daughters, she gets out of the wheelchair and walks, limping badly on her left leg. . . .

"See, she's fallen ill," remarks someone from the crowd. "She's lost the use of her legs. . . ."

"If Grishka were here," giggles someone in the crowd, "she'd get well in a hurry."[48]

Deafening laughter resounds.

To laugh at a sick and unfortunate person, no matter who he might be, is vulgar and vile. The Russians are laughing, the same ones who five months ago feared and

trembled before the Romanovs, although they understood
—vaguely—their role in Russia. But what matters is not
that happy people laugh at the misfortune of a woman but
that the article is signed with the Jewish name of Ios.
Kheysin.

I consider it necessary to remind Mr. Kheysin of a few
lines from the article by Professor Baudouin de Courtenay
in the collection *Shchit* (The Shield):

"A suitcase was stolen in a railway car. The thief
turned out to be a Pole. However, it was not said that a
'Pole' had stolen it but only that a 'thief' had stolen it.

"The next time the thief turned out to be a Russian.
This time also it was not a Russian who was accused of
stealing but simply a 'thief.'[49]

"But had the suitcase been found in the hands of a Jew,
it would have been said that a 'Jew had stolen it,' not just
a 'thief.' "

I think the moral should be clear to Kheysin and to
similar "local colorists," for example, to David Ayzman[50]
and others. Regarding their works one may also say that
they are written not simply by people embittered to the
point of stupidity, but by "Jews."

It is doubtful that you could find anybody so stupid as
to suspect me of anti-Semitism because of what I have
said.

I deem it necessary—considering the conditions of the
times—to point out that nowhere is such tact and moral
sensitivity required as in the relation of Russians to Jews
and of Jews to the manifestations of Russian life.

This does not mean at all that there are some facts in
Russia which should not be mentioned critically by the
Tartar or the Jew, but one must keep in mind that even an
involuntary mistake—not to speak of deliberate mean-
ness, even though it may have sprung from a sincere desire
to gratify the instincts of the crowd—can be interpreted in

a way harmful not only to one angry or stupid Jew but to all of Jewry.

One should not forget this if one lives among people who can laugh at a sick and unfortunate person.


## UNTIMELY THOUGHTS

*Novaya Zhizn, No. 92,
August 4 (17), 1917*

*Rech* (Speech) has been very attentive to me; almost every day in its bluish columns I come across a few words about me.[51]

Several dozen times *Rech* has noted the "latest repentance of Gorky," although I have never repented of anything to anybody—least of all to *Rech*—for I have an inherent loathing for this kind of occupation, which the Russians like very much. And there is nothing for me to repent; I do not feel that I am more sinful than the rest of my countrymen.

No less often *Rech* repeats my words that, taking some part in organizing the newspaper *Luch* (Ray), I and my colleagues intentionally imposed upon ourselves "restraints" unavoidable under the conditions of the old regime[52] for every person who wished to work honestly in the interests of democracy and who was repelled by the idea of playing up to the despicable power of the government, which was destroying the country economically as well as morally.

And yesterday *Rech* again mentioned:

"We have heard from the lips of a writer, who considers himself called upon to defend cultural values, that he now sees no basis for restraint."[53]

This, of course, is incorrect; I did not say that now, i.e., after the revolution, "I see no basis for restraint." Intelligent and unbiased people clearly see that *Novaya Zhizn,* for which I have the honor and pleasure to write, is trying in every way and to the best of its ability to suggest the necessity of "restraint" to adventurers of the left as well as adventurers of the right. I say this not for the sake of controversy with *Rech*—"you can't convince a polecat that the hen doesn't belong to him"—but I nonetheless deem it necessary to remind the honorable public figures from *Rech* that sometimes "restraint" may be equivalent to moral suicide or to self-distortion to the point of completely losing one's identity.

For example, when one of the leaders of the Cadet party declared it to be "His Majesty's Opposition," that was "restraint," wasn't it?

And when the "Party of the People's Freedom" formed a bloc with the Octobrists (the party which had applauded the hangman Stolypin) wasn't that also "restraint?"[54]

And when the "Party of the People's Freedom" apologized to Stolypin because the eloquent Rodichev tactlessly mentioned Stolypin's predilection for "hemp neckties"[55] with which he strangled the people's freedom, that was also "restraint," was it not?

Dozens of similar acts of "restraint" could be restored to the memory of the contributors to *Rech.* The party of the "people's freedom" used to restrain itself extremely immoderately and, so to speak, intemperately. Everyone knows and remembers that, except the newspaper *Rech,* of course.

But even the honorable contributors to this organ will be—I am sure—very much amazed if they, upon reading "The Program of the Constitutional-Democratic Party," clearly realize the extent to which this party has "restrained itself."

Hence it is understandable why *Rech* preaches the need

for "restraint" so frequently and persistently—it does this out of habit.

People who believe in the sincerity of *Rech* can afford the luxury of hoping that, having restrained themselves on the left to the greatest possible extent, *Rech* and its party will soon begin to restrain themselves also on the right. I do not believe this.

But I see that the example of the Cadet party in the business of "restraint" is finding imitators among other parties' organizations and that this process in essence is already becoming the process of the revolution's suicide, the restraining of the legal rights of democracy.

## ONE MUST NOT BE SILENT![56]

*Novaya Zhizn, No. 156,*
*October 18 (31), 1917*

Rumors are more and more persistently being spread that some "action by the Bolsheviks" will take place on October 20; in other words, the disgusting scenes of July 3-5 may be repeated. This means, again, trucks tightly packed with people holding rifles and revolvers in hands trembling with fear—and these rifles will fire at the windows of stores, at people, at anything! They will fire only because those armed with them want to kill their fear. All the dark instincts of the crowd irritated by the disintegration of life and by the lies and filth of politics will flare up and fume, poisoning us with anger, hate, and revenge; people will kill one another, unable to suppress their own animal stupidity.

An unorganized crowd, hardly understanding what it wants, will crawl out into the street, and, using this crowd as a cover, adventurers, thieves, and professional murderers will begin to "create the history of the Russian revolution."

In a word, there will be repeated that bloody and senseless slaughter which we have already witnessed and which has undermined the moral meaning of the revolution in the whole country and has shaken its cultural significance.

It is very likely that this time events will assume an even more bloody and destructive character and will deal an even more serious blow to the revolution.

Who needs all this, and why? The Central Committee of the Social-Democratic Bolsheviks is, apparently, not taking part in the intended adventure, for until today it has in no way confirmed the rumors about the forthcoming action, even though it has not refuted them.

It is appropriate to ask: Are there really adventurers who, seeing a decline in the revolutionary energy of the thinking part of the proletariat, hope to stimulate this energy by means of a profuse blood-letting?

Or do these adventurers wish the counterrevolution to deal its blow sooner, and are they striving, with this end in mind, to disorganize the forces which are being organized with such difficulty?

The Central Committee of the Bolsheviks is obliged to refute the rumors about the action of the 20th. It must do this if it is really a strong and freely acting political body capable of guiding the masses, and not a weak-willed toy of the moods of the wild crowd, not an instrument in the hands of utterly shameless adventurers or crazed fanatics.[57]

## TO THE DEMOCRACY

*Novaya Zhizn, No. 174,*
*November 7 (20), 1917*

The socialist ministers released by Lenin and Trotsky from the Peter and Paul Fortress went home, leaving their colleagues M. V. Bernatsky, A. I. Konovalov, M. I. Tereshchenko,[58] and others in the hands of people who have no conception of the freedom of the individual or of the rights of man.

Lenin, Trotsky, and their companions have already become poisoned with the filthy venom of power, and this is evidenced by their shameful attitude toward freedom of speech, the individual, and the sum total of those rights for the triumph of which democracy struggled.

Blind fanatics and dishonest adventurers are rushing madly, supposedly along the road to the "social revolution"; in reality this is the road to anarchy, to the destruction of the proletariat and of the revolution.

On this road Lenin and his associates consider it possible to commit all kinds of crimes, such as the slaughter outside St. Petersburg,[59] the destruction of Moscow,[60] the abolition of freedom of speech,[61] and senseless arrests —all the abominations which Pleve[62] and Stolypin once perpetrated.

Of course, Stolypin and Pleve went against democracy, against all that was live and decent in Russia. Lenin, however, is followed by a rather sizeable—for the time being —portion of the workers; but I believe that the good sense of the working class and its awareness of its historical tasks will soon open the eyes of the proletariat to the utter impossibility of realizing Lenin's promises, to all the depth of his madness, and to his Nechaev and Bakunin brand of anarchism.[63]

The working class cannot fail to understand that Lenin is only performing a certain experiment on their skin and on their blood, that he is striving to push the revolutionary mood of the proletariat to its furthest extreme and see— what will come of this?

Of course, he does not believe in the possibility of the victory of the proletariat in Russia under the present conditions, but perhaps he is hoping for a miracle.

The working class should know that miracles do not occur in real life, that they are to expect hunger, complete disorder in industry, disruption of transportation, and protracted bloody anarchy followed by a no less bloody and gloomy reaction.

This is where the proletariat is being led by its present leader, and it must be understood that Lenin is not an omnipotent magician but a cold-blooded trickster who spares neither the honor nor the life of the proletariat.

The workers must not allow adventurers and madmen to heap shameful, senseless, and bloody crimes on the head of the proletariat, for which not Lenin but the proletariat itself will pay.

I ask:

Does the Russian democracy remember the ideas for the triumph of which it struggled against the despotism of the monarchy?

Does it consider itself capable of continuing this struggle now?

Does it remember that when the Romanov gendarmes threw its ideological leaders into prisons and hard-labor camps, it called this method of struggle base?

In what way does Lenin's attitude toward freedom of speech differ from the same attitude of a Stolypin, a Pleve, and other half-humans?

Does not Lenin's government, as the Romanov government did, seize and drag off to prison all those who think differently?

Why are Bernatsky, Konovalov, and other members of the coalition government[64] sitting in the fortress? Are they in any way more criminal than their socialist colleagues freed by Lenin?

The only honest answer to these questions must be an immediate demand to free the ministers and other innocent people who were arrested, and also to restore freedom of speech in its entirety.

Then the sensible elements of the democracy must draw further conclusions, they must decide: is the road of conspirators and anarchists of Nechaev's type also their road?[65]

## FOR THE ATTENTION OF THE WORKERS

*Novaya Zhizn, No. 177,
November 10 (23), 1917*

Vladimir Lenin is introducing a socialist order in Russia by Nechaev's method—"full steam ahead through the swamp."

Both Lenin and Trotsky and all the others who are accompanying them to their ruin in the quagmire of reality are evidently convinced, along with Nechaev, that "the easiest way to make a Russian follow you is to give him the right to act dishonorably," and so they cold-bloodedly dishonor the revolution and dishonor the workng class by forcing it to organize bloody slaughter and by inciting it to outrages and the arresting of completely innocent people such as A. V. Kartashev, M. V. Bernatsky, A. I. Konovalov, and others.[66]

Having forced the proletariat to agree to abolish freedom of the press, Lenin and his cronies thus gave the enemies of democracy the legitimate right to shut its mouth. Threatening with hunger and violence all who do not agree with the despotism of Lenin and Trotsky, these "leaders" justify the despotism of authority against which all the best forces of the country fought so painfully long.

"The obedience of schoolboys and fools"[67] who together follow Lenin and Trotsky "has reached the highest point"; cursing their leaders behind their backs, now leaving them, now joining them again, the schoolboys and fools, in the end, humbly serve the will of the dogmatists and arouse more and more the unrealizable hope for a carefree life among the most unenlightened masses of soldiers and workers.

Imagining themselves to be Napoleons of socialism, the Leninists rant and rave, completing the destruction of Russia.[68] The Russian people will pay for this with lakes of blood.

Lenin himself, of course, is a man of exceptional strength. For twenty-five years he stood in the front rank of those who fought for the triumph of socialism. He is one of the most prominent and striking figures of international social democracy; a man of talent, he possesses all the qualities of a "leader" and also the lack of morality necessary for this role, as well as an utterly pitiless attitude, worthy of a nobleman, toward the lives of the popular masses.

Lenin is a "leader" *and* a Russian nobleman, not without certain psychological traits of this extinct class, and therefore he considers himself justified in performing with the Russian people a cruel experiment which is doomed to failure beforehand.

The people, worn out and impoverished by war, have already paid for this experiment with thousands of lives and will be compelled to pay with tens of thousands, and this will deprive the nation of its leadership for a long time to come.

This inevitable tragedy does not disturb Lenin, the slave

of dogma, or his cronies—his slaves. Life in all its complexity is unknown to Lenin, he does not know the popular masses, he has not lived with them; but he—from books—has learned how to raise these masses on their hind legs and how—easiest of all—to enrage their instincts. The working class is for a Lenin what ore is for a metalworker. Is it possible, under all present conditions, to mold a socialist state from this ore? Apparently it is impossible; however—why not try? What does Lenin risk if the experiment should fail?

He works like a chemist in a laboratory, with the difference that the chemist uses dead matter, but his work produces a valuable result for life; Lenin, however, works with living material and he is leading the revolution to ruin. Sensible workers who follow Lenin should realize that a pitiless experiment is being performed on the Russian working class, an experiment which will destroy the best forces of the workers and will arrest normal development of the Russian revolution for a long time to come.

## UNTIMELY THOUGHTS

*Novaya Zhizn, No. 178,*
*November 11 (24), 1917*

A well-known Russian student of the Sudan tribes, Yunker, said:

"Miserable savages turn away from human flesh with horror, whereas people who have attained a relatively high cultural level fall into cannibalism."

We Russians have undoubtedly attained "a relatively high cultural level"; this is best of all evidenced by that greediness with which we tried and still try to devour tribes politically hostile to us.

Almost from the first days of the revolution a certain

portion of the press attacked democracy with the fury of
cannibals of the "Yum-yum" tribe, and began daily to
gnaw the heads of soldiers, peasants, and workers, fiercely
exposing their passion for "seeds,"[69] their lack of love for
their native land, their lack of a sense of responsibility for
the fate of Russia, and all their deadly sins. No one will
deny that laziness, seed-chewing, the people's social inertness, and all else for which they were reproached are bitter
truths, but we ought to "say the same word but in a different way" and we ought to remember that the people in no
way can be better than they are, because we cared little
about making them better.

A sickly and hysterical irritability, which has replaced
"holy wrath" among us, has made use of the entire lexicon
of insulting words without considering the consequences
that these words must inevitably produce in the hearts of
those who are judged.

It would seem that the "cultured" leaders of certain
organs of the press ought to have understood what excellent help would be rendered to the adventurers by the
furious abuse of democracy, and how much this would
help the demagogues in their striving to conquer the
psychology of the masses.

This simple thought did not occur to the wise politicians, and if we now see before us people who have completely lost their human likeness, then half the blame for
this depressing manifestation must be assumed by those
honorable citizens who tried to inculcate cultural feelings
and thoughts in people by means of verbal punches and
whips.

Is it too late to talk about this? No, it isn't. The throat
of the press has been temporarily squeezed by the "new"
regime which is so shamefully using the old means of
strangling freedom of speech. Soon the newspapers will
again begin to talk, and, of course, they will have to say

everything that we all need to know in order to be shamed and instructed.

But if we, parading in front of each other in pitifully wretched vestments of impotent wrath and pettily malicious vengeance, are again to continue the venomous work of arousing evil impulses and dark feelings, then we must acknowledge in advance that we assume responsibility for every way in which the people may respond to the insults thrown at them.

Anger is unavoidable; it is, however, within our power to make it less disgusting. Even a fist-fight has its own laws of propriety. I know it is ridiculous to speak in Holy Russia of the chivalrous feeling of respect for one's enemy, but I think it will be very useful to couch our sickly wrath in more decorous verbal forms.

Let everyone grant to his enemy the right to be worse than himself, and then our verbal battles will acquire more force, persuasiveness, even beauty.

Frankly speaking, I would like to say:

"Be more humane in these days of general bestiality!"

But I know there is not one heart that would accept these words. Well, let us be at least more tactful and restrained in expressing our thoughts and feelings; we should not forget that, in the final analysis, the people learn wickedness and hate from us. . . .


UNTIMELY THOUGHTS

*Novaya Zhizn, No. 179,*
*November 12 (25), 1917*

I am already being reproached for "removing my mask" and betraying my people "after serving democracy for twenty years."[70]

Their Bolshevik lordships have the legal right to define
my conduct anyway they please, but I must remind these
gentlemen that I was never blinded by the superb inner
qualities of the Russian people; I did not genuflect before
democracy, and to me it is not something so sacred as to
be above criticism and censure.

In 1911, in an article about "The Self-Taught Writers,"
I said: "Abominations must be exposed, and if our
muzhik is a beast, we must say so, and if a worker says:

'I am a proletarian!' in the same repulsive tone of a
man of caste, in that tone in which a nobleman says:

'I am a nobleman!' this worker must be mercilessly
mocked."[71]

Now—when a certain portion of the working masses
aroused by its crazed masters is manifesting the spirit and
methods of a caste, employing terror and coercion, that
coercion against which its best leaders, its perceptive comrades, so long and so courageously fought—now, of
course, I cannot march in the ranks of this portion of the
working class.

I think that to gag with a fist the mouth of *Rech*
(Speech) and other bourgeois newspapers only because
they are hostile to democracy is disgraceful for democracy.[72]

Does democracy really feel it is wrong in its actions and
does it fear the criticism of its enemies? Are the Cadets
really so strong ideologically that they can be defeated
only by means of physical coercion?

Denial of freedom of the press is physical coercion, and
this is unworthy of democracy.

To keep in prison an old man, the revolutionary
Burtsev, a person who dealt the monarchy no small number of powerful blows, to keep him in prison only because
he is carried away by his role of cesspool cleaner of political parties is a disgrace to democracy.[73] To keep in

prison such honest people as A. V. Kartashev, such talented workers as M. V. Bernatsky, and such promoters of culture as A. I. Konovalov, who has done no small amount of good for his workers, is disgraceful to democracy.

To frighten by terror and violence those who do not wish to participate in Mr. Trotsky's frenzied dance on the ruins of Russia is disgraceful and criminal.

All this is unnecessary and will only increase the hatred for the working class. It will have to pay for the mistakes and crimes of its leaders—with thousands of lives and torrents of blood.

## UNTIMELY THOUGHTS

*Novaya Zhizn, No. 185,*
*Nov. 19 (Dec. 2), 1917*

The following appeared in *Pravda* (The Truth):

"Gorky has begun to speak in the language of the enemies of the working class."

That is not the truth. Addressing myself to the most intelligent representatives of the working class I say:

Fanatics and thoughtless dreamers, having aroused in the working masses hopes which cannot be realized in present historical conditions, are luring the Russian proletariat to utter defeat and ruin; and the defeat of the proletariat will call forth in Russia a prolonged reaction of blackest hue.

It is further stated in *Pravda:*

"It is inevitable that every revolution, in the process of its progressive development, should also include a number of negative features which are connected with the break up of the previous thousand-year-old state system. A mighty young hero, creating a new life, brushes with his muscular arms against someone else's decrepit comfortableness, and the petty bourgeoisie, the very people of whom Gorky used to write, begin to howl about the ruin of the Russian state and culture."

I cannot regard as "inevitable" such facts as the plundering of national wealth in the Winter Palace, the Gatchina Palace, and others. I do not understand what connection there is between "the break up of the thousand-year-old state system" and the vandalism in the Maly Theater in Moscow or the thievery in the dressing room of our famous actress M. N. Ermolova?

Without wishing to enumerate the known acts of senseless destruction and looting, I assert that the responsibility for this shame perpetrated by hooligans falls also on the proletariat, which, evidently, is powerless to eradicate hooliganism in its midst.

Further: "The mighty young hero, creating a new life," is making the printing of books increasingly impossible, for there are printing plants where the typesetters are fulfilling only thirty-five percent of an already childishly low norm established by the printers' union.

The proletariat, being heavily outnumbered by one hundred million semiliterate inhabitants of Russian villages, must understand how important a possible lowering of book prices and an increase in a number of books published would be. The proletariat, to its own disadvantage, fails to understand this.

It must also understand that it is sitting on bayonets, and this, as is well known, is not a very stable throne.

And, in general, there are many other "negative features," but where are the positive ones? They are not noticeable if one leaves out of the account "the decrees" of Lenin and Trotsky, but I doubt that the proletariat participated consciously in the creation of these "decrees." No, if the proletariat had been fully aware of the nature of

these paper creations, they would have been impossible in
the form in which they now exist.

The article in *Pravda* concludes with the following
lyrical question:

"At the bright festival of the peoples of the world,
where those who had formerly been unwilling enemies will
unite in a brotherly embrace, will Gorky, who quit the
ranks of the genuine revolutionary democracy in such
haste, be a welcome guest at this banquet of peace?"[74]

Of course, neither the author of this article nor I will
live to see "the bright festival." It is far away. There remain decades of persistent, everyday cultural work to
bring about this festival.

But at a festival where the despotism of the semiliterate
masses will celebrate its easy victory and—as before, as
always—human personality will remain oppressed, I will
have no part because such to me is not a festival.

No matter in whose hands power rests, I retain my
human right to be critical of it.

And I am especially suspicious, especially distrustful, of
a Russian when he gets power into his hands. Not long
ago a slave, he becomes the most unbridled despot as soon
as he has the chance to become his neighbor's master.


## UNTIMELY THOUGHTS

*Novaya Zhizn, No. 194,*
*December 6 (19), 1917*

Having expended an enormous amount of energy, the
working class has created its own intelligentsia of little
Bebels, who play the role of true leaders of the working
class, true spokesmen for its material and spiritual interests.

Even under the trying conditions of a police state, the

workers' intelligentsia, not sparing itself and daily risking
its freedom, knew how to fight with honor and success for
the triumph of its ideas, consistently bringing the light of
social consciousness to the dark working masses and
showing them the way to freedom and culture.

At some future time the impartial voice of history will
tell the world how great, heroic, and successful the work
of the proletarian intelligentsia was during the period from
the beginning of the 1890's to the beginning of the war.

The accursed war has exterminated tens of thousands of
the best workers, replacing them at their workbenches by
people who went to work "for the defense" in order to
avoid military service. These are all people alien to proletarian psychology, politically backward, devoid of class
consciousness, and lacking the natural propensity of the
proletarian for the creation of a new culture; they are
concerned only with their Philistine desire to achieve personal prosperity as soon as possible and at whatever cost.
These are people organically incapable of accepting and
embodying in life the ideas of pure socialism.

And so the remnant of the workers' intelligentsia, that
part which was not wiped out by war and internecine
struggle, found itself hemmed in by the masses, by people
psychologically alien, by people who spoke the language
of the proletarian but could not feel the way the proletarian felt, by people whose moods, desires, and actions
doomed to disgrace and destruction the best, the topmost
stratum of the working class.

The inflamed instincts of these ignorant masses have
found spokesmen for their animal anarchism,[75] and these
leaders of rebellious Philistines are now, as we see, putting
into practice the pitiable ideas of Proudhon, but not those
of Marx; they develop Pugachevism[76] and not socialism,
and they propagandize in every way a general leveling
based on moral and material poverty.

It is difficult and painful to speak about this, but it is
necessary to speak because it is the class-conscious seg-
ment of the proletariat that will have to answer for all
the sins and outrages committed by a force alien to it.

Recently the representatives of one of the local factory
committees told the director of the factory about their
own workers:

"We are surprised that you were able to get along with
this crazy gang!"

There are factories in which the workers are beginning
to steal and sell the copper parts of machines; there are
many facts which point to the wildest anarchy among the
working masses. I know there are phenomena of a different
kind: for instance, in one factory the workers bought material for the work with their own wages. But examples of
this type are very few, while examples of the opposite
character are counted in hundreds.

The "new" worker is a person alien to industry and
unaware of its cultural significance in our peasant land. I
am sure an intelligent worker cannot sympathize with
facts such as the arrest of Sofya Vladimirovna Panina. In
her "People's House" in Ligovka hundreds of proletarians
learned to think and feel, just as they did in the Nizhny
Novgorod "People's House" which was built with her
help. The entire life of this enlightened woman was devoted to cultural activity among the workers. And now she
is in prison.[77] Long ago Turgenev pointed out that a good
deed never meets with gratitude; well, I am not speaking
about gratitude but about the fact that one must be able to
appreciate useful work.

The workers' intelligentsia should possess this ability.

Former minister A. I. Konovalov, a man of irreproach-
able honesty, built at his factory in Vichuga[78] a "People's
House" which is a model building of this type. Konovalov
is in prison. The responsibility for these absurd arrests

will, in time, be placed on the conscience of the working class.

A multitude of all sorts of swindlers, former minions of the Secret Police, and adventurers have been introduced into the midst of people who are supposedly "expressing the will of the revolutionary proletariat." A. V. Lunacharsky, lyrically inclined but muddleheaded, forces the proletariat to accept Yasinsky, a writer of evil reputation, as its poet.[79] This means soiling the banners of the working class, corrupting the proletariat.

They want to kick the Cadets out of the Constituent Assembly. Without mentioning the fact that a considerable portion of the country's population wants these very Cadets to express its opinions and desires in the Constituent Assembly and that therefore the expulsion of the Cadets would be a violation of the will of hundreds of thousands of people—without mentioning this disgrace, I should point out that the Constitutional-Democratic party is uniting the most cultured people of the country, the most skillful workers in all fields of intellectual endeavor.[80] It is extremely useful to be faced with an intelligent and steadfast enemy; a good enemy educates his opponent, making him more intelligent and stronger. The workers' intelligentsia should understand this. And, once again, it should keep in mind that all that is being done now is being done on its behalf; it is on the intelligentsia, on its reason and conscience that history will pass its stern judgment. Not everything is just politics, it is necessary to preserve some conscience and other human feelings.

# UNTIMELY THOUGHTS

*Novaya Zhizn, No. 195,*
*December 7 (20), 1917*

"The proletariat is the creator of a new culture"—a wonderful dream of the triumph of justice, reason, and beauty,
a dream of man's victory over brute and beast is contained
in these words; thousands of people of all classes have
perished in the struggle for the realization of this dream.

The proletariat is in power; now it has an opportunity
for free creativity. It is appropriate and timely to ask: In
what way is this creativity expressed? The decrees of the
"Government of the People's Commissars" are newspaper
feuilletons, no more. This is literature which is written
"with a pitchfork in water," and although there are valuable ideas in these decrees, contemporary reality will not
provide the conditions for the translation of these ideas
into life.

What will the revolution offer that is new, how will it
change the bestial Russian way of life, and will it bring
much light into the darkness of the people's life?

Up to ten thousand "mob trials" have already been
counted during the revolution. Here is how democracy
tries its sinners. A thief was caught near the Aleksandrovsky Market, the crowd there and then beat him up and
took a vote—by which death should the thief be punished:
drowning or shooting? They decided on drowning and
threw the man into the icy water. But with great difficulty
he managed to swim out and crawl up on the shore; one of
the crowd then went up to him and shot him.

The middle ages of our history were an epoch of
abominable cruelty, but even then if a criminal sentenced
to death by a court fell from the gallows, he was allowed
to live.

How do the mob trials affect the coming generation?

A thief, beaten half to death, is taken by soldiers to the Moyka[81] to be drowned; he is all covered with blood, his face is completely smashed, and one eye has come out. A crowd of children accompanies him; later some of them return from the Moyka and, hopping up and down, joyfully shout:

"They sunk him, they drowned him!"

These are our children, the future builders of life. The life of a man will be cheap in their estimation, but man— one should not forget this!—is the finest and most valuable creation of nature, the very best there is in the universe. The war has valued man cheaper than a tiny piece of lead; we were justly indignant at this evaluation and reproached the "imperialists" for it—but whom shall we now reproach for the daily, brutal massacre of people?

———— • ————

Due to a number of circumstances our printing and publishing of books has almost completely ceased, and, at the same time, the most valuable libraries are being destroyed one after another. Only recently muzhiks plundered the estates of Khudekov and Obolensky, as well as a number of other estates. The muzhiks took home everything that had value in their eyes, but they burned libraries, chopped pianos to pieces with axes, and tore up pictures. Objects of science and art and instruments of culture have no value in the eyes of the village—one may doubt whether they have any value in the eyes of the urban masses.

A book is the principal disseminator of culture, and to enable the people to obtain help from an intelligent and honest book, those in the book trade ought to be able to make some sacrifices—for they, more than anybody, are especially interested in creating an ideological environment around them which would further the development and realization of their ideals.

Our teachers, the Radishchevs, Chernyshevskys,[82] and Marxes, the spiritual producers of books, sacrificed both freedom and life for their books. How are the physical producers of books facilitating the development of the book trade at the present time?

———— • ————

Every night for almost two weeks crowds of people have been robbing wine cellars, getting drunk, banging each other over the head with bottles, cutting their hands with fragments of glass, and wallowing like pigs in filth and blood. Over this period, wine worth several tens of millions of rubles has been destroyed, and, of course, hundreds of millions of rubles worth will continue to be destroyed.

If this valuable commodity were sold to Sweden, we could receive for it gold or goods vital to our country, such as textiles, medicine, and machinery.

The people from Smolny,[83] who started to think about it somewhat late, are threatening drunkards with severe penalties, but the drunkards are not afraid of threats and continue to destroy a commodity which should long ago have been requisitioned, declared the property of the impoverished nation, and sold at a profit for the benefit of all.

During the wine riots people are being shot down like mad wolves, while others are being gradually taught to exterminate their neighbors without qualms.

*Pravda* writes about the drunken riots as a "provocation of the bourgeois" which, of course, is a lie, an "eloquent phrase" that can increase bloodshed.[84]

———— • ————

Thievery is spreading, robberies are increasing, shameless people engage in bribery just as cleverly as the officials of the Tsarist regime; shady persons, who gather around Smolny, try to blackmail the frightened citizen. The coarseness of the representatives of the "Government of the People's Commissars" provokes general censure that is justified. Various small fry, taking delight in power, treat the citizen like the vanquished, that is, just as the Tsar's police treated him. They yell at everyone, they yell like policemen in Konotop or Chukhloma.[85] All this is done on behalf of the "proletariat" and in the name of the "social revolution," and all this represents the triumph of an animal way of life, a development of that Asiaticism which is causing us to decay.

But where and how is that "idealism of the Russian worker" expressed, about which Karl Kautsky wrote so flatteringly?

Where and how is the socialist ethic, the "new" ethic, being put into practice?

I expect that one of the "realistic politicians" will exclaim with disdain for all that has been pointed out:

"What do you want? This is a social revolution!"

No, I do not see any vividly expressed elements of a social revolution in this outburst of animal instincts. This is a Russian rebellion without the socialists-in-spirit, without participation of the socialist psychology.[86]

# UNTIMELY THOUGHTS

*Novaya Zhizn, No. 198,*
*December 10 (23), 1917*

Not so long ago I was accused of having "sold myself to the Germans" and of "betraying Russia";[87] now I am accused of having "sold myself to the Cadets" and of "betraying the cause of the working class."

These accusations do not offend or bother me personally, but they suggest unhappy and unflattering thoughts about the morality of the accusers' feelings and about their social consciousness.

Listen, gentlemen, aren't you throwing all these nasty accusations of betrayal, treason, and moral vacillation in each other's faces a little too freely? If one is to believe you, then all of Russia is inhabited by people who are only concerned with selling out the country, people who think only of how to betray each other!

I understand: the abundance of informers and adventurers in the revolutionary movement must have cultivated in you a natural feeling of distrust of one another and of man in general, I understand that this shameful fact must have afflicted even very healthy people with the agony of acute suspicion.

But nonetheless, in hurling at each other so carelessly accusations of betrayal, treason, self-interest, and hypocrisy, you apparently imagine all of Russia to be a country inhabited from one end to the other by dishonest and vile people, but then you, too, are Russians.

As you see, this is quite amusing, but—even more—it is dangerous, because those who play this dirty game may gradually and unwittingly suggest to themselves that all Russia indeed is a country of dishonest and mercenary people, and therefore we, too, are "cut from the same cloth."

Just think: the revolution in our country is made now
with Japanese, now with German money; the counterrevolution, with the money of the Cadets and the British;
but where is that Russian unselfishness, where is our glori-
fied scrupulousness, our idealism, our heroic legends about
honest champions of freedom, our Don Quixotism, and all
the other good qualities of the Russian people which are
so loudly extolled in both oral and written Russian literature?

Is all this a lie?

Understand that in accusing one another of baseness,
you accuse yourselves, the whole nation.

When I read an angry letter from some accuser, I cannot help recalling the words of a peasant from the Orel
province:

"Our whole village is drunk: there is one righteous
man, but he is a fool."

And I recall that beautiful and legitimate indignation
which I observed among the workers at the time when
*Russkoe Znamya* (Russian Banner) of the Black Hundreds[88] accused *Rech* (Speech) of some kind of involvement with the money of the Finns or Eskimos.

"The scoundrels have nothing to say, so they say the
nastiest thing they can think of."

It seems to me that I write simply and clearly enough
and that the thinking workers should not accuse me of
"betraying the cause of the proletariat." I consider the
working class to be a mighty cultural force in our ignorant
peasant country, and with all my heart I wish the Russian
worker a quantitative and qualitative development. I have
repeatedly said that industry is one of the foundations of
culture, that the development of industry is vital to the
salvation of the country, to its Europeanization; that the
factory worker is not only a physical but a spiritual force,
not only one who fulfills somebody else's will, but a man
who realizes his own will, his own reason. He is not as

dependent on the elemental forces of nature as is the peasant, whose heavy labor is not seen and does not remain over the ages. All that the peasant produces he sells or eats, his energy is completely absorbed by the land, whereas the labor of a worker remains on earth, beautifying it and contributing to the further harnessing of natural forces for the benefit of man.

In this difference of working activity is rooted a profound difference between the souls of a peasant and a worker, and I look upon the intelligent worker as the aristocrat of the democracy.

Exactly: an aristocracy among the democracy—that is the role of the worker in our peasant country, that is how the worker should feel. Unfortunately, he does not feel this way yet. It is clear how high my evaluation of the role of the working class in the development of Russia's culture is, and I have no reason to change this evaluation. Besides, I have a love for the working man, I feel I have blood ties with him, and I have love and respect for his great work. And, finally, I love Russia.

The People's Commissars will smile contemptuously and say, "Oh, of course!" But that won't kill me. Yes, I love Russia with fear and with torment and I love the Russian people.

We Russians are a people who have not yet worked freely, not yet developed all our strength and abilities; and when I think that the revolution will give us an opportunity to work freely and to create fully, my heart fills with great hope and joy, even in these accursed days drenched in blood and wine.

Here begins the line of my resolute and irreconcilable disagreement with the senseless activity of the People's Commissars.

I consider ideological maximalism very useful for the undisciplined Russian soul; it must cultivate great and bold demands in this soul; arouse a long-needed capacity for action, and an aggressiveness; develop initiative in this sluggish soul, and, in general, shape and enliven it.

But the practical maximalism of the anarchistic communists and visionaries from Smolny is fatal to Russia and, above all, to the Russian working class.

The People's Commissars treat Russia as material for an experiment; to them the Russian people is that horse which bacteriologists inoculate with typhus so that the horse produces antityphoid serum in its blood. Just such a cruel experiment, which is doomed to failure beforehand, is being performed by the Commissars on the Russian people, without considering that the worn-out, half-starved horse may die.

The reformers from Smolny do not care about Russia; they are cold-bloodedly sacrificing her to their dream of world or European revolution.

There is no place for a social revolution in the present conditions of Russian life, for it is impossible, just by a wave of the wand, to make socialists out of the eighty-five percent peasant population of the country, among whom are several tens of millions of non-Russian nomads.

The working class will be the first to suffer from this utterly insane experiment, because it is the vanguard of the revolution and it will be the first to be wiped out in a civil war. And if the working class is crushed and destroyed, that means the best forces and hopes of the country will be destroyed.

Therefore I say to the workers who are aware of their cultural role in the country: a politically literate proletarian must examine thoughtfully his attitude toward the Government of the People's Commissars. He must take a very cautious approach to their social creativity.

My own opinion is this: the People's Commissars are destroying and ruining the working class of Russia, they are terribly and absurdly complicating the workers' movement; by directing it beyond the bounds of reason, they are creating conditions which are insuperably difficult for the entire future work of the proletariat and for the entire progress of the country.

I do not care what I shall be called for my opinion of the "Government" of experimenters and visionaries, but I do care about the fate of the working class and Russia.

And as long as I am able, I shall tell the Russian proletarian again and again:

You are being led to ruin, you are being used as material for an inhuman experiment, and in the eyes of your leaders you are still not human beings![89]

## UNTIMELY THOUGHTS

*Novaya Zhizn, No. 205,*
*December 19, 1917 (January 1, 1918)*

The revolution goes deeper. . . .

The reckless demagoguery of people who are "deepening" the revolution is bearing its fruits, which are obviously poisonous for the more intelligent and culturally advanced representatives of the social interests of the working class. A vicious struggle between common laborers and skilled workers is already gradually beginning in mills and plants; the common laborers are beginning to assert that metalworkers, turners, smelters, etc., are "bourgeois."

The revolution is continually going deeper to the glory of those who are performing an experiment on the living body of the working people.

And the workers who realize the tragedy of the moment feel the greatest anxiety for the fate of the revolution.

"I am afraid," one of them writes to me, "that the day

is not far off when the masses, dissatisfied with Bolshevism, will become forever disillusioned about a better future, will forever lose faith in socialism, and will turn their eyes back to the past, to black monarchism, and then the cause of the liberation of nations will have perished for hundreds of years.

"I think this will happen, because Bolshevism will not fulfill all the aspirations of the uncultured masses, and I don't know what we, who find ourselves among these masses, must do to prevent the extinguishing of faith in socialism and in a better life on earth."

Another reports: "The position of a half-way educated worker in the midst of the stultified masses is getting similar to the position of one who becomes a stranger to his own kind."

These complaints are being heard more and more frequently, foreshadowing the possibility of a deep split in the core of the working class. But other workers are saying and writing to me:

"You should rejoice, comrade, the proletariat has conquered!"

There is nothing for me to rejoice about; the proletariat has conquered nothing and no one. Just as the proletariat itself was not conquered when the police regime had it by the throat, so now, when it has the bourgeoisie by the throat, the bourgeoisie is not yet conquered. Ideas are not conquered by means of physical force. Conquerors are usually magnanimous, perhaps because of weariness; the proletariat is not magnanimous, as is evidenced by the cases of S. V. Panina, Boldyrev, Konovalov, Bernatsky, Kartashev, Dolgoruky,[90] and others who were put in prison for reasons unknown.

Besides those named, thousands—yes, thousands!—of workers and soldiers are starving in prison.

No, the proletariat is neither magnanimous nor just,

even though the revolution was supposed to establish all possible justice in the country.

The proletariat has not conquered; an internecine slaughter is taking place all over the country; hundreds and thousands of people are killing one another. In *Pravda,* insane people are egging us: "Smite the bourgeois, smite the Kaledinites!" But the bourgeois and the Kaledinites are just ordinary peasant-soldiers and worker-soldiers; it is they who are being wiped out and it is they who are shooting the Red Guards.

If only the internecine war consisted of Lenin's seizing the petty bourgeois hair of Milyukov and of Milyukov's pulling the luxuriant curls of Lenin, then—

All right! Go to it, Masters!

However, it is not the masters but the serfs who are fighting, and there is no reason to believe that this fight will end soon. One cannot rejoice at the sight of the healthy forces of a country perishing in mutual extermination. Yet thousands of people roam the streets and, as if mocking themselves, they shout: "Long live peace!"

Have the banks been seized? It would be good if the banks contained bread with which children could be fed their fill. But there is no bread in the banks, and day after day the children don't get enough to eat, they are becoming ever more exhausted and the death rate is increasing.

The internecine slaughter is totally destroying the railroads; even if the peasants gave their grain, it could not be transported quickly.

But what surprises and frightens me most of all is that the revolution carries no sign of man's spiritual rebirth, is not making people more honest, more straightforward, and is not increasing their sense of their own value and the moral evaluation of their work.

There are, of course, people who "strut about" like

circus wrestlers who have successfully "pinned" their opponents; these people are not worth talking about. But in
the masses, on a general scale, it is not noticeable that the
revolution has revived the social sense in man. Man is
valued just as cheaply as before. Habits of the old way of
life are not disappearing. The "new authorities" are just as
crude as the old, but with even less appearance of being
courteous. They yell and stamp their feet in today's police
stations just as they yelled before. And they grab bribes
just as the former bureaucrats did, and they drive people
in herds to prison. At the moment all that is old and nasty
is not disappearing.

This is a bad sign: it indicates that only a transfer of
physical power has taken place, but this transfer does not
accelerate the growth of spiritual power.

Nevertheless, the meaning of life and the justification of
all its abominations lie only in the development of all our
spiritual powers and abilities.

"It is premature to speak about this, first we must take
power into our hands."

There is no poison more foul than power over people;
we must keep this in mind so that power will not poison
us, turning us into cannibals even more abominable than
those against whom we have fought all our lives.

## UNTIMELY THOUGHTS

*Novaya Zhizn, No. 207,*
*December 21, 1917 (January 3, 1918)*

A small group of people is standing on the shore of the
Fontanka[91] and, looking into the distance at a bridge
packed with a dark crowd, they talk calmly and indifferently:

"They're drowning thieves."

"Did they catch many?"

"Three, they say."

"They beat one, a youngster."

"Killed him?"

"What else did you expect?"

"They've got to beat them to death, otherwise they'll make your life a misery. . . ."

An impressive gray-haired man, red-faced, and looking in some ways like a butcher, says confidently:

"There are no courts now, that means we should be tried by ourselves. . . ."

A shabby man with sharp eyes asks:

"But wouldn't that be too simple if we did it ourselves?" The gray-haired man answers lazily and without looking at him:

"The simpler the better. It's faster, that's the main thing."

"Hey, he's howling!"

The crowd became silent, straining to hear. From far away, from the river, a wild anguished cry is heard.

———— • ————

Having abolished the old courts in the name of the proletariat, their lordships the People's Commissars have thereby strengthened in the consciousness of the "street" its right to "mob trials," a bestial right. And earlier, before the revolution, our street liked to beat people, indulging in this loathsome "sport" with delight. Nowhere is man beaten so often, with such zeal and joy, as in our Russia. "To smack in the teeth," "to punch up the throat," "in the bread basket," "in the kidneys," "to give a drubbing," "to cuff around the ears," "to bloody the nose"—all these are our nice Russian pastimes. We brag about this. People have become too accustomed to being "knocked about from time they were small"; they are knocked about by their parents and masters; they used to be knocked about by the police.

And it looks as if these people, brought up on torture, have now been given the right to torture one another freely. They are exercising their "right" with evident sensuality and unbelievable cruelty. "Trials" by street mob have become a "way of life," and we must keep in mind that every one of these increases in depth and extent the dull, morbid cruelty of the crowd.

The worker Kostin tried to defend those who were being beaten; he, too, was killed. No doubt anyone who dares to protest against the street "trials" will be severely beaten.

Do I have to say that "mob trials" frighten no one and that street robberies and thievery are becoming more and more brazen?

But the most terrible and ignoble thing is that the cruelty of the street is growing, and the blame for this will be placed on the working class, since it will inevitably be said that the "government of the workers has let loose the savage instincts of the dark masses of the street." No one will mention how terribly the heart of an honest and intelligent worker aches because of all these "mob trials" and because of all the chaos of disrupted life.

I do not know what can be done to combat the abominable manifestation of this bloody justice of the street, but the People's Commissars must immediately do something very decisive. They cannot help but realize that the responsibility for the blood shed by the brutalized street will fall both on them and on the class whose interests they try to serve. This blood soils the banners of the proletariat, it stains its honor, kills its social idealism.

The worker understands better than anybody else that

thievery, robbery, and mercenary murder are all the deep sores of the social order; he understands that people are not born murderers and thieves but become such. And it goes without saying that the intelligent worker must fight with greater effort against the street's "trying" of people who are driven by need to crimes against the "sacred institution of property."

## FRUITS OF DEMAGOGY

*Novaya Zhizn, No. 208,
December 22, 1917 (January 4, 1918)*

The following letter was received by the editors of *Novaya Zhizn*:*

The Cannon Section of the Putilov Works.

Has resolved to censure you, the writers of *Novaya Zhizn*, both Stroev, who was once a writer, as well as Bazarov, Gimmer-Sukhanov, Gorky, and all compilers of *Novaya Zhizn*. Your Organ does not correspond to our present general life, you are the following the defensists. But remember do not touch our working Life of the proletarians, with *the demonstration which occurred on Sunday, the demonstration was not conducted by you so it is not for you to criticize it.* And in general our party is the Majority and we support our political leaders, real socialists, liberators of the people from the oppression of the Bourgeoisie and capitalists, and if such counterrevolutionary articles are written in the Future then we workers swear that we will shut your newspaper just get that into your skull, and if you wish ask your Socialist the so-called neutralist he was at our Putilov Works with his backward speeches ask him whether he was allowed to speak but no,

* The grammatical and stylistic peculiarities of this letter are retained.

but soon you will be prohibited and your organ is beginning to be like that of the Cadets, and if you bitter,[92]
backward writers *continue your polemic also with the government organ Pravda* then know that we will quit selling
in our Narva-Petergof district. the address
   The Putilov Works the Cannon Section write an answer
otherwise there will be Reprisals.

   Ferociously written!
   Children talk with such ferocity after reading a great
many of the frightening books of Gustave Aimard and
imagining themselves to be terrible Indians.
   Of course, children ought to be taught. And, for the
edification of the author—or authors—of the angry letter,
I say:
   One should not reason the way you do:
   "The demonstration was not conducted by you, so it is
not for you to criticize it."
   Political and economic oppression of the working class
has also "not been conducted by us," but we have always
criticized and we will go on criticizing any system of oppression of man no matter by whom this system is "conducted."
   The people whose names are mentioned in the letter did
not fight against the autocracy of swindlers and scoundrels
to have it replaced by an autocracy of political savages.
   We are threatened that if we "continue the polemic with
the government organ *Pravda,*" then. . . .
   Yes, we will continue the polemic with a government
which ruins the working class; we regard this polemic as
our duty, the duty of honest citizens and independent socialists.

## UNTIMELY THOUGHTS

*Novaya Zhizn, No. 209,*
*December 23, 1917 (January 5, 1918)*

They want to arrest Irakly Tsereteli, a talented politician
and an absolutely honest man.[93]

For his struggle against the monarchy, for his defense of
the interests of the working class, and for propagating
ideas of socialism, the old government rewarded Tsereteli
with penal servitude and tuberculosis.

Now the government, which supposedly acts on behalf
of and according to the will of all the proletariat, wants to
reward Tsereteli with prison. Why? I do not understand.

I know Tsereteli is dangerously ill, but it goes without
saying that I would not dare to insult this courageous man
by appealing for compassion for him. And anyway, to
whom would I appeal? Serious, sensible people, who have
not lost their heads, now feel that they are "in the wilderness" which—alas!—is not "uninhabited." They are powerless in the turbulence of inflamed passions. Life is
governed by people who are in a state of continuous "ex-
citability and irritability." This state is recognized by law
as one of the reasons which give a criminal the right to
leniency, but this is nonetheless a state of "sanity."

The "civil war," that is, the self-destruction of our
democracy to the malicious delight of its enemies, was
contrived and is being kindled by these people. And now it
is already clear, even to the proletariat which is bewitched
by their demagogic oratory, that they are guided not by
the practical interests of the working class, but by the
theoretical triumph of anarcho-syndicalist ideas.[94]

These sectarians and fanatics are gradually arousing the
instincts and hopes of the ignorant masses—vain and un-

realizable under present conditions—and are isolating the proletarian, truly socialist, and consciously revolutionary intelligentsia. They are tearing off the head of the working class.

And if they dare to play with the fate of the entire class, what then do they care about the fate of one of their finest old comrades, about the life of one of the most honorable knights of socialism?

Just as for the half-witted archpriest Avvakum, dogma is for them higher than man.

How will all this end for our Russian democracy which they are trying so persistently to de-personalize?

## [UNTITLED]

*Novaya Zhizn, No. 210,*
*December 24, 1917 (January 6, 1918)*

Yes, we are going through a storm of dark passions; the past has laid bare before us its very depths and shows us how repulsively deformed man is; a blizzard of greed, hatred, and vengeance rages about us; a wild beast, enraged by long captivity and worn out by centuries of torment, has opened wide its vengeful jaws and in triumph roars out its rancor and malice.

But all that is vile and despicable on earth has been and is being done by us, and all that is beautiful and intelligent, for which we are striving, lives within us.

Yesterday's slave today sees his master reduced to dust, powerless and frightened—a sight of supreme joy for the slave who has not yet experienced a joy more worthy of man, the joy of being free from the feeling of enmity toward one's neighbor.

But this joy will also be experienced; it is not worth

living if it is impossible to believe in the brotherhood of
men; life has no meaning if there is no confidence in the
victory of love.

Yes, yes, we live up to our necks in blood and filth;
thick fogs of detestable vulgarity surround us and are
blinding many; yes, at times it seems that this vulgarity
will poison and stifle all the beautiful dreams to which we
have given birth in labor and torment, all the torches
we lit on the way to rebirth.

But man, nevertheless, is man, and ultimately only that
which is human triumphs; in this lies the great meaning of
the life of the whole world, and there is no other meaning
in life.

Perhaps we shall perish?

It is better to burn in the flames of the revolution than
to rot slowly in the garbage pit of monarchy as we did
before February.

We, Russia, have apparently reached the time when all
our people, stirred to the depths of their souls, must wash
away, fling off from themselves the filth of life which has
accumulated for centuries, must kill our Slavic laziness,
and must reexamine all our customs and habits, all our
evaluations of the phenomena of life and our evaluations
of ideas and man; we must arouse in ourselves all our
strength and abilities and, finally, we, as new, bold, and
talented workers, must join in mankind's work of organizing our planet.[95]

Yes, our situation is deeply tragic, but it is in tragedy
that man is supreme.

Yes, to live is difficult, too much petty malice has come
to the surface of our life, and there is no righteous wrath
against vulgarity, wrath which might kill it.

But as Synesius, the Bishop of Ptolemais, said:

"Tranquility of the soul is necessary for the philosopher;
the skillful helmsman is reared only by storms."

Let us believe that those who do not perish in the chaos and storm will get stronger and will develop in themselves the unshakeable strength to resist the age-old, bestial principles of life.

Today is the day of the birth of Christ, one of the two greatest symbols created by man's striving toward justice and beauty.

Christ is the immortal idea of mercy and humaneness, and Prometheus is the enemy of the gods, the first rebel against Fate—man has created nothing more majestic than these two embodiments of his desires.

The day will come when, in the people's souls, the symbols of pride and mercy and of meekness and reckless courage in attaining a goal will both fuse into one great feeling, and all people will realize their own significance, the beauty of their aspirations, and the blood ties of everyone with everyone else.

In these days of revolt, blood, and hostility, days which are terrifying for many people, one should not forget that, through great torments and unbearable trials, we are marching toward the rebirth of man, and that we are doing the earthly job of liberating life from the heavy, rusted chains of the past.

Let us believe in ourselves, let us work stubbornly. All is within our will and there is no other lawmaker in the universe besides our rational will.

To all who feel lonely amidst the storm of events, whose hearts are gnawed by evil doubts, and whose spirit is oppressed by weighty grief—heartfelt greetings!

And heartfelt greetings to all who have been wrongly shut up in prison.

## [UNTITLED]

*Novaya Zhizn, No. 214,*
*December 31, 1917 (January 13, 1918)*

What will the New Year bring us? All that we are capable of doing.

But in order to become people capable of action, we must believe that these frenzied days smeared with filth and blood are the great days of the birth of a new Russia.

Yes, now, at this very moment when people, deafened by the preaching of equality and brotherhood, are robbing their neighbor in the streets, stripping him bare; when the struggle against the idol of property does not prevent people from brutally torturing and murdering the petty violators of the law of the sanctity of property; when "free citizens," engaging in petty trade, fleece one another mercilessly and shamelessly; in these days of monstrous contradictions a new Russia is being born.

It is a difficult birth—in the noise of the destruction of the old forms of life, amidst the decaying remains of the filthy barracks in which the people suffocated for three hundred years and which made them pettily spiteful and utterly mediocre.

In this outburst of all the baseness and vulgarity accumulated by us under the leaden weight of the most despicable monarchy, in this eruption of the filthy vulcano, the Russian of former days, the idler and dreamer in love with himself, is perishing, and his place shall be taken by the bold and sturdy worker, the builder of a new life.

The Russian is now no good, worse than ever before. Not sure of the durability of his conquests and not experiencing the joy of freedom, he has bristled up with petty spite and is still trying to discover—is he really free? These trials are costly both for him and the objects of his experiments.

But life, our stern and merciless teacher, will soon capture him with the noose of necessity, and this will force him to work, force him to forget, in united toil, all the petty, slavish, and shameful things which possess him now.

New people are created by new conditions of existence; new conditions create new people.

A man who has not experienced the torments of slavery, who has not been deformed by oppression, is coming into the world—this will be a man incapable of oppressing others.

Let us believe that this man will feel the cultural significance of work and will learn to love it. Work performed with love becomes creation.

If only man would learn to love his work, all the rest would be added unto him.

## THE FRUITS OF DEMAGOGY

*Novaya Zhizn, No. 3 (217),*
*January 5 (18), 1918*

A "group of employees" of Petrograd public institutions writes me the following:*

> Getting acquainted with your previous literary works, we imagine you to be most sensitive to the demands of the moment and to have an especially kind heart for the oppressed peoples. Knowing also how authoritative your opinion among the people was, we expected to hear from you now a strong word uniting all toilers, but not at all what you write in your "fruits of demagogy" (*Novaya Zhizn,* No. 208). Reading these lines, we don't understand

* The grammatical and stylistic peculiarities of this letter are retained.

what you wanted to say in them to the children of the
Putilov Works; we think that much was left unsaid by you
on this important question; you either did this intentionally
so that the average person wouldn't immediately understand what was the matter or you simply don't feel like
answering the question more clearly and in more detail.
We think that if you want to teach these children and if a
child asks, then the teacher should answer all their questions clearly, exactly, and—what is especially important—
impartially, but you, it seems, didn't do this, you just
polemicize.

I do not understand the bewilderment of the "group of
employees"; it seems to me I replied quite convincingly
and clearly to the authors of the letter from the Putilov
Works. They wrote to me: "If you are going to criticize
the Government of the People's Commissars, we shall
close down *Novaya Zhizn.*"
I replied: "*Novaya Zhizn* will criticize the Government
of the People's Commissars just as it will any other government." For further edification I added: "The people
working at *Novaya Zhizn* did not fight against an autocracy of scoundrels and swindlers to have it replaced by an
autocracy of savages."
Since a threat of physical violence is a threat of savages,
free citizens should not resort to such means in an ideological struggle.
Everything is as clear as it could possibly be—what is it
then that the "group of employees" doesn't understand?
The "group of employees" writes further:

We still cannot understand by what means and how, in
your opinion, the Government of Soviets, in which the
working class predominates, can "ruin the working class!"
That is just like taking yourself by the hair and lifting
yourself up.

From the fact that the "working class predominates in the Government" it still does not follow that the working class understands all that is done by the Government. The "Government of Soviets" is putting into the heads of the workers the notion that the establishment of a socialist system is possible in Russia.

*Novaya Zhizn,* in a number of articles which met no objections as to their substance from the government organs, asserted—and will assert in the future—that the necessary conditions for the introduction of socialism are nonexistent in our country and that the Smolny government treats the Russian worker like brushwood: it kindles the brushwood in order to see—will a European revolution be ignited by the Russian bonfire?

This means "playing long shots," not sparing the working class, not thinking about its future or about the fate of Russia—let Russia be burned up senselessly, let it be reduced to ashes, if only the experiment is carried out.

That is how fanatics and utopians act, but the intelligent and cultured part of the working class cannot act this way.

Therefore I keep on saying: an experiment is being conducted with the Russian proletariat for which the proletariat will pay with their blood, life, and, worst of all, a prolonged disillusionment with the very ideal of socialism.

One should keep in mind that if the "recklessness of the Tsars is capable of destroying entire generations," then all people who are intoxicated with the poison of power are not lacking in this "recklessness."

The letter of the "group of employees" is written maliciously and is adorned with various quibbles such as the reference to my "own villa," etc.

Once and for all I declare to this "group" and other lovers of quibbles that I never had and do not have my "own villa"; I live on the capital of my experience of life and on my knowledge, which I wish with all my heart to the group of employees as well as to all other people who sincerely hate "property" until they come into possession of it. But if I had my own villa, I would not feel like a sinner.

I would like to ask the "group" and all the other authors of angry epistles to me: Why are you, citizens, all angry, why are your letters saturated with such irritation, such petty quibbles and gibes?

After all, you are no longer "oppressed peoples," but victors; you should experience the joy of victory, the calm confidence of people whose sacred hopes are being realized. You waited so long and so patiently to be treated with justice, now it is your obligation to be just to all, to concern yourselves with the triumph, throughout the whole world, of that justice we desire.

But you keep getting angry, you keep shouting and cursing. What for?

You will not change the abominable conditions of life without changing your feelings and your attitude toward yourselves and your neighbor.

## JANUARY 9—JANUARY 5

*Novaya Zhizn, No. 6 (220),*
*January 9 (22), 1918*

On January 9, 1905, when the downtrodden, ill-treated soldiers were firing into unarmed and peaceful crowds of workers by order of the Tsarist regime,[96] intellectuals and workers ran up to the soldiers—the unwilling murderers—and shouted point-blank in their faces:

"What are you doing, damn you? Who are you killing?

Don't you see they are your brothers, they are unarmed, they bear no malice toward you, they are going to the Tsar to beg his attention to their needs. They are not even demanding, but begging without threats, without anger, with humility. Come to your senses, what are you doing, idiots!"

It seemed that these simple, clear words which were provoked by anguish and pain for the innocently killed workers should find their way to the heart of the dear "meek" Russian peasant in a gray overcoat.

But the dear meek peasant either beat these people of conscience with the rifle butt or stabbed them with the bayonet, or shouted, quivering with rage:

"Break up, we'll shoot!" They did not break up and then he fired accurately, piling tens and hundreds of corpses on the pavement.

However, the majority of the Tsar's soldiers answered the reproaches and persuasions with dismal and slavish words:

"We've got our orders. We know nothing, we've got our orders. . . ."

And, like machines, they fired at the crowds of people. Reluctantly, perhaps with a heavy heart, but—they fired.

On January 5, 1918, the unarmed Petersburg democracy—factory and white-collar workers—demonstrated peacefully in honor of the Constituent Assembly.

For almost a hundred years the finest Russians have lived by the idea of a Constituent Assembly, a political institution which would give the entire Russian democracy the opportunity freely to express its will. In the struggle for this idea, thousands of the intelligentsia and tens of thousands of workers and peasants have perished in prisons, in exile and at hard labor, on the gallows, and by soldiers' bullets. Rivers of blood have been spilled on the sacrificial altar of this sacred idea, and now the "People's

Commissars" have given orders to shoot the democracy which demonstrated in honor of this idea. I shall remind you that many of the "People's Commissars" themselves, throughout all their political careers, kept inculcating in the working masses the need to fight for the convocation of a Constituent Assembly. *Pravda* lies when it writes that the demonstration of January 5 was organized by the bourgeois, the bankers, etc., and that it was precisely the "bourgeois" and "Kaledinites" who marched on the Tauride Palace.[97]

*Pravda* lies, it knows full well that the "bourgeois" have no reason to rejoice over the opening of the Constituent Assembly, they can do nothing among 246 socialists of one party and 140 Bolsheviks.[98]

*Pravda* knows that the workers of the Obukhov, Patronny, and other factories took part in the demonstration, that the workers of the Basil Island, Vyborg, and other districts marched on the Tauride Palace under the red banners of the Russian Social-Democratic party.

It was precisely these workers who were shot, and however much *Pravda* lies, it cannot hide this shameful fact.

The "bourgeois" probably rejoiced when they saw how the soldiers and Red Guards tore the revolutionary banners out of the workers' hands, trampled them with their feet, and burned them on bonfires. But perhaps even this pleasant spectacle no longer enthused all the "bourgeois," for even among them there are honest persons who sincerely love their people and their country.

One of these was Andrey Ivanovich Shingarev, who was basely murdered by some beasts.[99]

Thus, on January 5, the Petrograd workers were mowed down, unarmed. They were mowed down without warning that they might be fired on, they were mowed down from ambush, through cracks in fences, in a cowardly fashion, as if by real murderers.

And just as on January 9, 1905, people who had not lost their conscience and reason asked those who were shooting:

"What are you doing, idiots? Aren't they your own people marching? You see there are red banners everywhere, and not a single poster hostile to the working class, not a single utterance hostile to you!"

And—like the Tsarist soldiers—these murderers under orders answered:

"We've got our orders! We've got our orders to shoot."

And just as on January 9, 1905, the man in the street, indifferent to everything and always merely a spectator of the tragedy of life, exclaimed admiringly:

"They are shooting like hell!"

And he shrewdly reflected:

"They will quickly finish each other off this way!"

Yes, quickly. Rumors are circulating among the workers that the Red Guards from the Erickson factory shot at the workers from the Lesnoy factory and the workers of the Erickson factory were fired upon by the Red Guards from some other factory.

There are many of these rumors. They may not be true, but this does not prevent them from having a very definite affect on the psychology of the working masses.

I ask the "People's" Commissars among whom there must be decent and sensible people:

Do they understand that by putting the noose around their own necks they will inevitably strangle the entire Russian democracy and ruin all the conquests of the revolution?

Do they understand this? Or do they think, on the contrary: either we have power or let everyone and everything perish?

## TO THE INTELLECTUAL OF THE PEOPLE

*Novaya Zhizn, No. 7 (221),*
*January 11 (24), 1918*

You conclude your article in *Pravda* with the following
words:

"One would like to believe that Gorky has turned away
from the social revolution, which we are experiencing,
only because he failed to see its true beautiful face during
the first troubled days, but that he is already beginning to
see it and soon will rejoice and grieve together with all
who live with the joys and griefs of our October Revolution."[100]

No, esteemed comrade, I shall not "rejoice" with you
and I do not believe that you are rejoicing. What is there
to rejoice about? That the truly revolutionary but numeri-
cally insignificant Russian proletariat is being wiped out in
the internecine slaughter in the South? That they have
begun to shoot down the proletariat in the streets of
Petersburg? That the working intelligentsia of the proletariat, the flesh of its flesh, is being terrorized by the dark
masses and is drowning in them, powerless to influence
them? That the country's industry—destroyed to its very
foundations—makes a further growth of the working class
impossible?

A social revolution without the proletariat is an absurdity, a senseless utopia, and in a short time the proletariat
will disappear, slaughtered in the internecine struggle and
corrupted by that rabble about which you speak. The proletariat without democracy hangs in the air; you are pushing democracy away from the proletariat.

With what are you going to make the social revolution
—with the peasantry? With the soldiers? With bayonets
and bullets? Understand—what is going on now is not a

process of social revolution, but the devastation, for a long time to come, of the soil which might have made this revolution possible in the future. The leaders of the proletariat, as I have said more than once, are using it as a fuel to ignite an all-European revolution.

Before we succeed in doing this, the Russian working people will be crushed by the European soldier. Do you really believe that Germany, England, France, and Japan will allow you, powerless and unarmed, to fan the flames which might devour them?

Do not believe that, dear comrade.

We are alone and shall remain so until our madness compels us to exterminate each other.

And our friends abroad?

Abroad there are excellently disciplined and patriotic-minded soldiers, some of whom consider us traitors and betrayers, and others an impotent people, absolutely incapable of creative work in the field of government.

No, there is nothing to rejoice about, comrade, but it is time to come to our senses! If it is not too late.

## UNTIMELY THOUGHTS

*Novaya Zhizn, No. 9 (223),*
*January 13 (26), 1918*

"The war has undoubtedly played an enormous role in the development of our revolution. The war has materially disorganized absolutism, brought demoralization into the army, and given boldness to the man in the street. But, fortunately for us, the war created no revolution; fortunately, because a revolution created by war is an impotent revolution. It arises from extraordinary conditions, it is supported by external forces, and, finally, turns out to be incapable of holding the positions captured."

These intelligent and even prophetic words were spoken by Trotsky in 1905; I took them from his book *Our Revolution,* where they appear in all their beauty on page 5. Quite some time has passed since then, and now Trotsky very likely thinks differently—in any case, he is probably no longer prepared to say that "a revolution created by war is an impotent revolution."

These words, however, have not lost their meaning and truth. The current events, in all their power and all their impetus, affirm the truth of these words.

The war of 1914-1917 put power into the hands of the proletariat, precisely—"put"; no one will say that the proletariat itself seized power with its own hands; it fell into its hands because the Tsar's defender, the soldier, worn out by the three-year war, refused to defend Romanov's interests which he so zealously stood up for in 1906, wiping out the revolutionary proletariat. It is necessary to keep in mind that the revolution was begun by the soldiers of the Petrograd garrison and when these soldiers, having taken off their greatcoats, go to their villages, the proletariat will find itself in an isolation not very comfortable for it.

It would be naïve and ridiculous to demand that the soldier, who has become a peasant again, should accept the proletarian idealism as his religion and that he should introduce proletarian socialism into his rural way of life.

The peasant acquired something during the war, as did the soldier in the course of the revolution, and they both know well that in Russia money ensures man's freedom best of all. Just try to destroy this conviction or even shake it.

One should remember that in 1905 the proletariat was stronger both in numbers and in quality than it is now, and that at that time industry was not destroyed to its very foundation.

The revolution created by the war will inevitably turn out to be impotent if the proletariat, instead of devoting all its energy to creative social work, begins, in obedience to its leaders, to destroy to the roots the "bourgeois" technical organizations, the mechanism of which it should master and the operation of which it ought to control.

The revolution will perish from internal exhaustion if the proletariat, submitting to the fanatic implacability of the People's Commissars, continues to widen its rift with democracy. The ideology of the proletariat is not the ideology of class egotism; its best teachers, Marx, Kautsky, *et al.*, impose on its honest strength the obligation to liberate all people from social and economic slavery.

The life of the world is governed by social idealism— the great dream of the brotherhood of all. Does the proletariat think that it is realizing this very dream while coercing its ideological enemies? A social struggle is not a bloody smashing of faces, as the Russian worker is being taught by his frightened leaders.

The revolution is a great and honorable cause, a cause necessary for our rebirth, and not senseless riots destroying the national wealth. The revolution will turn out to be impotent and will perish if we do not give it all that is best in our hearts and if we do not eliminate, or at least mitigate, the cruelty and malice which, intoxicating the masses, are discrediting the Russian revolutionary worker.

## UNTIMELY THOUGHTS

*Novaya Zhizn, No. 11 (225),*
*January 17 (30), 1918*

Everything that is cruel and senseless will always find a way into the feelings of an ignoramus or a savage.

Recently the sailor Zheleznyakov,[101] translating the ferocious speeches of his leaders into the crudely elementary language of the mass man, said that, for the welfare of the Russian people, even a million persons could be killed.

I do not consider this statement to be braggadocio and, though I resolutely refuse to recognize any circumstances that might justify mass murder, I still believe that a million "free citizens" can be killed in our country. Even more can be killed. Why shouldn't they be killed?

There are many people in Russia and there are plenty of murderers, but when it comes to prosecuting them, the regime of the People's Commissars encounters certain mysterious obstacles, as it apparently did in the investigation of the foul murder of Shingarev and Kokoshkin.[102] A wholesale extermination of those who think differently is an old, tried method of the domestic policy of Russian governments. From Ivan the Terrible to Nicholas II this simple and convenient method of combating sedition was freely and widely used by all our political leaders; why, then, should Vladimir Lenin renounce such a simple method?

And in fact he does not renounce it when he frankly declares that he will shrink from nothing to eradicate enemies.

But I think that as a result of such statements we shall have a lengthy and extremely cruel struggle of all the democratic forces and the best part of the working class against that animal anarchy which the leaders from Smolny are so actively fostering.

This is what Russia is threatened with by the simplified translations of anarcho-communistic slogans into our plain backwoods language.[103]

———— • ————

Pr. Roman Petkevich—praporshchik [ensign] or professor?—writes to me:

> Your dispute with Bolshevism is an extremely serious error, you are fighting against the national spirit which is striving for a revival. The peculiarity of the Russian spirit, its uniqueness, is expressed in Bolshevism. Note well the saying: "To each his own!" Each nation creates its own particular and individual modes and methods of social struggle which are characteristic of that nation only. The French and Italians are anarcho-syndicalists, the English are more strongly inclined toward the trade unions, and the social democratism of the Germans, patterned after their military establishment, is the clearest possible reflection of their lack of talent.

> We, on the other hand, according to the prophecy of our great teachers—for instance, Dostoevsky and Tolstoy—are a messianic people entrusted with the task of outpacing and outdistancing all others. It is precisely our spirit that will liberate the world from the chains of history.

And so on, in the tone of that Moscow Neo-Slavophilism which squealed so loudly at the beginning of the war.

What a footloose man the Russian is!

## UNTIMELY THOUGHTS

*Novaya Zhizn, No. 13 (227),*
*January 19 (February 1), 1918*

Every government, whatever it calls itself, strives not only
to "govern" the will of the popular masses, but also to
mold this will in accordance with its own principles and
aims. The most demagogic and shrewd governments usually embellish their aspirations to govern and mold the
people's will with the words: "We represent the will of the
people."

These, of course, are not sincere words, for, in the final
analysis, the intellectual force of the government overcomes the instincts of the masses, and if the ruling bodies
do not succeed in accomplishing this, they use physical
force to suppress the people's will, hostile to their aims.

Whether by means of a resolution drafted beforehand in
an office, or by bayonet and bullet, the government strives
constantly and inevitably to master the will of the masses,
to convince the people that it is leading them along the
one right road to happiness.

This policy is an inevitable obligation of every government: being confident that it is the mind of the people, the
government is compelled by its position to instill in the
people the conviction that they have the wisest and most
honest government of all, one sincerely devoted to the
interests of the people.

The People's Commissars are striving precisely for this
goal, having no scruples (just as any other government)
about shooting, murdering, and arresting those who disagree with them, and having no scruples about any kind of
slander and lies aimed at the enemy.

But in trying to inspire popular confidence in themselves, the People's Commissars, who are in general

poorly acquainted with the "Russian element," do not
take into account at all that frightening psychological atmosphere which was created by the fruitless torment of
nearly four years of war, and because of which the "Russian element"—the psychology of the Russian masses—
has grown even more somber, sharp-edged, and embittered.

Their lordships the People's Commissars completely fail
to realize the fact that when they put out slogans of "social" revolution, the spiritually and physically exhausted
people translate these slogans into their own language with
a few brief words:

"Smash, plunder, destroy. . . ."

And they destroy the thinly scattered nests of advanced
agriculture in Russia; they destroy the cities of Persia, her
vineyards, orchards, and even the irrigation system;[104]
they destroy everything, everywhere.

And when the People's Commissars shout too eloquently and in a panic about the necessity of fighting the
"bourgeois," the ignorant masses take this as a direct call
to murder, and this they have already demonstrated.

Saying that the People's Commissars "fail to realize"
what echo their hysterical outcries about the gathering
counterrevolution call forth in the people, I am deliberately making an assumption which explains, to some extent, the insane way in which they act, but I am by no
means excusing them. If they got into "government," they
must know over whom and under what circumstances they
govern.

The people went through long torment and suffering,
they are indescribably exhausted, they are full of vengeance, anger, and hate, and these emotions continue to
grow, organizing, in proportion to their strength, the will
of the people.

Do their lordships the People's Commissars consider

themselves called upon to express the destructive urges of this diseased will? Or do they consider themselves to be in a position to cure and organize that will? Are they strong enough and independent enough to fulfill this second urgent task?

They must put this question to themselves with all the directness and resoluteness of honest people. But there is no reason to believe that they are capable of putting this question on trial in their minds and consciences.

Surrounded by the disturbed Russian element, they have become blind intellectually and morally, and they are already powerless victims in the paws of a beast worn out by the past and now aroused by them.

### "SOMETHING FUNNY"

*Novaya Zhizn, No. 15 (229),*
*January 21 (February 3), 1918*

A man arrived from Moscow and, chuckling, related the following:

"A certain worker was walking along the street at night when suddenly two heroes, in soldiers' greatcoats and with rifles, appeared from around the corner and started toward him:

'Halt!' they shouted. 'Do you have weapons?'

"He drew a revolver from his pocket and, thinking quickly, took aim at them:

'Yes I have,' he said. 'Hands up!'

"The heroes got scared—their rifles, apparently, were not loaded—and he ordered:

"Put your rifles down. Take off your coats. Now—take off your boots. Now—your pants. Right, now—run along the street and shout 'Help!'

"The heroes did all this obediently. They ran, barefoot and without pants, through the snow and shouted conscientiously:

'Help!'

"The worker left their clothes on the pavement, took their rifles to the commissariat, and there related this funny adventure. . . .

"Another similar event occurred near the Pushkin;[105] two thieves attacked an artel worker who was walking from his factory to the station. They attacked him and ordered:

'Hand over your weapons!'

"He handed them an unloaded revolver, but another, with cartridges, remained in the back pocket of his trousers. They took off his fur coat, relieved him of fifty-two thousand in cash, and wanted to go on their way, after telling him:

'You should thank God you're still alive!'

"With another man it might have ended with this, but the artel worker was no fool. He begged them:

'Brothers, I'm a working man; that money's not mine, it belongs to the factory, to the boss, it's the workers' wages; they won't believe you've robbed me, they'll say I stole the money myself. There are no marks on me, I ask you—look—I have two thousand more of my own money; I'll give it to you, and you shoot up my jacket, so it'll be clear that I was attacked!'

"The thieves—kindhearted lads—understood his idea, they even cheered up and started pumping bullets into his jacket; he held the flap out to the side and they blasted away point blank at the jacket, so that the material even smoldered.

'Well,' they said. 'That's enough!'

"But he asked them:

'Just once more!'

'No more cartridges,' they said.

'No more?'

'Not one.'

'Well, in that case,' said the artel worker, drawing the loaded revolver, 'give back the money, the coat, otherwise.
. . .'

"What could they do? The lads became frightened, gave everything back to him, and he, noticing a sledge in the distance, near a watchman's hut, said to them:

'Bring the sledge here and drive me to the station.'

"They drove him. You've got to drive, if you're waiting for a bullet in the back of your head."

———— • ————

More and more of these and similar anecdotes are appearing; people tell them almost without indignation, in a jolly tone. Do they want to conceal behind it that frightening element which permeates the anecdote, or are they concealing their own savagery of which they are vaguely conscious?

I do not understand this, but it is clear to me that the robbers rampaging in the streets are the most ordinary Russians and, perhaps, even nice people, from that group who are accustomed to "living haphazardly" from day to day. And the most frightening thing is the very fact that these people are "ordinary."

I think that these street exploits originate in this way: two ordinary people sit in a corner somewhere and chat unhurriedly:

"You know, we've lived to see absolute freedom."

"Ye-es; no police, no courts. . . ."

"Amazing."

And after talking about this new, unaccustomed way of life, these people—who have no idea of rights, of culture, of the value of life—people who were brought up in a country where government ministers behaved like professional thieves—these people say:

"How about getting out on the street and relieving a bourgeois of a couple of things?"

"Take his fur coat?"

"All right?"

"Why not—I've read in the papers you can strip them!"

"Shall we go?"

"Let's go. Maybe we'll earn something."

They go out and work. Sometimes they have to kill a disobedient bourgeois, sometimes they are caught and, by "mob law," are beaten to death.

And both these facts—murder and mob law—startle one by their terrifying "simplicity."

So life rushes on: some rob and kill, others drown and shoot the robbers, still others speak and write about this. And everything is "simple." Even funny, at times.

But when you recall that all this is going on in a country where human life is ridiculously cheap, where there is no respect for the individual and his work, and when you think that the "simplicity" of killing becomes a "habit," an "everyday occurrence," you grow fearful for Russia. And such events become somehow fearfully comprehensible. Three people visited an acquaintance; but the guests took a dislike to something about their host, so they cut him into twelve pieces, put the parts into sacks, and threw them into the Obvodny Canal. Simple.

And then there was the murder of Shingarev and Kokoshkin. There is something unspeakably foul in this murder of sick men worn out by prison.

Granted, they understood the good of their native land more narrowly than others do, but no one will dare to say that they did not work for the people, did not suffer for them. These were honest Russians, and we do not have many honest people.

And now they have been murdered, murdered foully and "simply."

I ask myself: if I were a judge, could I try these "simple people?"

And, it seems to me, I could not. Or defend them? Nor could I do this.

I have the strength neither for trying nor for defending these people,[106] created by our accursed history to our shame and as an object of derision for the whole world.

## UNTIMELY THOUGHTS

*Novaya Zhizn, No. 43 (258),**
*March 16 (3), 1918*

Studying Russian native creativity by the German method, a certain part of our intelligentsia very quickly came to Slavophilism, Panslavism, and "Messianism," and infected with the harmful idea of a Russian originality another part of the thinking people who, thinking in a European way, nevertheless felt in a Russian way—and this led them to a sentimental semi-adoration of the "people," a people brought up in slavery, drunkenness, and the dark superstitions of the church and alien to the beautiful dreams of the intelligentsia.

The Russian people, because of the conditions of their historical development, are a huge flabby body lacking the taste for governmental organization and almost impervious to the influence of ideas which might ennoble acts of will; the Russian intelligentsia is the head, malignantly

* It should be No. 42 (256). *Novaya Zhizn* of March 8 (February 23) was misnumbered and this affected the numeration of all subsequent issues.

swollen with an abundance of foreign thoughts and connected with the torso not by a strong backbone of unified
aspirations and aims, but by some barely perceptible and
very thin neural thread.

The Muscovites—beaten senseless by cruel reality,
drunk, repulsively forebearing, and, in their own way,
rather cunning—have always been and yet remain completely alien in their psychology to the Russian intellectual, rich in bookish knowledge but poor in knowledge of
Russian reality. The body lies flat on the ground, but the
head has grown high up into the heavens—from far away,
as we all know, everything looks better than from up
close.

Of course, we are conducting an experiment in social
revolution, an occupation very pleasing to the maniacs
expounding this beautiful idea and very useful to crooks.
As is well known, one of the loudest and most heartily
welcomed slogans of our peculiarly Russian revolution has
been the slogan: "Rob the robbers!"

They rob amazingly, artistically; no doubt history will
tell of this process of Russia's self-robbery with the greatest inspiration.

They rob and sell churches and war museums, they sell
cannons and rifles, they pilfer army warehouses, they rob
the palaces of former grand dukes; everything which can
be plundered is plundered, everything which can be sold is
sold; in Feodosiya, the soldiers even traffic in people—
they bring Turkish, Armenian, and Kurdish women from
the Caucasus and sell them for twenty-five rubles a piece.
This is very "original," and we can be proud—there was
nothing similar even in the era of the Great French Revolution.

Honest people, of whom we have always had a shortage, are today almost completely extinct; I recently heard
an invitation of this sort:

"Come visit us, comrade; except for three workers, there is not a single honest person here!"

And this weak, ignorant people, with an inborn inclination toward anarchism, is now called to be the spiritual leader of the world, the Messiah of Europe.

It would seem that this curious and sentimental idea should not disturb the tragic game of the People's Commissars. But the "leaders of the people" do not conceal their intention to kindle a fire from green Russian logs, a fire whose flame would light up the Western world, that world where the fire of social creativity burns brighter and more sensibly than in our Russia.

The fire is kindled; it burns poorly, it stinks of Russia, filthy, drunk and cruel. And this unfortunate Russia is being dragged and shoved to Golgotha to be crucified for the salvation of the world. Isn't this "Messianism" with a hundred horsepower?

But the Western world is stern and mistrustful, it is completely devoid of sentimentalism. In this world the business of evaluating a man is very simple: do you like to work and do you know how to work? If so, you are a man the world needs, you are just that man by whose strength everything valuable and beautiful is created. You don't like to work and don't know how to work? Then, with all your other qualities, however superlative they may be, you are a superfluous man in the workshop of the world. That's all.

And since we Russians do not like to work and do not know how to work, and since the Western European world knows this characteristic of ours very well, we shall fare very poorly, worse than we expect. . . .

———— • ————

Our revolution gave full play to all the evil and brutal instincts which had accumulated under the leaden lid of the monarchy, and at the same time it cast aside all the intellectual forces of democracy, all the moral energy of the country. We see that bribe takers, profiteers, and swindlers are continually caught among the employees of the Soviet regime, while honest, efficient people, in order to keep from starving, sell newspapers in the streets or do physical labor, thus increasing the masses of the unemployed.

This is a nightmare, this is a purely Russian absurdity, and—it is no sin to say—this is idiocy!

All existing conditions dictate imperatively the necessity of uniting the forces of democracy. It is clear to every sensible man that only the unity of democracy can save the revolution from complete destruction, can help it overcome the internal enemy and fight the external one. But the Soviet regime does not realize this, being occupied exclusively with the business of its own salvation from inevitable destruction.

Turning its eyes to the future, the Soviet regime forgets that the future is created out of the present. At the present time, the country has a disorganized working class which is being wiped out in an internecine slaughter, an industry razed to the ground, and a state plucked bare and given to people of bestial instincts for looting and pillage.

The Soviet regime is powerless in the battle with these people, it is powerless irrespective of how many absolutely innocent people it "accidentally" shoots.

And it will be powerless in this battle until it dares to enlist all the intellectual forces of Russian democracy in the cause of building life.

## UNTIMELY THOUGHTS

*Novaya Zhizn, No. 44 (259),*
*March 17 (4), 1918*

Today is "Forgiveness Sunday."[107]

On this day, according to ancient custom, people asked each other's forgiveness for mutual sins against the honor and dignity of man. This was when conscience existed in Russia, when even the ignorant provincial Russian people vaguely felt in their souls an inclination toward social justice which perhaps was narrowly understood, but understood nonetheless.

In our nightmarish days conscience is dead. Everyone remembers how the Russian intelligentsia, all of it—unaffected by the ugliness of party distinctions—was outraged by the shameless Beylis affair,[108] the despicable shooting of the Lena workers,[109] the pogroms against the Jews, and the slander by which all the Jews to a man were accused of betraying Russia. Remembered also is the stirring of conscience brought about by the trial of Polovnev, Larichkin, and the other murderers of Iollos and Gertsenshteyn.[110]

And now Shingarev and Kokoshkin, innocent and honest people, lie dead, but our authorities lack both the strength and conscience to bring their murderers to trial.[111]

Six young, absolutely innocent students were shot; this vile act did not disturb the conscience in a disintegrated community of cultured people.[112]

Scores of "bourgeois" are massacred in Sebastopol and Evpatoriya,[113] and no one dares to ask the creators of "social" revolution: are they not the moral inspirers of mass murder?

Conscience is dead.[114] The sense of justice is directed toward the distribution of material wealth. The idea of this "distribution" is especially well understood in that place where the beggar sells to the beggar spruce logs disguised as bread by being baked in a thin coating of dough. The half-starved beggars cheat and rob each other; the present day is full of such things. And for all this—for all the filth, blood, vileness, and vulgarity—the lurking enemies of the working class will eventually put the blame on that working class, on its intelligentsia, which is powerless to cope with the moral disintegration of the masses run wild. Where there is too much of politics, there is no place for culture; and if politics is permeated with fear of the masses and flattery of the same—as is the politics of the Soviet regime—then, perhaps, it is already absolutely useless to speak of conscience, of justice, of respect for man, and of everything else which political cynicism calls "sentimental," but without which it is impossible to live.

## UNTIMELY THOUGHTS

*Novaya Zhizn, No. 47 (262),*
*March 21 (8), 1918*

Citizen Mikh. Nadezhdin asks me in *Krasnaya Gazeta* (Red Gazette):
"Tell me whether there was a living conscience—and whose conscience—under serfdom when peasants were flogged to death in hundreds?"[115]
Yes, in that accursed period, simultaneously with the extension of the right to use physical violence on man, a beautiful flame of conscience flared up and brightly illumined the stifling gloom of Russian life. Mikh. Nadezhdin probably recalls the names of Radishchev and Pushkin, of Herzen and Chernyshevsky, of Belinsky and Nekrasov, of the enormous constellation of talented Russians who

created a literature exceptional in its originality, exceptional because it was all devoted to problems of social justice. This was the literature that nurtured the revolutionary energy of our democratic intelligentsia; the Russian worker is indebted for his social idealism to the influence of this literature.

So "conscience" was not simply "hammered in" with "clubs and whips," as M. Nadezhdin asserts, but it existed in the people's soul, as the Tolstoys, the Turgenevs, the Grigoroviches,[116] and many others whom we ought to believe asserted, for they knew the people and loved them in their own way, even somewhat embellishing and exaggerating their qualities.

Citizen Nadezhdin, apparently, also loves his people with that somewhat sentimental and flattering love which, in general, is peculiar to the Russian admirers of the people. In our country today, this love is even more corrupted by reckless and repulsive demagogy.

Nadezhdin reproaches me:

"It is inexcusable especially for you, Aleksey Maksimovich, as a teacher who emerged from the people, to hurl such accusations at your own brothers."

I have the right to speak the painful and bitter truth about the people, and I am convinced that it will be better for the people if I am the first to speak this truth about them, and not those enemies of the people who are now silent and who store up revenge and malice so that, at some moment auspicious for them, they can spit this malice in the face of the people, as they did after 1905 and 1906.

It should not be assumed that the people are holy and righteous simply because they are martyrs; even during the early centuries of Christianity many were martyrs through their own stupidity. And we should not close our eyes to the fact that now when the "people" have won the right to use physical violence on man, they have become torturers no less savage and cruel than their own former torturers. Mikh. Nadezhdin's manner of reasoning leads him in an endless circle: since the people were tortured, they also have the right to torture. But in this way he gives them the right to avenge torture by torture, violence by violence. How can one get out of this circle?

No, it will be better for us to speak the truth, for the truth is healthful and only it can cure us.

Unworthy are the people who, seeing their village neighbors starving, will not sell them bread, but will make kvass and moonshine out of it because this is more profitable. One cannot praise a people who resolves: every fellow villager who sells this or that product not in his own but in a neighboring village shall be subject to imprisonment for three months.

No, let us speak plainly and directly: the Bolshevik demagogy, bringing the egotistic instincts of the peasant to a white heat, snuffs out the embryo of his social conscience.

I understand that it is unpleasant for *Krasnaya Gazeta, Pravda,* and the like to hear this, especially unpleasant just now when Bolshevism is gradually putting over the helm to the right, trying to gain the support of the "village poor" and forgetting the interests of the working class.

Let me remind Mikh. Nadezhdin of a few phrases from Lenin's Moscow speech:

"Concluding the peace, we betray the Estonian workers, the Ukrainian proletariat, etc. But can it be that if our comrades perish, then we must perish along with them? If detachments of our comrades are surrounded by substantial enemy forces and cannot resist, then must we also fight? No and again no!"

Probably Mikh. Nadezhdin will agree that this is not a working class policy, but a policy of ancient Russia, of an appanage, of Suzdal itself.

Later Lenin speaks even more cynically:

"In a trembling, strained voice Martov called us to battle. No, he did not call us to battle, he called us to death, he called us to die for Russia and the revolution. The majority of the Congress—the *peasant masses* comprising one and a half thousand men (there were an insignificant number of workers at the Congress)—*were utterly indifferent to Martov's appeals. They did not want to die for Russia and the revolution, they wanted to live in order to conclude peace.*"[117]

These words signify the complete subjugation of the entire "people" and a death sentence for the working class.

This is a quite appropriate ending for the repulsive demagogy that has corrupted the "people."


## UNTIMELY THOUGHTS

*Novaya Zhizn, No. 48 (263),*
*March 22 (9), 1918*

The right of criticism imposes on us the obligation to criticize mercilessly not only the actions of enemies but also the shortcomings of friends. From both the moral and tactical viewpoint, it is much better for the development of a feeling of social justice in man if we ourselves honestly admit our shortcomings and errors, before our enemy seizes the opportunity to point them out with malicious joy. And in this case, of course, the enemy will not fail to exclaim triumphantly:

"Aha!"

But the malice of triumph will be dulled and the poison of that malice will have no effect.

We should not forget that enemies are frequently right in accusing our friends, and truth intensifies the enemy

blow. To tell a sad and painful truth about friends, before
the enemy tells it, is to render the enemy attack powerless.

———— • ————

The fledgling Bolsheviks tell me almost every day that I
"have broken away" from the "people."[118] I have never
felt myself "pinned" to the people to such a degree that I
could not notice their shortcomings, and since I am not
bucking for a high position, I have no desire to hush up
these shortcomings and to sing demagogic litanies to the
dark masses of the Russian people.

If I see that my people have an inherent propensity for
equality in nullity, a propensity arising from the rotten
Asiatic notion that it is simpler, easier, and less of a responsibility to be null—if I see this, I must say it.

If I see that the policy of the Soviet regime is "profoundly national," as even the enemies of the Bolsheviks
ironically admit—and it is precisely the "orientation towards
poverty and nullity" in which the nationalism of the
Bolshevik policy is expressed—then I must admit with
bitterness that these enemies are correct, that Bolshevism
is a national calamity, for, in the chaos of crude instincts
that Bolshevism aroused, it threatens to destroy the weak
germs of Russian culture.

We are all a little afraid of criticism, and self-criticism
provokes almost an aversion in us.

We love to excuse no less than to condemn, but in this
love of excusing there is much more concern for oneself
than for one's fellow man; in this love a desire to excuse
one's own future sin is always noticeable—this is very
prudent, yet nasty.

The favored hero of Russian life and literature is the
unlucky and pitiful failure. Heroes are not a success
among us. The people love prisoners when they are
marched to hard-labor camps, and they readily help the

strong man from their midst to put on the garb and fetters of a criminal.

The strong man is not loved in Russia, and it is partly because of this that the strong man does not live long in our country.

Life does not love him, neither does literature, trying in every possible way to entangle his will in contradictions, to drive it into the dark corner of the insoluble, to reduce it, in general, to the level of life's disgraceful conditions, to reduce it and break it. It is not the fighter, the builder of new forms of life, who is sought out and loved, but rather the righteous man, who would take upon himself the petty disgusting sins of humdrum people.

From this material—from the ignorant and flabby village people—the dreamers and those who learn from books want to create a new socialist state, new not only in form but in essence, in spirit. It is clear that the builders must work taking into account the peculiarities of the material, and the most important and the least irradicable peculiarity of village folk is a fierce property-owning individualism which inevitably must declare a cruel war on the socialist aspirations of the working class.

It was the peasants who stabbed the Paris Commune to death—this is what the worker must keep in mind.

His leaders forgot about it.

## UNTIMELY THOUGHTS

*Novaya Zhizn, No. 51 (266),*
*March 26 (13), 1918*

Among the government's decrees and actions published recently in some of the newspapers, I read, with the greatest amazement, a bombastic proclamation of the "Special

Meeting of Sailors of the Red Fleet of the Republic." In this proclamation the sailors notify us:

"We, the sailors, have resolved: if killing of our best comrades continues in the future, then we shall turn out, weapons in hand, and for every one of our murdered comrades we shall answer with the death of hundreds and thousands of the rich, who live in bright and luxurious palaces and who organize counterrevolutionary gangs against the toiling masses, against those workers, soldiers, and peasants who, in October, carried the revolution forward on their shoulders."[119]

Well, what is this—a cry of indignant justice?

But then I, as any other citizen of our republic, have the right to ask the citizen-sailors:

What proof do they have for the assertion that Myasnikov and Zabello perished by the "treacherous hand of the tyrants"? And, if such proof is available, why has it not been published?

Why has the government found it necessary to include in its "actions and decrees" the dreadful roar of the "beauty and pride" of the Russian revolution?[120]

Does this mean that the government is in agreement with the method which the sailors promised to employ in their actions? Or is it powerless to prevent them from using this method?

And, finally, was it not the government itself that put into the sailors' heads such a savage idea of physical retribution?

I think that the government, in all conscience, should answer to this last question with an admission of its guilt.

Probably everyone remembers that after a certain joker or bored idler had punctured with a penknife the body of the automobile used by Lenin, *Pravda,* regarding the damage to the car's body as an attempt on the life of Vladimir Ilich, sternly declared:

"For each of our heads we shall take a hundred bourgeois heads."[121]

Apparently this arithmetic of madness and cowardice had its due influence on the sailors—already they demand not a hundred, but thousands of heads for one.

The self-evaluation of the Russian is rising. The government can put this down to its own credit.

But to me—as, probably, to all those who have not yet completely lost their minds—the stern proclamation of the sailors represents not a cry for justice but the wild roar of unbridled and cowardly beasts.

———— • ————

I address myself directly to the sailors, the authors of this sinister announcement.

There can be no doubt, gentlemen, that you, who are armed, can batter or stab to death as many "bourgeois" as you please. Of this there can be no doubt. Your comrades have already tried to carry out mass murders of the bourgeois "intelligentsia"; after having slaughtered several hundred educated people in Sebastopol and Evpatoriya,[122] they proclaimed:

"What's done is done, and we cannot be tried."

These words sound half-repentant and half-threatening, and in these words, my dear sailors, is fully preserved and triumphant the spirit of the bloody despotism of that very same monarchy whose external forms you have destroyed, but whose soul you cannot kill—it lives on in your breasts, compelling you to roar like beasts and robbing you of human likeness.

You, gentlemen, should remember well that you were brought up on violence and murder, and when you say "we cannot be tried," you say this not because you have recognized your right to power, but only because you know that, under the monarchy, no one was tried or punished for mass murder. No one was tried for the murder of thousands of people on January 9, 1905, for the shooting of the Lena and Zlatoust workers,[123] for the massacre of your *Ochakov* comrades,[124] for all the mass murders which were so abundant in the time of the monarchy.

It was this atmosphere of unpunished crimes in which you were brought up, and this bloody belch of the past is also heard in your roar.

Just as the monarchist government, slaughtering sailors, workers, peasants, and soldiers by the hundreds, testified to its own moral impotence, so the sailors of the Red fleet admit by their stern proclamation that they have no means, except for bayonet and bullet, of fighting for social justice. Certainly, it is simpler to kill than to convince; and this simple method, as it seems, is very well understood by people brought up on killing and trained to kill.

I ask you, my dear sailors: Where and in what is the difference between the brute psychology of the monarchy and your psychology? The monarchists were sincerely convinced that happiness was possible for Russia only with the complete extermination of all those who expressed dissent. You think and act in exactly the same way.

I repeat: to kill is simpler and easier than to convince, but was it not the acts of violence committed against the people which brought about the destruction of the power of the monarchy? Just because you divide among yourselves the material wealth of Russia, she will become neither richer nor happier, nor will you be better, more humane. New forms of life demand a new spiritual content —are you capable of working this spiritual innovation? Judging by your words and deeds, you are still not capable of doing this; you are the savage Russians corrupted and beaten down by the old regime which imparted to your flesh and blood all its horrible maladies and its senseless despotism.

By acting the way you do, you give future reactionary forces the right to point at you, the right to tell you to your face: under the socialist government, when power was in your hands, you killed masses of people, just as we did before the revolution.

And in this way you have given us the right to kill you.

My dear sailors! You must come to your senses. You must try to be human. This is difficult, but this is necessary.

## UNTIMELY THOUGHTS

*Novaya Zhizn, No. 53 (268),
March 28 (15), 1918*

More and more often various people write to me: "We do not believe in people," "I have lost faith in people," "I cannot believe in people, I do not believe parties and leaders."

All these are sincere cries of people stunned by the heavy blows dealt by this fantastic and murky Russian life, these are cries from the heart of people who want to love and believe. But—and here forgive me, my esteemed correspondents!—their voices do not seem to me to be the voices of people who desire to know and work. This is the sighing of that very same Russian people in whose capacity for spiritual rebirth and creative work my correspondents refuse to believe. My esteemed correspondents must admit that they are flesh of the flesh of that same people who have always manifested (and who manifest now even more convincingly) an utter lack of faith in themselves.

These are the people whose whole life was built on living
"haphazardly" from day to day and on dreams of help
from somewhere without: from God and Saint Nicholas,
from "foreign kings and sovereigns," from a "master"
who will "come" from somewhere and "settle our disputes."[125] Even now when the people are the physical
"masters of life," they nonetheless continue to put their
hopes on the "master." For one part of the people this
master is the "European proletariat"; for another part it is
the German, the organizer of an iron order; some think
that Japan will save them; and no one has any faith in his
own strength.

Faith—this is always very good for the comfort of one's
soul, for its tranquility; faith somewhat blinds a man,
allowing him to ignore the agonizing contradictions of life.
It is natural that all of us strive to come quickly to believe
in something, in some "master" capable of "settling our
disputes" and of organizing a benevolent order within us
and without. We believe very easily: the Populists painted
the village peasant as attractively as a cake, and we readily began to believe that our peasant is good, a real Chinese, no comparison to a European peasant.

It was very comfortable to believe in the exceptional
spiritual qualities of our Karataevs[126]—they are not simply peasants but all-round men! Gleb Uspensky dealt a
serious blow to this belief with his *Power of the Soil*,[127]
but the believers did not notice him; Chekhov, whom we
so tenderly love, showed us "The Peasants" in an even
gloomier light, and he was chided for lack of faith in the
people. Ivan Bunin courageously emphasized the dark
colors—they told Bunin that he was a landlord blinded by
class hatred of the peasant. And, of course, they did not
notice that the peasant writers—Iv. Volny, Semen Pod-
yachev, and others—depict the peasant in gloomier colors
than did Chekhov and Bunin, and in even gloomier colors

than did such obvious and real enemies of the people as, for example, Rodionov, the author of the sensational book *Our Crime*.[128]

In our country people believe not because they know and love, but just for peace of mind—this is the fruitless and impotent faith of the contemplatives, it is "dead." We do not have that faith capable of moving mountains. Now, when our people have freely revealed before the world all the riches of their psyche conditioned by centuries of savage darkness, abominable slavery, and beastly cruelty, we begin to shout:

"We do not believe in people!"

It is appropriate to ask the non-believers:

But in what and why did you believe before? Don't you see that everything which alienates you from the people was within them in the time of Stepan Razin and Emelyan Pugachev,[129] in the years of the potato and cholera riots,[130] in the years of the Jewish pogroms, and during the reaction of 1907-1908? In what did you believe then?

A good and honest craftsman, before making this thing or that, has studied and knows the material with which he wants to work.

Our craftsmen of social affairs undertook the construction of a temple of the new life, having, perhaps, a fairly precise idea about the material conditions of the people's existence, but completely lacking a knowledge of the spiritual environment, of the spiritual qualities of the material.

We have to learn and, in particular, we have to learn to love work, to understand its redemptive power.

To have faith is very pleasant, but to have knowledge is necessary. Politics is like bad weather, unavoidable, but in order to ennoble politics cultural work is needed, and it's high time to introduce the emotions of beauty and goodness into the sphere of angry political emotions. One should believe in himself, in his own ability for creative work, and the rest will be added unto him.

"We have come into the world in order to disagree," in order to argue with the abominations of life and overcome them.

To believe is comfortable, but it is much better to have a well developed sense of personal dignity and not to moan over those things for which we are all equally to blame.

## UNTIMELY THOUGHTS

### *Novaya Zhizn, No. 56 (271),*
### *March 31 (18), 1918*

A man came to me from the provinces, one of those indomitable optimists who, being "as stubborn as a mule," do not lose heart, do not whine, and of whom, unfortunately, there are few in our Russia.

I asked him:

"Well, do you know anything new or interesting?"

"Quite a few things, my dear sir, quite a few; but the most interesting and significant is that the bourgeois is growing! You are amazed, you laugh? I too was amazed at first, but I did not laugh, I was sad because—how can this be? A socialist fatherland—and suddenly the bourgeois is growing! And, you know, he grows as abundantly as toadstools in a wet summer. A sort of petty bourgeois, but strong and vigorous, as I see it. I took a close look and resolved: what can you do? A trick of fate which you cannot get round, the wall of history which you cannot smash."

"But if you please! Where are these bourgeois from?"

"From all over. From the peasant who during the war

made a bit of money, just a bit—about three or five thousand and, in some cases, twenty! He robbed the landowner —you can't say this income is honest, but it's good. And all the things you gentlemen say and write about the peasant allegedly becoming a drunkard and gambler are wrong. Those drink who are worse off than others, who are not destined to live; the village trash drinks, good-for-nothing people who have been poisoned by vodka long since; it is all the same to these people, under any regime they are doomed to degeneration and death! They really drink all sorts of awful stuff and therefore die very quickly, in this very way freeing the village from hooliganism and all kinds of trash. A pretty stern law governs here: just as cholera is a test for determining whether one has a good stomach, so alcoholism is a test of the general resistance of the body. Yes, the human trash is dying out; it's a pity, of course, but comforting, nonetheless! And it's true that they play cards something cruel! Everyone has lots of money and, naturally, they have fun. But bear in mind that the cooler and more calculating player always wins, so that no harm is done here. A natural selection is taking place; the strong overcomes the weak.

"A soldier arrived; he also brought quite a bit of money with him and increased it successfully, putting it into circulation. The soldiers formed their own sections and this is very profitable for them: the running of a volost committee cost us 1,500 rubles, but the soldiers are now collecting fifty-two thousand. And, in general, to put it simply, unbelievable robbery goes on in the village, but, as you shall see, this is not so very frightening. . . . Add a woman to this—she became an unbelievably sly and clever money-grabber.

"A sailor appeared, also a man of means; I saw two of them who didn't mind saying that they'd 'accumulated' thirty thousand each. How did they do it? You see, after the army left, they transported Turkish Armenians on torpedo-boats to Russian ports, collecting a thousand rubles for every head of Armenian."

"But what is today's money worth?"

"Don't worry, that's been taken into account! They don't value money, they don't hoard it; they carry small, negotiable bills with them, but convert all large sums into property. They buy everything that has a more or less stable value. And you should see how the new peasant is taken up with the acquisition and breeding of stock. Especially the women! Oh, these are amazing people in their greed for gain! Moreover, right now there are people so farsighted that they are already beginning to consider the possible demands of the future. Thus, for example, in the neighboring volost nine soldiers and peasants and an odd sailor started a brick factory. Our province is not very heavily wooded, but all the same it is not bare—why do they need a factory here, far from the railroad? 'But, you see, comrade, we figure that when everything calms down, people will begin to build brick houses because many now have piled up a great deal of valuable possessions, so that a hut is no longer good enough!' In our town a cavalry sergeant major established a stud farm; he acquired three stallions and he is thinking of expanding his business to the size of a real horse ranch. And ventures of this kind are many, you hear about them everywhere.

"Well, yes, of course, it's a long way from here to socialism, but it would be naïve indeed to count on village socialism in our Russia. Did we count on it? Well, we were mistaken, and 'anyone can make an honest mistake.' But the point is that the village breeds a bourgeois who is very strong and knows his own worth. This, my dear sir, will be, from all the evidence, a real master of his land, a man with a 'patrimony!'[131] Just try to take from this gentleman a thing which he considers his own! He'll show

you something, for now he is armed. And if at first he
happens to grab cheap German goods, that won't last
long; some ten years will pass, and he will realize the true
cultural value of his cheap goods and he won't have any
scruples about starting a new fight with the German.

"Yes, that's just how it's turned out: socialism has bred
the bourgeois! Of course, much was destroyed or stolen in
Russia; what was stolen, however, has not yet left Russia,
but has only been shared among a larger number of her
inhabitants. The 'bourgeois' have become more numerous in our land, and I'm telling you that petty bourgeois
they may be but they are very strong—they will make
their presence felt!"

"And the working class?"

"And the working class will feel their presence if the
worker does not take the road of peasant policy, does not
want to understand the full importance of village interests."

. . . All this sounds somewhat ironic and grotesque; it
seems to me, however, that in this story there is a very
significant grain of truth, and any truth should, for our
edification, be spoken out loud.


## UNTIMELY THOUGHTS

*Novaya Zhizn, No. 59 (274),
April 4 (March 22), 1918*

My little article concerning the proclamation of a group of
sailors about their readiness for mass-murder of unarmed
and absolutely innocent people has provoked the supporters of that group to write several letters in which various shameless or mad persons try to frighten me with
horrible punishments.

This is stupid, for threats cannot render me dumb, and however they threaten me, I will always say that brutes are brutes and idiots are idiots, and that one cannot achieve the triumph of social justice by resorting to murder, violence, and similar methods.

But here is a letter which I consider it necessary to publish as the sole human response to my little article.

> Having read your article "Untimely Thoughts" in the newspaper *Novaya Zhizn,* No. 51 (266), I want to believe that you do not consider all wearers of sailors' greatcoats unruly savages. But permit me to ask what am I to do on meeting you or, in general, any citizen in civilian dress who agrees with your opinion and your view of the sailors, and not only I, but a hundred individuals living with me in an intimate circle and whom I know very well, and I know that they, as I, have never even given a thought to the slightest mischief, let alone killing. How can we look others in the eye, since we wear sailors' greatcoats.
>
> Reading your article I was sick at heart not only for myself but also for those many innocent comrades who are put in the pillory of public opinion. I live with them, I know them as I know myself; I know them as unspectacular but honest toilers whose thoughts do not reach the judgment of the broad public, and therefore I ask you to speak about them your loud and heartfelt word, for their sufferings and mine are undeserved!
>
> Sailor: signature illegible.
> Kronstadt, March 27, 1918.

It goes without saying that I am far from wishing to accuse all sailors of being inclined toward brutal killing. No, I meant only those who made themselves known by the killings in Sebastopol and Evpatoriya and by the murder of Shingarev and Kokoshkin, and I meant that group which composed and signed the well-known insane proclamation published among the "Decrees and Actions of the Government."

———— • ————

I shall not deny that in Russia there are a great many people with "conscience" even among professional thieves and murderers—everyone knows that; a man robs or kills his neighbor and then his "soul languishes," that is, his conscience bothers him. A great many kind-hearted Russians find much comfort in this "languishing of the soul" —it seems to them that the limp sensitivity of conscience is a sign of spiritual health while, in all probability, it is really a sign of a sickly lack of will in those people who, before they kill, admire the modest beauty of a field flower and are able to combine in themselves a sincere revolutionary and a no less sincere informer, as has happened among us too frequently.

I think that all of us—sailors and writers, "bourgeois" and proletarians alike—are weak-willed and cowardly, but this does not prevent us at all from being the cruelest kind of physical and moral torturers of each other. As proof of this sad truth I suggest that the reader compare the psychology of the mob law with the methods of newspaper "polemics." In each case, both in the newspapers and on the streets, he will see equally blind and mad people whose main purpose and greatest delight is in hitting their neighbor in the "mug" or in the heart as painfully and cruelly as possible.

This is the psychology of people who still cannot forget that fifty-six years ago they were slaves—and that every one of them could be whipped with birch rods—and that they are living in a country where mass pogroms and murders can go unpunished and where a man is worth nothing. Nothing.

Where there is no respect for man, people capable of respecting themselves are seldom born and do not live long.

And where should this respect come from?

In *Pravda* various little beasts egg on the proletariat against the intelligentsia; in *Nash Vek* (Our Age) sly-minded rats egg on the intelligentsia against the proletariat. This is called "class struggle" in spite of the fact that the intelligentsia is thoroughly proletarianized and is already prepared to starve to death together with the proletariat. You say the intelligentsia is engaged in sabotage? But the moral sense of the intellectual cannot permit him to work with a government which includes in its "actions and decrees" the well-known threat of the group of sailors and similar disgusting things. Whatever the sages of Bolshevism say about the "sabotage" of the intelligentsia and however eloquently they say it, the fact remains that it is from shortage of intellectual power that the Russian revolution is perishing. In this revolution there is a great deal of morbid irritability, but there is a lack of culturally developed, trained reasoning.

Now the Bolsheviks have come to their senses and are calling the representatives of intellectual power to cooperate with them. This is late, but not bad, nonetheless.

In all probability, however, haggling will begin in which some will ask too much and others will gradually back down, whilst the country will be destroyed still further, and the people will become corrupted all the more.

UNTIMELY THOUGHTS

*Novaya Zhizn, No. 61 (276),*
*April 7 (March 25), 1918*

"Don't hit a man when he's down" is an excellent rule, and we would all be much nicer both to ourselves and to each other if we honestly adhered to this rule.

But when a man who is down raises his head and quietly slithers up behind you with the insidious intention of hitting you in the back of the head, then it is necessary to talk about him in that tone which his Jesuitic schemes deserve. This task is just as unpleasant as the cause of it is repulsive.

There can be no argument that in the process of social struggle the man who is down has suffered not only what he deserved but more. What is to be done? As the soldier is conditioned by barracks life, so each one of us is conditioned by that class milieu in which he is placed by history. Meekly submitting to the influence of facts, we have always cared too little for self-education, for the cultivating of our will and our feelings. We are all much worse and coarser than we should be, and some of us try especially hard to show as much coarseness and cruelty as possible, hoping in this way to hide a lack of talent and a lack of strength.

And so the man who is down raises his head, slithers up, and hisses; this is heard very clearly not only in Izgoev's article about "Tragedy and Guilt,"[132] not only in all the writings of *Novy Vek* (New Age), *Sovremennoe Slovo* (The Modern Word)[133] and the like; this evil, vindictive hissing sounds louder and louder among the "Cadets." The "Cadets" are the very best politicians in Russia; they are convinced of this and also of the fact that they are the only force capable of saving Russia from the threat of destruction. In the difficult struggle for freedom they played the role of Krylov's fly which, as is well known, somewhat over-estimated its own work.[134] They are very smart people, the Cadets; they not only are careful not to criticize sharply the actions of the Soviet regime, but even indulge it somewhat, and for this have been repeatedly awarded flattering approval by the Soviet press. They know very well that Soviet "communism" discredits

more and more not only the ideas of social democracy but
any hopes at all of radical democracy, and they no longer
wish to hide their sincere hatred of a democratic Russia.
A good Cadet is first of all a politician—or, more exactly, a politico—he is the same sort of fanatic about his
idea as is the Bolshevik "communist"; he believes in the
same blind sectarian way in the possibility of the complete
destruction of socialism, as the Bolshevik believes in the
necessity of an immediate realization of socialist ideas.

The leader of the Constitutional-Democratic party, P. N.
Milyukov, proudly told Petko Todorov, a Bulgarian
writer, in 1905:

"I have organized in Russia the first political party
which is completely free from socialism."

And now the Cadets are proud of this "freedom from
socialism," and since democracy cannot be other than socialist, it is natural that Cadetism and democracy are inherently hostile to each other.

After 1906 the Constitutional-Democratic party was
that spiritual ulcer of the country which for ten years ate
away at the intelligentsia by its Jesuitic politicking, oppor-
tunism, and most shameless hounding of the defeated
workers. "His Majesty's Opposition"[135]—they did not
disdain any means in trying to elbow their way into
power. That did not happen then; the Cadets hope
that it will happen now. They are beginning their
work from the same point that they began in 1907, from
the persecution of democracy, and now, as then, they are
striving anew to organize all the renegades and cowards,
all the enemies of the people and haters of socialism.
Gradually loosening their tongues, they once again intend
to resume that repulsive howl of revenge and offended ego
with which they deafened Russia after the first revolution.
This wail of the "insulted and injured" is already rising,
and soon democracy will be presented with an exception-

ally lengthy indictment, carefully and maliciously prepared, in which all the crimes will be magnified and all the mistakes will be treated as deceit. These people know very well that slander is a magnifying glass through which an insect may be seen as a monster, and a mosquito's bite as a deep wound.

The "Cadets" consider themselves the thinking apparatus of the bourgeoisie and its tongue, but in reality they are simply a group of the intelligentsia who overestimate their strength and their significance in the country, and who have completely lost the living spirit of democracy.

People who "serve" the bourgeoisie are more dangerous than the bourgeoisie itself; they are more power-hungry and less efficient. The difference between commerce and politicking is that the merchant includes in his inventory everything that may be bought and sold—including conscience—while the politico trades in people and his own conscience. They are literate, well versed in tricks of politicking, not very squeamish in their choice of the methods of struggle, and they are able to entangle in the nets of Jesuitical eloquence people who are less literate but more sincere and capable of positive work. They are fully capable of creating again that gloomy atmosphere of moods which depress the soul, the moods which so firmly supported the terrible reaction of 1908-1916.

These people are all the more dangerous, since it is impossible to understand what exactly is dear to them, to whom their love and their hearts belong.

Democracy has two enemies: their "communist" lordships who crushed it physically, and the Cadets who are already starting the work of killing its spirit.

## UNTIMELY THOUGHTS

*Novaya Zhizn, No. 62 (277),*
*April 9 (March 27), 1918*

Recently I received the following letter and I highly recommend it to the attention of my comrades who are convinced that they are building a "socialist fatherland:"*

> In your last article you wrote that the soldiers bring a great deal of money into the village and you wonder where this capitol [sic] comes from. Well, here is an example for you: my brother, a soldier who was not in the war and saw light service in Petrograd, then found work as a guard on the railroad, and there passed trains loaded with alcohol which he and others had to guard. And so after serving there two months he brought home five thousand rubles. And he earned it onestly [sic]: when a train stopped they would open a car they would drill into a barrel (maybe they did it some other way) they simply would fill bottles with alcohol (he was not alone) they would lock the car again the sealer would seal the car, and everything would be in order. They would split the money according to rank and so it went for two or three months. He returned home last week, put the money in the bank, everyone was so happy, all the neighbors vied with each other in inviting him to their homes and he got himself a rich bride, since money likes money. *Not a single person blamed him, only I his sister a plain peasant woman was ashamed and hurt because my brother was a thief, an embezzler of the public purse. And there are hundreds of thousands of his kind.*
>
> [signed] A peasant woman from X province, X county, and the village I won't write."

"A plain peasant woman," an honest person, she apparently "won't write" the village because she is afraid that her neighbors would tear off her head.

---

* The grammatical and stylistic peculiarities of this letter are retained.

Comrade builders of a socialist paradise in Russia: "Behold the fowls of the air: for they sow not, neither do they reap, nor gather into barns." Behold and say honestly: are these birds of paradise? Are these not black ravens and will they not peck to death the urban proletariat?

I know that the letter of a "plain peasant woman" cannot shake the rocklike confidence of the "socialism-now brigade" in their rightness. It will not be shaken by scores and hundreds of similar testimonials about the current sentiments of the "village poor," and it will not be shaken by such testimony as a short scene by Ivan Volny published in the No. 12 issue of *Delo Naroda* (The People's Cause).

Ivan Volny is a peasant himself, a participant in the events of 1905-1906, a beaten and martyred man who was marched off to prison by his school friends. He endured a great deal, but he retained his living, passionately loving soul, and managed to write, ungrudgingly and truthfully, the dark epic of the Black Hundreds' movement in the countryside after 1906. He is an honest, truthful witness, and I know how difficult it is for him to speak the bitter truth about his own people—his heart burns with sincere love for them. This is a man whom we can and must believe.

Yet reality, which is always more truthful and talented than anyone (even writers of genius), depicts the Russian countryside of our times even more cruelly.

I especially recommend to Mr. Gorlov of *Pravda* these sources for understanding the present-day village. He is a very hot-tempered man and being, probably, an honest person, he ought to know well what he speaks about, what he defends. He does not know this.

He has no right to talk nonsense about my allegedly scornful spitting in the face of the people. That which he likes to call "scornful spitting" is my conviction formed over dozens of years.[136] If Mr. Gorlov is literate, he ought to know that I was never carried away by the Russian village and that I cannot be carried away by the "village poor" who are inherently inimical to the psychology, ideas, and aims of the urban proletariat.

It is, of course, quite natural that, pushing the working class ever farther from themselves, the "socialism-now brigade" must find support in the village. They will be the first to howl from its bear-like embrace, and numerous Gorlovs who ought to learn before they teach will also howl with bitter tears.

Mr. Zinoviev[137] "challenged" me to a verbal and public duel. I cannot satisfy Mr. Zinoviev's desire; I am not an orator, I do not like public appearances, I am not sufficiently skilled to compete in eloquence with professional demagogues.

And why is this duel necessary? I write; every literate person has the opportunity to read my articles just as he has the right not to understand them or to pretend that he does not understand.

Mr. Zinoviev asserts that by condemning the acts of cruelty, coarseness, and so forth, which the people perpetrated, I am "scratching the back of the bourgeoisie."

This attack is crude, not clever—but nothing else can be expected from Zinovievs. He, however, should have said in front of the workers that, condemning some of their actions, I tell them all the time:

that demagogues, like Zinoviev, corrupt the workers;

that the reckless demagogy of Bolshevism, arousing the dark instincts of the masses, puts the workers' intelligentsia in the tragic position of strangers in their native surrounding;

and that Soviet policy is a treacherous policy in regard to the working class.

This is what Mr. Zinoviev should have told the workers.

## UNTIMELY THOUGHTS

*Novaya Zhizn, No. 80 (295),
April 30 (17), 1918*

It is natural that the attention of thinking people is focused on politics—on the area of violence and despotism, anger and lies, where various parties, groups, and figures, having gathered allegedly for the "last and decisive battle," cynically scorn the ideas of freedom, gradually losing their human likeness in the struggle for physical power over people. This attention is natural, yet it is one-sided and therefore abnormal and harmful. The process of social growth is not limited to the phenomenon of political class struggle, at the base of which lies the crude egoism of the instincts. Along with this inevitable struggle there is developing more and more powerfully another, higher form of struggle for existence, a struggle of man against nature, and only in this struggle will man develop the forces of his spirit to perfection, only here will he acquire the uplifting awareness of his own significance, and here will he conquer that freedom which will destroy in him the animal traits and which will allow him to become intelligent, kind, honest—really free.

I would like to tell everyone who is worn out by the cruel torments of reality and whose spirit is depressed that even in these days which are threatening Russia with destruction, the intellectual life of the country has not dried up, has not even died down, but on the contrary is developing vigorously and on a broad front.

The country's highest academic institution, the Academy of Sciences, is working strenuously; its investigation of Russia's productive forces goes on without let-up; a number of very valuable reports and treatises are prepared for printing or are printed; soon there will appear a survey

of the success of Russian science, a book which will enable us to be proud of the great works and achievements of
Russian talent.

The University intends to give free science courses in
the spirit of the Sorbonne; many learned societies are
functioning regardless of crude handicaps which the ignorance of politics and the policy of ignoramuses place upon
them.

The modest devotees of pure knowledge, overlooking
nothing that can be useful for their devastated and tormented motherland, draw up projects for establishing
various institutes necessary for the revival and development of Russian industry. In Moscow, "The Scientific Institute" founded with Mrs. Mark's resources and directed
by Professor Lazarev is taking up its work; in Petrograd,
"The Free Association for the Development and Dissemination of the Positive Sciences" is organizing research institutes of chemistry, biology, etc.

The limitations of a newspaper article do not allow me
to enumerate all the undertakings initiated among our
scientists during the revolution, but without exaggerating
the significance of these undertakings, one can state with
confidence that the scientific forces of Russia are developing a vigorous activity and that this great and pure work of
the country's best brains is a pledge for and a beginning of
our spiritual revival.

If only those who consider themselves the political
leaders of Russia understood rightly the needs of the people and the interests of the state, if only they had enough
tact not to hinder the great cause of scientific creativity
and enough sense to promote the work of scientists!

——— • ———

But unfortunately the creative process in the area of pure and applied science remains almost unknown to broad strata of the democratic intelligentsia who need to follow the development of this process, since knowledge is fully capable of curing tormented souls, of comforting the exhausted, and of increasing their working energy.

The Academy of Sciences would accomplish a fine and useful task by undertaking the publication of a small journal which would inform literate people about everything that occurs in the area of Russian science. An information journal such as this would undoubtedly have a profound educative significance both socially and nationally; I did not slip up saying "national" significance, for I find it is time for us—the people whose strength was so skillfully and extensively used by our "friends" in the struggle against their enemies—to understand that we have no other friends than ourselves.

Finally it is time for us, people thoroughly uncultured, to understand also that for a long time we have lived in the conditions determined by science without the participation of which you cannot make a good brick, or a button, or anything that makes our life easier, brightens it, and tries to save our energy from useless waste and to overcome the forces which destroy life. It is time for us to understand that scientific knowledge is a force without which the revival of the country is impossible.

"We are lazy and incurious,"[138] but we should hope that the cruel, bloody lesson given to us by history will shake off our laziness and make us think seriously why, why we—Russia—are more unfortunate than others? I repeat that the Academy of Sciences by taking upon itself the publication of an information journal which, in brief essays and reports, would relate everything that occurs in the mysterious field of science, a field hidden from the uninitiated, would accomplish the nationally important

and necessary task of bringing to reason and humanizing a
country which is losing faith in its own strength and is
being brutalized by the cynical tortures of stupidity, the
most frightening enemy of the people.


## UNTIMELY THOUGHTS

*Novaya Zhizn, No. 81 (296),*
*May 1 (April 18), 1918*

Culturally more advanced groups of the working class
have begun to realize how necessary it is for a worker to
possess scientific and technical knowledge. Intelligent
workers feel that industry is their concern, that it is the
basis of culture, a guarantee of the well-being of the country, and that for the revival and development of industry
the worker needs a sizeable fund of scientific knowledge.
This, to us, new appraisal of knowledge and work is supported by the testimony of such facts as those adduced by
trade union members in memoranda calling for the establishment in our country of museums and institutes for
various branches of production, for example, glass, ceram-
ics, and porcelain.

It is very characteristic that, first of all, the workers
point to the quickest possible development of artistic
production. One may see in this a manifestation of emotional creativity and of "mother wit" of the people, who, it
seems, understand that the Germans, ready to inundate
Russia with cheap and trashy goods, will be unable to
compete with us in the realm of artistic production.

It has been said of the Germans:

"The German, disciplined to the perfection of a mechanical apparatus, an obedient tool in the hands of whatever force controls him, can produce marvelous imitations

of everything, from philosophy to rubber, but he has no understanding of the poetry of labor." And there is more than a little truth in this.

We Russians are anarchists by nature, we are cruel beasts; in our veins there still flows the dark and evil blood of slaves, the poisonous inheritance of the Tartars and of serfdom—that is also true. There are no words that one could not use in cursing the Russian, one weeps blood but one continues cursing, for he, wretched soul, has always justified and still justifies our baying at him drearily, our howling at him like dogs whose love is inaccessible and incomprehensible to their wild master, who is also a beast.

The most sinful and filthy people on earth, senseless both in good and evil, drunk with vodka, deformed by cynical violence, hideously cruel and, at the same time, incomprehensibly kind-hearted—that, when all is said and done, is a talented people.

Now—when the putrescent boil of the police and bureaucratic system has burst and the poisonous pus, accumulated for centuries, has flowed all over the entire country—is when we must all endure stern and painful retribution for the sins of the past, for our Asiatic stagnation, for that submissiveness with which we bore oppression.

But this outburst of spiritual filth, this hurricane of pus, will not last long, for this is the process of purification and recuperation of a sick organism. "The illness has declared itself," has appeared in all its ugliness.

But one refuses to believe that this is a fatal illness and that we will perish from it. No, we will not perish if we begin our cure all together and pursue it stubbornly.

The Russian intelligentsia must once more take upon itself the great labor of the spiritual healing of the people. Now it is able to work under conditions of greater freedom, and there is no doubt that the labor of the country's

spiritual resurrection will be shared by the working proletarian intelligentsia, by the more culturally advanced part
of it which is sinking and choking among the ignorant
masses.

The task of the democratic and proletarian intelligentsia
is to unite all the intellectual forces of the country on the
basis of cultural work. But in order to succeed in this
work we should reject party sectarianism, we should
understand that the "new man" cannot be formed by politics alone, that by turning methods into dogmas we do not
serve the truth but only increase the number of ruinous
delusions which fragment our forces.

Our forces are not large; we must spare them, we must
economize on the use of our energy, coordinate the separate undertakings and efforts of individuals, groups, and
organizations, and create a single organization that would
head all cultural-educative work aiming at the restoration
of spiritual health and at the revival of the country.

It seems that the part of the intelligentsia which is less
sectarian-minded and not yet slashed to death by factional
and party "politics" is beginning to feel the necessity of
wide-spread cultural work dictated imperatively by the
tragic conditions of reality.

This is seen in the attempt of representatives of various
political views to organize a non-party society under the
motto, "Culture and Freedom";[139] and there is no doubt
that if this society understands the task of the moment in
sufficient depth, it will be able to fulfill the difficult role of
organizer of all the individuals and groups who are the
most capable and who sincerely wish to work for the good
of the country.

But even here, as the first condition for successful work,
one must effect the publication of an information journal
which would give a more or less accurate picture of the
whole progress of the cultural-educative undertaking. It is

necessary to count our strength, it is necessary to know who does, or intends to do, what—and where; it often happens with us that people working in the same area know nothing of one another.

If the country has two publications, one of which sets itself to the task of reporting in detail everything that takes place in the fields of pure and applied science, and the other which assumes the responsibility of telling about cultural-educative work, then these publications will be enormously useful to the cause of shaping thought and feeling. We must work, honorable citizens, we must work, for in this alone is our salvation and in nothing else.

The sadistic delight with which we, standing on the brink of destruction, tear at each other's throats is a pettily base delight, although it comforts us in our endless sorrows.

But really, it is of no use to devote ourselves with especial zeal to the cause of mutual torture and extermination; we should remember that there are enough people who both wish to and, perhaps, actually can exterminate us.

Let us work for the sake of our salvation, and let us not perish "like the Avars of whom there is neither kith nor kin."[140]


# UNTIMELY THOUGHTS

*Novaya Zhizn, No. 82 (297),*
*May 3 (April 20), 1918*

Recently, some damned sages sentenced a seventeen-year-old youth to seventeen years of public labor because this youth frankly and honestly stated: "I do not recognize the Soviet regime!"

Without mentioning the fact that there are tens of millions of people in Russia who do not recognize the authority of the Commissars' regime and that it is impossible to slaughter all these people, I find it useful to remind the stern but unintelligent judges of the origins of this honest youth, who was so absurdly and severely punished by them.

This youth is flesh of the flesh of those straightforward and fearless people who for decades, living in an atmosphere of police surveillance, spying, and betrayal, tirelessly worked at destroying the leaden prison of the monarchy, bringing, with danger to their own lives and freedom, the ideas of freedom, right, and socialism to the dark masses of workers and peasants. This youth is a spiritual decendant of those who, captured by enemies and suffering in prisons, refused, out of contempt for the victorious enemy, to talk to the police interrogators.

This youth has been brought up on the lofty example of those finest Russians who perished in their hundreds and in their thousands in exile, in prisons, at hard labor, and upon whose bones we intend to build a new Russia.

This is a romantic, an idealist, with a natural aversion to the "realistic policy" of violence and deceit, a policy of fanatics of dogma who are surrounded—as they themselves admit—by swindlers and charlatans.

Bringing up a courageous and honest youth in the vile conditions of Russian life required an enormous expenditure of spiritual force, nearly a whole century of strenuous labor.

And now those people for whose freedom this labor was undertaken have failed to understand that an honest enemy is better than a base friend and have condemned the courageous youth because he, as it should be, cannot and does not want to recognize a regime which flouts freedom. There is a very clever fable of a pig under a centuries-old oak tree—perhaps the wise judges will find time to read it? They ought to become acquainted with the moral of this fable.[141]

———— • ————

They have arrested I. D. Sytin in Moscow. Here is a man who recently celebrated his fiftieth anniversary in the book-publishing business. He was a Minister of People's Education, much more real and useful for the Russian countryside than the Count Dm. Tolstoy and the other ministers of the Tsar. Undoubtedly, the hundreds of millions of Sytin calendars and leaflets cut down at least by half the number of relapses into illiteracy. All his life he struggled to attract to his work the best forces of the Russian intelligentsia, and it is not his fault that he was poorly understood by it in his sincere desire to "ennoble" the Sytin books. Nonetheless he managed to attract to his work the attention and help of such people as A. N. Tolstoy, A. P. Chekhov, N. A. Rubakin, Vakhterov, Klyuzhev, A. M. Kalmykova,[142] and scores of others. The publishing house "Intermediary"[143] was founded by him; he gave the Kharkov Committee for Literacy the idea of issuing the useful multi-volume *Agricultural Encyclopedia*. Over a span of fifty years Ivan Sytin, a self-taught man, accomplished an enormous work of undeniable cultural significance. In France or England—the "bourgeois" countries, as we know—Sytin would have been recognized as a man of genius, and on his death a monument would have been erected to him as a friend and educator of the people.

In "socialist" Russia, the "freest country in the world," they have put Sytin in prison, first destroying his enormous, superbly organized business and ruining the old man.[144] Of course, it would have been both more intelligent and more useful for the Soviet regime to attract Sytin,

as the best organizer in the book-publishing business, to
the work of restoring the broken-down book industry, but
this did not occur to them. Instead, they found it necessary to reward this rare worker for his life's labor with—
prison. Thus inveterate Russian stupidity piles whims and
absurdities on the roads and paths to the country's rebirth,
thus the Soviet regime expends its energy on the senseless
and harmful (both to itself and to the whole country)
excitation of anger, hatred, and gloating, with which
the natural enemies of socialism mark every false step,
every mistake, and every sin, intentional and uninten-
tional, of the Soviet regime.


### UNTIMELY THOUGHTS

*Novaya Zhizn, No. 86 (301),*
*May 10 (April 27), 1918*

In the May 3 issue of *Nash Vek* (Our Age) citizen D.
Filosofov published an article about Gorky who "is trying
to enlist scientists, writers, and artists in the service of the
Sovdeps."[145]

The event is insignificant. The article, however, is so
strangely written that it compels me to pose the author
several questions and to give the reader a few explanations.

First of all, what brought forth the following assertions
from citizen Filosofov:

"To argue with Gorky is very difficult. He cannot stand
being 'contradicted.' But such frightening and complicated
questions as the 'cultural contradiction' cannot be placed
on a personal basis. And can it be that we went through
the revolution just to return to the old autocratic ways
when it was forbidden to have one's own opinion? Gorky

appears and acts before the public.[146] Is it really necessary to agree with him about everything in order not to 'offend' him? It is time to give up these ways. Every opinion, every action is subject to free criticism."

Where did citizen Filosofov get the idea that I "cannot stand being 'contradicted'"?

Since I do appear before the public, I have given no one reason to assert that I "cannot stand" honest criticism of my opinions, however sharp this criticism may be. I like to learn, and an argument with an enemy is often more useful than a conversation with a friend.

Why does citizen Filosofov find it possible to assert that I "put public questions on a personal basis"?

If citizen Filosofov considers "personal" that feeling of inherent disgust which I have always experienced and still experience toward the morbidly inflated self-esteem of slackers by principle, toward people who have "a penny's worth of ammunition but a dollar's worth of ambition," then citizen Filosofov is right—I cannot stand "idlers by principle." I have always felt inimical toward the angry complaints of ungifted failures who do not have the strength and generosity to forgive or forget the cuts and bruises inflicted on them in the bustle of everyday life by their wild or careless fellowmen.

Filosofov speaks of "Gorky's plan to convert the Academy of Sciences into a Shanyavsky University."[147]

This is a lie. I said nothing of this sort, although I am a confirmed supporter of the need to popularize science. But, as goes without saying, the free development of science must precede its free dissemination, and it is vitally necessary that the country's highest scientific institution be completely independent in its creative activity.

Filosofov points out that Professors Kravkov and Pavlov left the Association, but he does not say when they left, for this is not to his advantage. He must have the reader think that the professors left after Gorky had begun to "make a match" between the Free Association and the Council of Commissars. Filosofov remains silent about the fact that the highly esteemed I. P. Pavlov left several months ago and that Kravkov had already left the Organizing Committee before the formation of the Association.

He says, for example, that Gorky's project "to compel the Academy to publish something on the lines of *The Messenger of Self-Education* is very nice and testifies to his good intention of teaching 'comrades' to read and write. But can we, with our poverty, squander our genuine scientists in this way?"

"By his works, the Academician Pavlov has earned the grateful admiration of all European science and has served all mankind. Gorky, however, wants to compel him to give a 'short course in physiology,' which any student can successfully give. And it turns out that Gorky, while concerned with the dissemination of science, shows very little respect for science itself and for its faithful servants."

This is cleverly done. By using twice the utterly inappropriate verb "to compel," Mr. Filosofov seems to whisper to the honorable representatives of free and pure science:

"Just think—Gorky is 'compelling' you, eh? See what he is? He'll show you!"

I am not "compelling" the Academy of Sciences to publish something on the lines of *The Messenger of Self-Education*. I only say that if the Academy took the trouble to acquaint the general public with the progress of its work in the "development of science," it would render a service important both nationally and socially. To suggest does not mean to compel.

Where did Filosofov get the idea that I want to "compel" I. P. Pavlov to give a short course in physiology? He places these words in quotation marks as if I actually said them.

He deliberately emphasizes that I am concerned only "with the dissemination of science" and omits mentioning its development; this omission is necessary so that he can say that Gorky is "ready to sell freedom and culture for the lentil soup" of a people's university and that I "am calling on the Russian intelligentsia to commit treason?"

That's how far things went! A call to work for the benefit of the state and people is a call to commit treason. What is this—the blindness of anger or Philistine stupidity?

But why did Filosofov not do anything about this before? Indeed, for many years I have been summoning the intelligentsia to work no matter what might happen and under all conditions. The madness of the brave is the madness of those who, disregarding each and every resistance of reality, all its painful tortures, strive unswervingly to assert their will, to carry through their ideas under actual conditions, however trying these may be. This is not only the madness of Garibaldi, but also that of Giordano Bruno and other martyrs of thought. Science is the most grandiose and striking of all mankind's madnesses, it is its noblest madness!

Let this sound like a paradox, but after thinking of the conditions in which pure science developed, even Mr. Filosofov will understand, I hope, how much truth there is in this—sad truth, maybe.

It would not be worthwhile to speak of Mr. Filosofov's tricks. His inventions are not so meaningful that they have to be refuted.

Nevertheless, his article was printed in *Nash Vek* not by the editor's "oversight," but, probably, by a unanimity of opinion.

What is the essence of this opinion?

Its essence is anger against democracy and, as is appar-

ent from Mr. Filosofov's article, this anger is becoming
ever more insolent. I have already pointed out that socialist democracy has no enemy angrier than the one who
hisses daily from the pages of *Nash Vek*.[148] The contributors to this publication blurt out their attitude toward the
revolution more and more frankly, they adopt an ever
stronger reactionary position, and undoubtedly they are
preparing themselves again to play that treacherous, corrupting role (in which they succeeded after 1905) of organizers of political and spiritual reaction.

Once again a festering sore is swelling on the body of a
tormented Russia.

A revolutionary democracy must know that the political
current which is being organized by *Nash Vek* is a most
hostile one. This is an implacable enemy, for it is an
enemy of the spirit.[149]


# UNTIMELY THOUGHTS

*Novaya Zhizn, No. 89 (304),*
*May 14 (1), 1918*

The Soviet regime has again throttled several newspapers
hostile to it.[150]

It is useless to say that such a method of fighting with
enemies is dishonest; it is useless to remind you that under
the monarchy respectable people unanimously considered
the closing of newspapers an underhand business; it is all
useless, since the concept of honesty and dishonesty is
apparently outside the competence and interests of a
regime foolishly confident that it can establish a new state
system on the foundations of the old—on arbitrariness
and coercion.

But the following ideas (not new, by the way) are

called forth by a new act of the Commissars' political wisdom.

The suppression of unpleasing public voices cannot have the practical effects desired by the regime, for the growth of moods hostile to their lordships the Commissars and to the revolution cannot be impeded by this act of faint-heartedness.

Their lordships the Commissars strike with all their might, without distinguishing between who is the opponent of their mad actions only, and who is, through his principles, the enemy of the revolution in general. Grabbing the former by the throat, they weaken the voice of revolutionary democracy, the voice of honor and truth; gagging the mouth of the latter, they create martyrs among the enemies of democracy.

Crowning the growing reaction with the halo of martyrdom, they feed it with a stream of new energy and provide justification for future vileness, a vileness which will turn not only against the entire democracy, but primarily against the working class; the working class will be the first to pay and it will pay more than anyone for the stupidity and errors of its leaders.

And so, suppressing freedom of speech, their lordships the Commissars will not gain any advantage for themselves and will be doing great harm to the cause of the revolution.

Why are they afraid, why are they faint-hearted? Realistic politicians, capable, as it seems, of evaluating correctly the importance of the forces that shape life—do they really think that they can destroy by mechanical means the power of the word? People experienced in underground activities must know that the forbidden word acquires a special persuasiveness.

And finally, have they really lost faith in themselves to such an extent that they are frightened by an enemy who speaks openly, out loud, and now they try to muffle him, even slightly?

A persecuted idea, even a reactionary one, acquires a certain tinge of nobility and elicits sympathy.

Give freedom to speak, as much freedom as possible, for when enemies speak a lot, they speak foolishly in the long run, and that's very useful.


## UNTIMELY THOUGHTS

*Novaya Zhizn, No. 91 (306),*
*May 16 (3), 1918*

N. N. Glebov's article[151] is the sincere outcry of a heart deeply disturbed by the gloomy confusion of life, and I know that now in Russia there are not a few who, as passionately as Glebov, are striving to break free from the bondage of this filthy and offensive reality and striving "Upward to Culture"—to genuine freedom, to light.

But it seems to me that Glebov, as well as those who, like him, painfully long for a better life, does not have an absolutely clear or sufficiently broad idea of what the concept "culture" or "being cultured" is.

The humanitarian, deeply idealistic content of these concepts somehow escapes these people. What do they really think about, what new forms of emotions and ideas do they imagine, dreaming of a new culture?

Look—around us we see quite a few so-called "cultured people"; these are people well-versed in politics and thoroughly saturated with various kinds of knowledge, but their everyday experience and their knowledge do not prevent them from being anti-Semites, anti-democrats, and even sincere defenders of a state system based on the oppression of the popular masses and the oppression of individual freedom. These people—personally respectable and sometimes even very sensitive in their private relationships—do not, in the struggle for the triumph of their ideas, i.e., in public activity, shrink from resorting to dishonest methods: to lies and slander against an enemy; to pettily mean, Jesuitical cunning; even to cruelty—the defence of capital punishment, the justification of executions, etc. And all this does not prevent them from considering themselves "cultured" people. Or let us take the German Social-Democratic party. It was considered very cultured and, indeed, its organizations contributed not a little to the cause of the development of Germany's external culture.

But for four years now, hundreds of thousands of German Social-Democrats, armed with the most abominable weapons of destruction, have been killing people like themselves on the ground, on the sea, in the air, and under the sea. They have been slaughtering the peaceful population, women and children. They have been destroying cities, vineyards, orchards, vegetable gardens, fields, temples, ships, and factories. They have been destroying the great, sacred, and centuries-old work of Belgium, France, and other countries.

I speak of the Germans because their disgusting actions during the entire war have been taking place on foreign soil, but it goes without saying that there are no innocents in this foul war. Everyone is to blame for it, and we were destined to suffer from it more than the others because we happened to be the weakest of all in regard to internal and external culture.

What is the essence of the matter and how must the true content of the concept of culture be understood, so that such disgraceful contradictions as those indicated above may become impossible?

Obviously we will only have the opportunity to elimi-

nate these disgraceful contraditions when we are capable
of cultivating our emotions and will.

It must be remembered that everything is within us, that
everything comes from us; it is we who create all facts, all
phenomena. Are we able to develop in ourselves an inherent aversion to the bestial half of our being, to those
animal elements in our psyche which allow us to be harsh
and cruel to each other? Can we instill in ourselves and
others an aversion to suffering, crime, lies, cruelty, and all
the nasty grime of which there is so much in the soul of
each of us, whoever he may be and however highly "cultured" he may be considered?

The true essence and meaning of culture lie in an inherent aversion to all that is filthy, base, false, and coarse,
to all that humiliates man and makes him suffer. We must
learn to hate suffering, for only then shall we eliminate it.
We must learn to love man such as he is, at least a little
bit, and we must passionately love man such as he will
be.

Now man is worn out, exhausted; his heart is torn into a
thousand pieces by longing, spite, disappointment, and
despair. Man is weary and he is pitiful, unpleasant, and
repulsive to himself. Some, hiding their pain because of
false shame, still continue to swagger, shout, and brawl,
pretending to be strong men, but they are all deeply unhappy, deathly tired.

What will cure us, what will revive our strength, what
can renew us from within?

Only faith in ourselves and nothing else. There are
things we need to remember, for we have forgotten too
much in the fight for power and a bite of bread.

We must remember that socialism is a scientific truth,
that the entire history of the development of mankind
leads us toward it, that it represents a perfectly natural
stage of the economico-political evolution of human soci-

ety. We must be confident of its realization—confidence
will calm us.

The worker should not forget the idealistic principle of
socialism; he will confidently feel himself to be both an
apostle of the new truth and a powerful fighter for its
triumph only when he remembers that socialism is necessary and salutary not only for the toilers, but that it liber-
ates all classes, all mankind, from the rusty chains of an
old, sick, incontinently lying and self-negating culture.

The propertied classes do not accept socialism, do not
sense the freedom and beauty in it, and do not realize how
high it can raise the individual and his creativity.

But do many workers understand this? For the majority
of them socialism is only an economic doctrine based on
the egotism of the working class, just as other social doc-
trines are based on the egotism of property owners.

In the struggle for class values one should not brush
aside the common human striving for the best.

A true sense of culture, a true understanding of it, is
possible only with an inherent aversion to everything
cruel, harsh, and base inside as well as outside oneself.

Are you trying to develop this aversion in yourselves?

Glebov, in response to my plan for publishing scientific
and cultural information magazines, exclaims:

"Does everything bad happen among us just because
our country does not have two additional publications?"

This exclamation is not in harmony with the intelligent
beginning of his article where he laments the "anarchic
and rebellious current of a derisive attitude toward books."

That we do not understand or that we undervalue the
power of knowledge is the most serious obstacle "on the
road upward to culture." Without knowledge and self-
awareness we can go nowhere from the rotten swamp of
the present. It is just now that we need publications which
would give us a more or less accurate idea about the good

things that we have—just the good things. A count of
negative features and facts has been made and is being
made daily with pleasure, but it is time to look closely—
aren't there any positive phenomena and facts around us?

## UNTIMELY THOUGHTS
*Novaya Zhizn, No. 92 (307),*
*May 17 (4), 1918*

Negative phenomena have always been immeasurably
more abundant than those facts in the creation of which
man invests his best feelings, his lofty dreams—this is a
truth as obvious as it is sad. The more realizable our
strivings for the triumph of freedom, justice, and beauty
seem to us, the more disgusting appears all that brutal
vileness which stands in the way of the victory of the
humanely beautiful. Filth and trash are always more noticeable on a sunny day, but it often happens that we,
fixing our attention too intensely on those facts irrecon-
cilably hostile to the thirst for better things, cease to see
the rays of the sun, and it seems that we do not feel its life-
giving force.

Three years ago we began to shout—with anguish, fear,
and anger—that Russia stands on the brink of ruin, but
long before that we spoke of the unavoidable ruin of our
native land in a whisper, in an undertone, in a language
distorted by the tortures of monarchist censorship. For
three years we have been incessantly going through a
catastrophe. The cries of Russia's ruin sound louder and
louder; the external conditions of her existence as a state
are growing more and more menacing. Her internal disintegration, supposedly, becomes more and more obvious
and it would seem she should have collapsed long since

into the abyss of political destruction. She has not collapsed, however, as of today; and she will not die tomorrow, unless we want this. We have only to remember that
everything that is repulsive, as well as everything that is
beautiful, is created by us; we have to kindle within ourselves an awareness, hitherto unknown to us, of personal
responsibility for the fate of our country.

It is superfluous to say that we live miserably and
shamefully, this is known to everybody—we have been
living so for a long time—and yet, under the monarchy,
we lived even more miserably and shamefully! We
dreamed then of freedom, not sensing its living, creative
force within ourselves, but now all the people sense this
force at last. They use it egotistically and brutally, stupidly
and abnormally—this is all true. It is time, though, to
understand and evaluate the enormously significant fact
that people brought up in the cruelest slavery are freed
from heavy, mutilating chains. Internally we have still
not overcome the heritage of slavery, we are still not sure
that we are free, we do not know how to use the gifts of
freedom appropriately, and because of all this—primarily
because of not being sure—we are so appallingly harsh
and morbidly cruel, and we so ridiculously and stupidly
fear one another and frighten one another.

And yet all of Russia to her very depths, to the last of
her savages, is not only externally free, but shaken internally in her foundations, and in the foundation of these
foundations: her Asiatic inertness, her Oriental passivity.

Those torments, those sufferings because of which the
Russian people howl like beasts and rush about, cannot
help but change their habits of mind, their prejudices and
biases, their spiritual essence. The people should quickly
understand that however strong and greedy the external
enemy may be, more frightening to the Russian people is

the internal enemy—they themselves—because of their own attitude toward themselves, toward man whom they have not been taught to value and respect, toward their country for which they have no feeling, and toward reason and knowledge, the power of which they have not known and have not valued, considering them a nobleman's invention harmful to a peasant.

They lived by ancient Asiatic cunning, not thinking about tomorrow, guided by the foolish saying: "Another day gone, thank God!" Now the external enemy has shown them that the cunning of a hunted animal is nothing compared to the calm, iron will of organized reason. Now they will have to devote the six-month winters to thinking and working, and not to half-asleep and half-starved inactivity. They have been compelled to understand that their native land is not limited by the boundaries of a province or a district, but that it is a huge country full of inexhaustible riches, capable of rewarding their honest and intelligent labor with fantastic gifts. They will understand that

> Laziness is stupidity of the body,
> Stupidity—laziness of the mind

and they will want to study in order to make both mind and body healthy.

A revolution is a convulsion, after which should follow a slow and measured movement toward the goal set by the act of revolution. The great French Revolution shook and tormented the heroic French people for ten years before they began to feel all of France as their native country, and we know how valiantly they defended her freedom against all the forces of European reaction. The people of Italy staged a dozen revolutions over a span of forty years before they established a united Italy.

Wherever the people have not taken a conscious part in the creation of their own history, they cannot have a feeling for their native land and cannot realize their responsibility for the misfortunes of their native land. Now the Russian people are all participating in the making of their own history—this is an event of tremendous importance and it should be the point of departure in evaluating everything bad or good that torments or gladdens us.

Yes, the people are half-straved, worn-out; yes, they commit a great many crimes, and they can be called "a bull in a china shop" not only with respect to the arts. They are an awkward force not organized by reason, a tremendous force, potentially talented, truly capable of all-round development. Those who so furiously and without a backward glance condemn and hound revolutionary democracy—seeking to wrestle from it its power and to subordinate it once again, even for a short time, to the narrowly selfish interests of the propertied classes—are forgetting the simple truth, unfavorable to themselves: "The greater the number of freely and intelligently working people, the higher the quality of work, the more rapidly develops the process of creating new, higher forms of social existence. If we compel all the brain-power of every given country to work vigorously, we shall create a country of miracles!"

Not accustomed to living with all the forces of heart and mind, we are tired of revolutions—a tiredness which is premature and dangerous for all of us. Personally, I do not believe in this tiredness, and I think that it will disappear if a cheerful, resurrecting voice sounds forth in the country—it must ring!

In one of the battles in the West, a French captain led his company in an attack on the enemy positions. He saw with despair how his soldiers fell one after another killed by bullets and more often by fear, by lack of faith in their

own strength, and by despair in the face of an objective
which seemed to them unattainable. Then the captain, as
befits a Frenchman, a man brought up on a heroic history,
shouted:

"Dead, arise!"

Those dead with fear rose up, and the enemy was defeated.

I passionately believe that the day is near when some
one who loves us very much and who can understand and
forgive everything will shout to us too:

"Dead, arise!"

And we shall arise. And our enemies will be defeated.

I do believe this.


## UNTIMELY THOUGHTS

*Novaya Zhizn, No. 93 (308),
May 18 (5), 1918*

We know only vaguely how the present-day village lives;
only rarely and accidentally do the voices of her living
people reach us "from the depths of Russia"—that is why
I find it necessary to publish the following letter which I
received the other day:

"My dear friend and comrade!" Then come several
lines of friendly outpourings, but the gist of the letter is as
follows:*

We have had plenty of news in our village recently,
especially during the last week. On April 3 and 4, all of us,
the inhabitants of Baska, went through a very hard time in
our lives, namely: on April 3, there came to our village
Baska about three hundred Red Guards who robbed all the
well-to-do householders, that is, they collected a levy—a

---

* The stylistic peculiarities of the following excerpt are retained.

thousand rubles from some, two to six thousand from others, all together they collected from our village 85,350
rubles which they took with them; and there is no possibility of drawing up an account of the various goods—
bread, flour, clothes, etc.—they stole from our citizens;
and they took a stallion from Sergey Timofeevich, but it
turned out that they did not get the use of it, as soon as
they reached the village of Tolstovka it died near the
church. And how they whipped people is difficult to describe, and they whipped them so hard that your hair
stands on end just remembering it, this is really horrible!
We Baskans spent these two days in such terror that I
haven't enough strength to describe all the horrors. It
seemed to everybody that it would be easier to survive the
torments of hell than the tortures of these brigands.

There is no more special news from our village, but in
Baranovka, Boldasievo, and Slavkino, after the departure
of the Red Guards and following the example of these
brigands, we ourselves, our poorest class, began to rob the
well-to-do citizens of our village, even to make raids on
other villages at night time. In a word, life here is becoming unbearable. Well, good-bye now, we are expecting you
to be our guest, and until then stay well.

The epic simplicity of the narrative could not testify
more convincingly to the author's truthfulness, revealing
in him a real Russian, one of those who have long since
become inured to everything, and if they speak of the
"torments of hell," it is more for the embellishment of
style than from indignation over robbery and beatings.
This is a man who has seen how the "poorest peasant,"
after serving in the army, returned to his village as the
"richest peasant"; now he observes how they turn this
"richest" one into the "poorest" once again; he knows that
when the Red Guards, having impoverished the "richest"
ones, then take their places, the Red Guards can be robbed
too.

He considers this leap-frogging "unbearable," though not

to the extent that he would refuse to see his friend as a guest. The leap-frogging stirs up his mind but does not seem to affect his sense of justice very deeply, and it is quite possible that he confidently awaits his turn to change the richest into the poorest. All this is like a cartoon, a farce, but unfortunately this is the "living truth" called forth from the depths of the village animality by the slogan "Rob the robbers!"

So they zealously rob "these poor villages" from which they collect eighty-five thousand rubles each. They rob because they have remembered all too well the sensible saying coined by the cynicism of plunderers and the dull despair of failures: "Pious works won't get you palaces of stone." Back-breaking peasant labor, which is wholly dependent on the favorable disposition of the elements, and is guided by ancient habits and not by the latest achievements of science, is incapable of developing a taste for a "pious," persistent, and honest work; but the historic course of economic development in Russia could convince even a cretin that "property is theft," indeed.

And so they rob and steal, encouraged from above by a wise regime which has proclaimed to the city and the world the allegedly latest slogan of social organization:

"Riff-raff to the bow!"[152]—which, translated into the language of the present day, means:

"Rob the robbers!"

The lines from a Shumakher[153] farce come to mind:

> Are we to blame the peasant for his
> ways?
> When he has been a peasant all his
> days?

The peasant should not be blamed. He only obediently follows the path predetermined for his dark will by wise people, people of reason.

## UNTIMELY THOUGHTS

*Novaya Zhizn, No. 94 (309),*
*May 19 (6), 1918*

To the question of who destroyed the army there exists a
quite definite answer in certain circles: the army was destroyed by socialists. This is one of the basic refrains to
the endlessly long song about the ruin of Russia which is
not yet ruined and which, apparently, does not want to be
ruined. This is one of the principal accusations leveled
against socialists by patriots who love Russia with the love
of hungry wolves, and this is one of those accusations
that are the least sincere, the most false.

That the army should inevitably collapse had already
been stated in the Defense Committee's memorandum
submitted to the Tsar in 1916, but this is forgotten, because to remember it is not to the advantage of the zealous
authors of the indictment against the socialists.

Recently I came across a bundle of letters received by
me from the front in 1916 and 1917; some of them should
be published for they speak very precisely about the
causes of the disintegration of the army. Here, for example, is a soldier's letter from March 1916:

> I am sending this letter secretly with a friend who is
> going on leave; you cannot write about anything in ordi-
> nary letters because they are read by the military censor-
> ship, and if they find two or three words about certain
> things, they immediately try to find out who wrote it, in
> what company and platoon, and they'll give you twenty-
> five lashes with the rod, or they will make you stand sentry
> on top of the trenches so that the German will fire at you.
> This was a frequent practice, but thanks be to him, he does
> not fire but shouts: "Don't be afraid, Russian; we shall not
> fire because your commanders put you there."

> We are a hundred paces away from the enemy so that we cannot get out at all, he shoots like hell; in 40 days our regiment lost 112 men without a fight. Mud up to the knees, cold, snow, sickness. . . . And they feed you only a miserable thin gruel, sometimes with meat in it, but more often without; and if you say you are hungry, they answer that they bring you bread all the time. So what—48 men are given 7 loaves per day of 11 pounds each. But we work all night digging trenches. True, you can buy bread in the supply train, but black bread costs 20 copecks a pound and white 45. There you are. Eat up.

In another letter from June of the same year, a noncommissioned officer, a volunteer decorated three times with the Order of St. George, complains:

> I am a simple soldier, I fight not because of egoism, but out of love for my native land, from anger against the enemy; all the same, even I have begun to understand that things are bad, that we can't hold out. Now, after returning from hospital, from Russia, I see what the reason for the disorder is; it is that the men at the front have exerted themselves to the utmost and there are not enough of them, but tens of thousands stay in the rear to no purpose; they loaf, they just gorge themselves, eating Russia to the bone. Who gives such outrageous orders?

The socialists did not give them.

An artilleryman, a youth, reports:

> The corps commander A. tells the officers whom he likes:
> "Take as much of this riff-raff as you please and get on with it. What are you waiting for?"
>   His favorites took a company or two and led the soldiers toward the German trenches without artillery support; the soldiers were killed, the officers received medals. One wounded infantryman told me:

"We are killed like lice—it's a disaster. Now they spread cholera, now they start a war. Oh Lord, to run away!"

What have the socialists to do with this?
I asked a wounded man, a holder of the St. George Cross:
"Is it hard in the trenches?"
He replied:
"It's hard for the soldiers. I don't see how they can bear it! Take me for example, I was a blanket but not bedding—a soldier was bedding. You see, in bad weather when water collected in the trenches, the privates would lie down in the mud, while we officers would cover them from above. They would get rheumatism, and we would get frost-bitten."

The well-known writer G—v[154] wrote in 1916: "From morning till night men are flogged for dodging work in the trenches; soldiers, refugees, Jews—all are flogged. But they cannot work—they are exhausted."

Soldiers in the rear knew how things were at the front they were told about them by wounded, crippled, frost-bitten, and tubercular warriors. And in the rear there arose a definitely hopeless mood with which one cannot win.

The masses in the rear sang ditties like the following:

> Young recruits don't feel so blue
> Germans will kill all of you!

> Great White Tsar, pray tell what for
> Did you start this sudden war?
> In a hurry rushed like mad
> To the slaughter are we led!

> Oh, we hate to be the crew
> Who Romanov's work will do
> Since Romanov's servants get
> Through the guts a bayonet.

And seeing off the boys doomed to death, the girls shouted in anger:

> Come ye tempest, come ye thunder
> Split the house of state asunder
> And within it may you slay
> Him who took my man away.

Reinforcements would come from the rear poorly armed, poorly trained, and already dispirited by what they knew about the front.

For all of this the socialists are not in the least to blame.

Here is an excerpt from the letter of an officer of the intelligentsia who in the main was very optimistic:

"These masses are so ignorant that many of them do not understand at all what is going on. They trust no one—neither Kerensky, nor the S.R.'s, nor the S.D.'s, nor the Provisional Government. All are empty noises to them. With my own ears I have heard such arguments that my tongue literally stuck in my mouth and I did not know how to answer such statements: 'God knows who this Kerensky is, maybe he wants to fight another three years!'

"The S.R.'s and S.D.'s are, in their opinion, soldiers at the rear who do not want to go to the front and who shout: 'War until victory!' "

Another officer writes:

"And yet these blind martyrs have something like an instinct for an organized state, otherwise you can't explain why they don't run away, sticking their bayonets into the ground."

Finally they ran away because their patience gave out, because the army knew and remembered such things as going into attack with clubs instead of rifles and repulsing attacks with rocks instead of shrapnel.

In 1914 and 1915 the entire press sang daily and thunderously of the Russian soldier's courage. In 1916, when the socialists were still silent, the praise had considerably toned down. Toward the end of that year some journalists very bravely began to doubt the fighting qualities of the victorious Russian army—not a very appropriate doubt after almost the entire regular core of the army had been destroyed by fighting, disease, and the appalling attitude toward the soldiers.

I am writing this not to defend the socialists, I do not think that they need defending; but it is utterly sickening to observe how a lie repeated a thousand times acquires for many the aspect of truth.

But the real, stern, and impartial truth is that all Russia, and not only her army, began to fall apart long before the socialists received the right to speak within her, and that now history has made the socialists responsible for the gigantic task of curing and reviving Russia.


## UNTIMELY THOUGHTS

*Novaya Zhizn, No. 95 (310),*
*May 21 (8), 1918*

We in Russia ought to discuss culture without end, and then endlessly again.

A self-taught poet came to me, a healthy, smooth fellow of about twenty, with eyes that were kind—though not without cunning. He read me about a yard of rather uncouth verse, and suddenly the following couplet rang in my ears:

> The cunning Teuton, under a clever disguise,
> Decided to bring culture to Russia!

I asked the poet:

"Won't you explain to me what is culture, in your opinion?"

His unfinished features assumed a condescending expression and the explained:

"I understand culture as any form of restraint on man such as organizations, parties, and, in general, everything that is against freedom of the individual."

"Are you an anarchist?"

"No, I fell out with them. They are a party, too, and make you read books."

"And you don't like to read?"

"I read novels and poetry, but not too much. It interferes with the writing of my own poetry: you read a lot, and you can't produce anything yourself. The poet must watch himself, yield to no one, and draw inspiration from his own soul."

"What poetry have you read?"

"Severyanin,[155] then several others . . . a lot! But I agree with one—I don't remember his name—who says:

> Do not learn from those books
> That you see around
> They've been written by hypocrites
> Exalted by the crowd. . . .

"This is put very well—do you agree?"

"There are different books . . ."

He swiftly interrupted me:

"No, everything foreign is harmful to a poet, he must live only by his own means. And generally all Russians must live by their own means, for we are a peculiar nation; look—no one can refuse to fight, but we did!"

"Did we really? We do beat each other, and very cruelly!"

"That's our internal affair. But all the same we won't accept German or French culture—see, they fight like beasts, it's all the same. Shame!"

"Are you a peasant?"

"Yes. Only I don't consider myself anybody; I don't like the village, or the muzhiks; they are people alien to me, they can't understand me."

His round, half-childish face became sad; his light-colored eyes screwed up as if he were hurt; he patted his hair—curled into ringlets at the ends—with his cleanly washed hand and sighed deeply. A real sufferer. A misunderstood soul.

When I told him that, in my opinion, he did not know how to write poems and that he should study, he did not believe me but did not seem to take it too much to heart.

"To study," he said, frowning thoughtfully, "that means —to be like everybody else? I'm not suited to that, I want to live in my own way. High-school and college students are all alike. No, I'll get there by myself somehow. . . ."

He left distressed, and I know that he will uselessly kill two, three, or maybe even five years, trying to "get" the opportunity, unrealizable for him, to become different from others.

And in five years he will squeeze himself into some kind of comfortable job, and will do it reasonably well, though not very willingly. He will live feeling terribly wronged by virtually everyone and harboring contempt for all who, in one way or another, will be dependent on him.

———— • ————

Mme. Z. G.[156] writes to me:

"I can imagine scores, even hundreds, of peasants capable of adopting culture, but when I think that every peasant man and woman will learn to clean their finger-

nails or blow their noses into handkerchiefs, this seems a
humorous utopia to me."

———— • ————

The veterinarian A. N. discusses culture as follows:
"In the very word 'culture' is clearly seen its meaning—
a cult, a religion. Culture can develop only on a religious
basis, and this will be a genuine culture. Everything else is
a culture of things, the external, and cometh of evil. In
these days when man has become a savage, he can be
saved only by a return to God, to the Temple, to a naïve
faith: 'Be like little children'—this is what must be said to
people, this is what they must be taught. But you are
teaching them: be like animals. This is a German influence, the influence of the foul books of Nietzsche, Marx,
Compte, and other Jesuits who invented all those ideas
just for us, the Russians, because the German knows that
we have a weakness for ideas like a carp for grubs."

———— • ————

"It is disgusting and repulsive to speak of culture when
the peasants are full and the intelligentsia goes hungry," a
woman teacher writes; and a "group of young people" is
convinced:
"It's for the best that everything external that people
took upon themselves to comply with duty, with the teaching of the holy fathers of literature, philosophy, and science
is falling from them; all this will fade, fall away, and man
will be really free. Perhaps he will once again take up the
very thing he has rejected, but he must live for a while
without ideas, principles, or any sort of tradition—there is
already enough of literature, culture, socialism, and all
that.

———— • ————

I could cite a dozen more such original opinions about culture, opinions attesting to the development of thought in the native Tambov-Kaluga[157] schools of philosophy; but those already quoted attest with sufficient persuasiveness to the fact that our perception of life is becoming sharper, while the understanding of its meaning and purposes grows dull. And as for those rules of social behavior, those usages of mutual relationships which can be based on the sharp animal perception of life, they do not promise us happiness. They will aggravate even more the general savagery to which not only the village but also the city, not only the people but also the so-called "semi-intelligentsia" succumb without resistance.

Once again and very obviously there arises the necessity for cultural-educational work—immediate, systematic, versatile, and persistent.

## UNTIMELY THOUGHTS

*Novaya Zhizn, No. 97 (312),*
*May 23 (10), 1918*

A man recently arrived from abroad relates the following:

"In Stockholm there are about sixty antique shops engaged in selling pictures, china, bronze, silver, rugs, and various other art objects exported from Russia. In Christiania I counted twelve such shops; there are many of them in Göteborg and other cities of Sweden, Norway, and Denmark. On some shops there are signs: 'Antiques and Art Objects from Russia,' 'Russian Antiquities.' In the newspapers you often see such announcements: 'We offer carpets and other items from the Russian imperial palaces.' "

There is no doubt that this story is the sad truth, as sad as it is disgraceful for us. To convince yourself that this is true, all you have to do is devote two or three days to observing what is going on in the galleries of the Aleksandrovsky Market,[158] in the antique shops of Petrograd, and in countless commission stores open on all streets of the city. People of American cut, well shaven but speaking Russian poorly, bustle around everywhere and buy endlessly; they buy everything that has even the slightest artistic value. With special zealousness and success they hunt for Oriental things: Chinese and Japanese porcelain, bronze, old lacquer, silk embroidery, drawings, enamel, cloisonné enamel, and so on. Foreigners know well that Russia is thickly sown with objects of Oriental art—especially after the march on Peking[159] where our warriors conducted themselves very unceremoniously with regard to the property of the Chinese, and from whence our war lords brought out valuable items by the box-car load. The Manchurian adventure[160] increased the flow of Oriental items even more substantially, and not a few of them were exported to Russia during the Russo-Japanese war. But, of course, China's being our immediate neighbor contributed most of all to the saturation of Russia with Oriental art.

Collectors and the experts in the trade who have studied the history of Oriental art assert that one can find in our country in marvelous abundance such rare and ancient items of the Orient as are no longer found either in China or Japan. Many foreigners are amazed that despite such a wealth of artistic treasures of the Orient, despite the spiritual link of Russian and Oriental art, we have no museum of Oriental antiquities and Oriental art.

Certainly this is the amazement of naïve people whose minds are absolutely incapable of understanding our Russian originality, our national distinctiveness. These people apparently do not know that we have the world's best ballet and the worst organized book publishing business, in spite of the fact that Russia is the world's largest book market. They do not know that the newspapers in Siberia, which is rich in forests, are printed on paper imported from Finland, and that we bring cotton from Turkestan to Moscow in order to take it back from Moscow to Turkestan, after processing it.

Generally, foreigners are naïve and ignorant people, and Russia is an enigma to them. To some Russians, as well, she is an enigma, and a very stupid one; but these Russians are simply people devoid of love for their native land, of patriotism, and of other things; they are heretics and, in the opinion of people with a wolfish patriotism, they are Hams who do not spare the nakedness of their fathers, supposedly because nakedness is disgusting when it is ugly and filthy.

But all joking aside. The point is that Russia is being robbed not only by the Russians themselves, but also by foreigners, which is much worse because a Russian robber remains in his own country with his loot, whereas a foreigner takes off for his home where, at the expense of Russian thoughtlessness, he adds to his museums and collections, that is, he increases the number of cultural treasures of his own country, treasures whose value is immeasurable, just as their esthetic and practical significance is. They not only develop taste and a love for the refined, not only elicit respect for the creative powers of man, but stimulate the striving to create new things, new forms of beauty, and in this way they influence the development of the art industry. And with the unavoidable change in social conditions, with the bringing of culture within the reach of democracy, the educative role of the art industry will be enormous and its development rapid.

Here also we will drag along behind the others, and our

wise men will moan, expressing belated and senseless regrets:

"How many beautiful things of the greatest significance,
both artistic and scientific, did we have in Russia and
look—it's all gone! How sad that it did not occur to us to
collect all of them in time, to build a museum—how nice
that would have been!"

They will moan and then calm down.

But, meanwhile, it is not too late yet, and it is possible
to save much that is valuable and necessary for Russian
culture.

———— • ————

Vera Alekseevna Petrova, a physician, a member of the
first graduating class of the Medical School for Women, is
dying of hunger. They wrote to me about her:

"I don't know whom to ask to help an old, sick person
*really dying of hunger*—a physician, who has devoted all
her life to the people, to Zemstvo work. Now she is dying,
helpless, covered with filth, in a dusty, awful room. If you
only could hear her words, the words of a person already
in the other world: 'What a horror hunger is!' She is dying
a slow and sure death, without anybody who would bring
boiling water or a bite of bread. We talked so much about
gentleness and love . . . where are they? An indifferent
beast, without kind feelings and impulses, a hungry belly
—this is what they have turned us into. . . ."

Help is needed. The address of V. A. Petrova: 8 Sixth
Rozhdestvenskaya St., room 46. Money can also be sent
to the editorial office of *Novaya Zhizn.*

# UNTIMELY THOUGHTS

## *Novaya Zhizn, No. 100 (315),*
## *May 26 (13), 1918*

Of the scores of letters I recieve from all over, the most interesting are those written by women. Devoted to impressions of the turmoil, these letters are saturated with longing, anger, and indignation; but feelings of helplessness and apathy are less often expressed in them than in letters from men. Every letter from a woman is an outcry of a living soul torn by the many varied tortures of these stern times.

Reading them, one feels in one's heart that they were all as if written by one woman, the mother of life, by her from whose womb all tribes and peoples came into the world, by her who bore and will bear all geniuses, by her who helped man to transform the crudely biological urge of an animal into the gentle and lofty ecstasy of love. These letters are the wrathful cry of a being who called poetry to life, who has served and will serve as the inspiration of the arts, and who forever suffers from an unquenchable thirst for beauty, love, and happiness.

A woman, in my view, is first and foremost a mother, though physically she may be a virgin; she is a mother in her feelings not only toward her children but also toward her husband, lover, and in general toward man, who came into the world from her and through her. As a being who incessantly replenishes the losses inflicted upon life by death and destruction, she must feel both more deeply and more acutely than I, a man, hatred and aversion for all that reinforces the work of death and destruction. Such, in my view, is the psychophysiology of a woman.

"Idealism!"

Perhaps. But if this is idealism, it is from the realm of

those beliefs which are naturally inherent in me and which apparently also constitute the basis of my psychophysiology. In any case I did not form these opinions yesterday— they have been with me since my youth; but I would not feel embarrassed if I had acquired them yesterday, for I find that social idealism is most necessary precisely in an era of revolution. I mean, of course, that healthy idealism which ennobles feeling, an idealism without which a revolution would lose its power to make man more socially conscious than he was before the revolution, an idealism without which a revolution would lose its moral and esthetic justification. Without the participation of this idealism, a revolution—and all of life—would turn into a dry, arithmetical problem of distributing material wealth, a problem the solution of which demands blind cruelty and streams of blood, a problem which, arousing savage instincts, kills man's social spirit, as we see in our time.

———— • ————

The letters that I am speaking of are filled to the brim with a mother's cries about the destruction of people, about the growing cruelty among them, about people becoming increasingly savage, base, and dishonest, about how terribly quickly manners are coarsening. These letters are filled with curses on the Bolsheviks, the peasants, and the workers—a woman calls down on their heads all evil machinations, scourges, and horrors.

"Hang them, shoot them, destroy them"—that is what is demanded by the woman, the mother and nurse of all the heroes and saints, the geniuses and criminals, the scoundrels and honest people, the mother of Christ but also of Judas, Ivan the Terrible, and the shameless Machiavelli, of the meek and kind Saint Francis of Assisi and of the gloomy enemy of joy, Savonarola; the mother of King Philip II, who laughed happily only once in his life—when he received news of the success of the St. Bartholemew massacre, that greatest crime of Catherine de Médicis, who was also born of woman, was a mother, and in her own way was sincerely concerned with the welfare of a great many people.

Condemning cruelty and inherently hating death and destruction, the woman and mother, the prompter of man's best emotions, the object of his admiration, the source of life and poetry—shouts:

"Slaughter them, hang them, shoot them. . . ."

Here there is a frightful and somber contradiction capable of destroying utterly that aura with which history has surrounded woman. Perhaps this contradiction is based on the fact that woman does not realize her great cultural role, that she is not aware of her creative powers and succumbs too easily to the despair caused in her mother's soul by the chaos of revolutionary days?

I shall not consider this question, but I shall permit myself to point out the following:

You women know very well that birth is always accompanied by pains, that a new man is born in blood—such is the cruel irony of blind nature. You howl like beasts at the moment of birth and you smile the happy smile of the Virgin, pressing the newborn to your breast.

I cannot blame you for your animal-like howl; I understand the torments causing this cry of unbearable pain. I myself am almost dying from that torment, though I am not a woman.

And I wish with all my heart, with all my soul that you should soon smile the smile of the Madonna, pressing to your breast the newborn man of Russia!

—————— • ——————

You women can speed the difficult process of birth, you can cut short the horrible pains experienced by the country. To do this you must remember that you are mothers and that the inexhaustible, living power of love is in your hearts. Do not yield to the evil influences of life, stand above reality. This requires strength—you will find it; now, in Russia, you are freer than anywhere else in the world—what prevents you from showing the best in you, your motherliness?

It must be remembered that a revolution is not just a succession of cruelties and crimes, but also a succession of feats of valor, honor, selflessness, and disinterestedness. Don't you see this? But perhaps you do not see this, just because you are blinded by hate and hostility?

And if, after looking closely, you nonetheless find nothing bright and cheerful in the chaos and turmoil of our times—then create something bright and good yourselves! You are free, you are strong with the charm of your love, you can make us men more like human beings, more like children.

The forty-year civil wars of the seventeenth century caused in France a revolting brutalization of morals, and developed a boastful cruelty—remember what a beneficial and healthy influence Julie Recamier had then for the whole country. You can remember scores of such examples of woman's influence on the development of human feelings and opinions. You mothers ought to be intemperate in your love for man and restrained in your hate for him.

The Bolsheviks? Well, imagine—they are people too. Like all of us, they are born of women, they are no more bestial than anyone of us. The best of them are excellent people of whom, in time, Russian history will be proud, and your children and grandchildren will also be fascinated by their energy. Their actions are subject to the severest criticism, even to caustic derision; the Bolsheviks have been rewarded with all this to a greater degree, perhaps, than they deserved. They are surrounded by the atmosphere of their enemies' suffocating hatred and, what is still worse, still more ruinous for them, by the hypocritical and base friendship of those who, making their way to power like foxes, use it like wolves and—let us hope! —will perish like dogs.

Am I defending the Bolsheviks? No, as far as my reasoning powers will allow, I am fighting them, but I am defending people the sincerity of whose convictions I know, whose personal honesty I know, just as I know the sincerity of their desire for the good of the people. I know that they are performing an extremely cruel scientific experiment on the living body of Russia. I know how to hate, but I prefer to be just.

Oh yes, they have made many very serious, depressing errors—God also erred in making all of us more stupid than necessary; nature also erred in many ways from the viewpoint of our desires contrary to her purposes or her purposelessness. But if you like, I can say something good about the Bolsheviks too; I will say that—not knowing toward what results their political activity will eventually lead us—psychologically the Bolsheviks have already rendered a tremendous service to the Russian people by moving all their masses from the dead center and by arousing in the masses a positive attitude toward reality, an attitude without which our country would have perished.

She will not perish now, for the people have come to life, and in them new forces are ripening, forces frightened neither by the madness of political innovators who had become too fanatical, nor by the greed of foreign robbers who are too sure of their invincibility.

———— • ————

Russia will not perish if you mothers will sacrificially pour everything beautiful, everything tender which is in your souls into the bloody and filthy chaos of these times. Stop shouting with hate and contempt, shout with love. Can it be that you, who give birth in suffering, do not understand the wonderful power of compassion for man! You have everything that can soften and humanize, for there is always more sunny warmth in the heart of a mother than in the heart of a man. Just remember those accursed men, the Bolsheviks and others, who have become savage and harsh in the work of destroying the rotten edifice of the old regime; remember them from when they were newborn babies—as with all babies, you had to wipe their noses, and they were helpless as all babies are. And can there be a man who is not indebted to you for the best days of his life?

You mothers should remember all that your love brings into life; this will save you from the tormenting oppression of hate which kills the greatest of feelings—maternal feeling.

Did you really try—try!—to assuage the cruelty of the embittered struggle, did you really try to reform the morals, to ennoble those human relations which arouse your righteous indignation? You are carried away by a futile hatred for grown men, but perhaps it would be more useful, more fitting to protect youth and children from the corrupting influence of the present day? You are wasting your attention and emotions on selecting things which actually discredit man and arouse a disgust for him; but would it not be better were you to look for, or try to create with your own powers, things which would elevate man in both his own and your eyes?

Physical mothers of the human world, you could be its spiritual mothers as well; indeed, if you disapprove of it, this means that you have reached a height which permits you to see more than others. So lift others up to this height!

Russia convulsively thrashes about in terrible labor pains—do you want the new, the marvelous, the good, the beautiful, the human to be born sooner?

Permit me to tell you mothers that anger and hatred are poor midwives.


## UNTIMELY THOUGHTS

*Novaya Zhizn, No. 103 (318),*
*May 30 (17), 1918*

More than once I have been approached by representatives of domestic servants with requests to "plead" for permission to publish in the newspapers job inquiries and job openings.[161]

Here is one of these requests stated in a letter:

"Try to explain to the present regime that it should choose any newspaper it wants and permit the publication of notices through which we could find employment as previously. Previously you would take a paper and could choose an offer according to your speciality; but now you haunt the doorsteps of all the unions and you get mean smiles and crude jokes, and there is no work. The Soviet regime should choose a newspaper for publishing work notices. The publishing of these will bring the regime a large income, and this is especially important for it since the Soviets have no money."

I do not know if it is true that job seekers encounter "mean smiles" in the offices of the trade unions; but willy-

nilly—in view of the unanimity of complaints—one cannot but believe that "crude jokes," and crudeness in general, have already become a habit with the new bureaucracy. The "bourgeois" wrote not a little about this, but it
is customary not to believe the bourgeois even when they
maintain with absolute sincerity that all brunettes have
brown hair. However, it is workers who are starting to
complain.

"I," writes one of them, "have performed no lesser service for the revolution than those boys on the Gorokhovaya
Street who bark at me like dogs. I've been a Bolshevik
since 1904 and not just since October; I stuck it out for
two years and seven months in prison; I served five years
in hungry exile. In my capacity as chairman of a volost
committee, I come to the authorities together with the
peasants; they shout at us and I'm ashamed to look my
comrade peasants in the eye, for all of a sudden they may
ask me: 'Why do they shout as if it were still Tsarist
times?' Influence these people somehow, so that they will
come to their senses!"

A worker arrested for reproaching a drunken Red
Guard with his coarseness was accused of "counterrevolutionary sentiments," and during the interrogation they,
in his words, "stuck a revolver in my mug, saying: 'Answer!' I answered: 'Are we comrades or not?' And they:
'Comrades like you should be punched in the teeth.' Let
me say that they smacked us in the teeth enough in the old
days, and if it continues this way, then the game's not
worth it."

Such accusations are heard more and more often, and I
do not see how people who provoke such shameful accusations and complaints can justify themselves. Under
the old regime, the contempt for a man of the working
class derived from the psychology of a pig that guzzled the
truth; after 1905 the pig grunted especially coarsely and

insolently as he felt himself victorious—he was celebrating his triumph.[162]

But in our days there are no victors, for although we fight ceaselessly, no one can celebrate a triumph—and who is to be humiliated? Can it be that we humiliate each other only out of habit, because we were humiliated in our time?

"I'm not responsible for the army!" replied one soldier to the familiar reproach heard among civilians.

The representatives of the regime, youths politically blond yesterday and intensely red-haired today, cannot use the soldier's answer to justify themselves. Each of them probably considers himself the bearer of a new, socially humane, and just rule; and each one is obliged to answer both for himself personally and for a whole army of builders of the new life. After all, this is their ideal mission, is it not? They it is who have replaced the old sowers of "the reasonable, the good, and the eternal?"[163] Exactly what of the new and how much of the reasonable and good do they bring directly into our daily round, into the hard life of hungry weekdays?

If they have no brains, then perhaps they have some conscience, and it will make them think about the accusations brought against them by the representatives of that class whose interests they supposedly serve.

With the greediness of a hungry man—this can be easily explained psychologically—*Petrogradskaya Pravda* (Petrograd Pravda) notes every kind word spoken about the "Bolsheviks." Whether Izgoev speaks about them with the irony of a Jesuit, or Klara Zetkin with many explanations that nullify the praise, *Pravda* immediately prints on its pages these doubtful compliments, thinking apparently that they refer to it, too.[164] It has also printed a few words from my answer to the letters of the women and accompanied them with this question:

"Does not Gorky agree now that many of the 'thoughts' expressed by him earlier really were 'untimely?' "[165]

No, I do not. Everything that I said about the Bolsheviks' savage crudeness, about their cruelty which approaches sadism, about their lack of culture, about their ignorance of the psychology of the Russian people, about the fact that they are performing a disgusting experiment on the people and are destroying the working class—all this and much more that I said about "Bolshevism" retains its full force.

## UNTIMELY THOUGHTS

### *Novaya Zhizn, No. 105 (320), June 1 (May 19), 1918*

The Obukhov hospital for men admitted "with symptoms of severe exhaustion due to malnutrition" a professor of the Technological Institute, the physicist Nikolay Aleksandrovich Gezekhus. In his time Professor Gezekhus was so popular as a scholar that talented physics teachers were called "Gezekhuses" in his honor. Now he is seventy-two years old; he is lying in the Obukhov hospital blown up with hunger, with swollen legs.

I don't think that this fact needs explanations and lamentations. I shall only remind you that the great French Revolution, having beheaded the chemist Lavoisier, did not starve its scholars. Since the general moral torpor makes everything possible among us, some cynic may say:

"The professor is seventy-two. . . ."

But even the vilest cynic will be disarmed if he finds out that in the men's section of the Obukhov hospital there lie 134 persons "ill from hunger," "stricken as a result of insufficient or abnormal diet"; 59 of them are under 30, and about 30 are under 20. All of these are people who do physical labor, people who for a normal life need food which would give their bodies 3,000 calories, and who, on the current food rations, receive 500 to 600 units, that is, less than a quarter of the number a person needs. In connection with this, we must keep in mind that far from all that is introduced into the stomach can be assimilated by the body; bread that's half straw, herring heads, cotton-cakes, and the like are not so much beneficial as harmful to people.

Famine in Petrograd has begun and is growing with dreadful strength. Almost daily they pick up people who have dropped from exhaustion right in the streets. Now you hear that a carter has collapsed, now a major general; here they picked up an officer who was selling newspapers, there a milliner.

But perhaps more frightening than the physical starvation is the ever more noticeable spiritual exhaustion. Recently the attention of physicians was arrested by the fact of a sharp decrease in weight among people who do intellectual work. Yet the people of this category eat better than the workers, and they need a thousand calories less than those who perform physical labor; nevertheless, emaciation is making steady progress among them. Medical research has shown that these people emit an enormous amount of phosphorus, which indicates an abnormal combustion of nervous tissue and which, ultimately, must bring people to the exhaustion of that spiritual, creative force needed by our country more than ever before.

Petrograd is dying as a city, it is dying as a center of spiritual life. And in this process of dying one senses a terrible submissiveness to fate, the passive Russian attitude toward life.

I was deeply touched by the unanimity with which

people of different classes rendered assistance to V. A. Petrova, a woman physician forgotten by all, dying of hunger and filth. But Mme. Z. Vvedenskaya and M. A. Berens inform me that Petrova "had been living in these awful conditions for several years." We were somewhat late with our help. And what state Petrova has reached is reported to me by Mme. Ek. Pugovko:

"Yesterday once again a nightmarish horror rose before my eyes—a senile body tormented by hunger and lice which teemed in swarms on its scabs.

"If one could convey what was reflected in the eyes of the physicians and even of the worldly wise maidservants who were present when Petrova took a bath.

"One of the maidservants asked me a question: 'Where did you find her?'

"I told where.

'Who is she?'

"Upon my reply that this woman was a physician, the maidservant looked at me wide-eyed and, pointing her finger at Petrova, who was sitting in the bathtub, almost shouted in disbelief:

'Who? Her—a physician?'

"The remark of a woman physician who was here rang with bitter reproach:

'Not all doctors, apparently, are well-to-do.' "

Something must be done. It is necessary to combat the process of physical and spiritual exhaustion of the intelligentsia; it must be realized that the intelligentsia is the brain of the country and that this brain has never been so necessary and valuable as in our times.

The intellectual forces of Petrograd must immediately organize themselves for the purpose of self-preservation, for the purpose of defense against hunger and nervous exhaustion. We could start with a small thing—the organization of dining halls—and at the same time look for ways and means of doing more important things.

We should not behave toward one another with such apathy and passivity; if hunger causes apathy, then apathy in turn can intensify hunger to the point of a natural catastrophe.

On the road to freedom, love and concern for man cannot be left somewhere along the way.

## UNTIMELY THOUGHTS

*Novaya Zhizn, No. 106 (321),*
*June 2 (May 20), 1918*

I received a batch of Semitophobe leaflets, some of them published by the "Central Committee of the Union of Christian Socialists" in Moscow on May 6, and the others by the "Petrograd Branch" of the same union. I do not know whether such a "Union" exists, but, if it does exist, then its members are, of course, neither Christians nor socialists but ordinary Russians from among those brutalized idlers and loafers who, being themselves responsible for all their misfortunes, shamelessly blame their nullity and inability to live on whomever they please, except themselves. That they are not Christians, and still less socialists, is attested by their nasty leaflets.

This is how they begin:

"Anti-Semites of all countries, all peoples, and all parties unite! 'The Union of Christian Socialists' addresses all Russian citizens with an appeal *to cleanse themselves from that Judaic foulness* which has permeated our land from the uppermost strata to the lowest levels of the masses. Markedly afflicted with this foulness is our intelligentsia, our so-called educated society brought up on the Judaic press *which preaches the false principles of equality and brotherhood of all peoples and races.* But every intelligent person knows that there is *not and cannot be either equality or brotherhood,* and, consequently, there cannot be a single attitute toward all people and toward all nationalities."

Aren't they the true followers of the loving Christ for whom there was "neither Jew nor Greek," who himself, with the Disciples, was a Jew and suffered, and who died an agonizing death for mankind as a whole, for people of all races and tribes? And aren't these "socialists" good who consider the principle of equality "false" and a notion of "Judaic foulness"?

Stupid and pitiable people, unfortunate people! Asserting that Russian citizens "from the uppermost strata to the lowest levels" are permeated with *"Judaic foulness," that is, the "principles of equality and brotherhood of races and nations"*—the sacred principles preached by nearly all religions, nearly all the greatest thinkers of all ages and countries—the authors of the leaflets reveal that they have an overly flattering but—alas!—completely wrong idea about Russian citizens. An example: the citizen-members of "The Union of Christian Socialists" themselves. They are not only not "permeated" with the high principles of equality, but simply, like the majority of Russian citizens, have no idea of the world-wide cultural value of these principles.

They write further:

"The Aryan race is a positive type from a physical as well as a moral viewpoint; the Jews are a negative type, standing on a lower stage of human development. If our intelligentsia, our 'salt of the Russian earth,' understands and realizes this, then it will throw away, like unusable old rags, the worn-out phrases about the equality of Jews and the necessity of treating equally both these pariahs of humanity and other people."

Just think—"and other people," excepting the Jews, cannot be treated equally! Who are these other people then?

Perhaps they are the Germans, the representatives of the
"Aryan race," a type "positive from the moral viewpoint,"
which does not prevent this "type" from shooting masses
of unarmed Russian peasants, and also Jews? Or perhaps
they are the meek Slavs, those Russians who are now so
senselessly and cruelly robbing and killing each other?

Or are the "other people" all those capable, in one way
or another, of disturbing the quiet development of the
wolfish patriotism of the authors of these leaflets? For
there is no doubt that the leaflets originated in the circles
of Russian predators who are accustomed to doubling
their money by skinning their own, ardently beloved
people for all they are worth.

Of course, the "other people" is an involuntary slip of
the tongue prompted in the "Christian socialists" by their
social savagery as well as by their moral and other illiteracy. In places, however, this illiteracy is very suspicious and, perhaps, utterly false.

The Petrograd leaflet is addressed to "workers, soldiers,
and peasants" and its composers obviously calculated on
the primitive minds and feelings of the addressees.

It asks:

"Do you know many Jews who are blacksmiths, yard
porters, hammerers, ploughmen, laundresses, cooks, dish-
washers? Have you seen our Jews begging for pennies in
the city streets? No."

Of course not; no one has seen Jewish yard porters in
Petrograd or Moscow, because this police duty could not
under any circumstances be performed by Jews, and the
reason is clear. But in Odessa, the majority of the dray-
men are Jews; ninety-two percent of the Jews living in the
Jewish pale are humble artisans and poor people.

It is quite true that no one has seen Jewish beggars
outside the pale, and this can be explained by the splendid
development of social relief work among the Jews, by the

fact that the police would not permit a Jew to beg, and I
think also by the fact that loving orthodox Christians
would probably shove a stone or serpent, and not bread,
into a Jewish beggar's hand. How false this all is, how
revolting is this anti-Semitism of these shiftless idlers!

When one reads all this stupid filth which springs from
the impotent and disgusting malice of these Russian
chowderheads, one becomes so ashamed and afraid for
Russia, the land of Leo Tolstoy, the land which created
the most humane, the most human literature in the
world.

The third leaflet is a provocative fabrication, even more
fraudulent and stupid.

It is entitled:

"Confidential. To the Branch Chairmen of the World
Israeli Union," and it advises the "chairmen" to exercise
every "caution." "We must firmly and unswervingly proceed along the road of destruction of foreign altars and
thrones," "we'll force Russia to her knees," "we are doing
everything to extol the great Jewish people"—but without
haste and with all due "caution."

Whom do the idiots want to frighten with these fabrications? They should have at least realized that a circular of
such exceptional importance addressed to the "Chairmen
of the World Israeli Union" would have been printed in
Hebrew, not in Russian. Or it should have at least occurred
to them to add: "translated from the Hebrew."

How unimaginative and disgraceful all this is!

The rest of the leaflets are no wittier than those cited.

I have already pointed out to the anti-Semites several
times that if some Jews succeeded in obtaining the more
advantageous and lucrative positions in life, this is because of their ability to work, the ecstasy which they bring
into the working process, their love for "doing," and their
capability of admiring work. A Jew is almost always a

better worker than the Russian; it is stupid to be angry at this—we should learn how to work. Both in the arena of personal gain and on the area of social service, the Jew displays more passion than the verbose Russian; and, in the final analysis, whatever nonsense the anti-Semites may talk, they dislike the Jew only because he is obviously better, more adroit, and more capable of work than they.

Now that we have realized with frightening clarity the extent to which the monarchy enfeebled us, spiritually emasculated us, and let us rot, we must especially value skillful workers, people of initiative who love their work—but we shout wildly:

"Smash them because they're better than we are!"

It is only because of this, my dear anti-Semites, it is only because of this—no matter what you say!

The leaflets, of course, devote no little attention to such Jews as Zinoviev, Volodarsky,[166] and other Jews who stubbornly forget that their tactlessness and stupidity serve as a basis for the indictment of all Jews as such. Well, so what? "It is a small flock that has not a black sheep," but the whole flock does not consist of black sheep and, of course, there are thousands of Jews who hate the Volodarskys with a hatred which is probably just as violent as that of the Russian anti-Semites. This, naturally, will not convince the anti-Semites that all Jews are not identical and that the class enmity among Jews is no less acute than it is among other nationalities; this will not convince them because for them it is absolutely necessary to be convinced of the opposite.

But perhaps those whom they want to set on the Jews like dogs, perhaps it is time for them to rebel against this new attempt to organize pogroms? Perhaps they will find it necessary and timely to tell the authors of the leaflets, to the "Camorras of People's Justice," and to other organizations of shady adventurers:

"Get out! We are the masters of the country. We won
its freedom without hiding our faces, and we shall not
allow shady people to control our intellect and our will.
Get out!"

## UNTIMELY THOUGHTS

*Novaya Zhizn, No. 107 (322),
June 4 (May 22), 1918*

Having won political rights, the people obtained the opportunity of freely creating new forms of social life, but
they still remain, both internally and externally, under the
influence of the mold and rust of the old way of life.
Among the masses there are no signs of a conscious striving to change radically the obsolete attitudes of man toward himself, toward his fellow man, toward life in general.

Life is saturated with a great number of valuable ideas
completely new to the masses, but these ideas penetrate a
sphere of instincts and emotions rude in kind and limited
in number; in this sphere the ideas are assimilated with
difficulty if they are assimilated at all, and this, unfortunately, may be doubted and ought to be doubted.

The revolution which is being created by the strength of
the most vigorous people exhausts and absorbs this most
valuable strength very quickly, but the process of ac-
cumulating and organizing a new strength is dangerously
slow.

It is necessary to accelerate the growth and development of this strength. It is necessary to establish, immediately, conditions for the education of the new man, for the
speediest accumulation of active reserves capable of continuing confidently and competently the work of reorga-
nizing Russia.

It is apparent that political propaganda alone is insufficient to create the new man—it is not enough to organize thought, it is necessary to organize the will, to educate, develop, and deepen the feelings.

We should be concerned with an uninterrupted development of the moral and esthetic education of the people, along with their political education—only given this condition will our people be completely freed from the oppression of their most unfortunate history, only in this way will they emerge from the bondage of the old mode of life, only with new emotions and new ideas will they understand and consciously set for their will clear, reasonable, and realizable goals.

It should be remembered that for centuries the people were brought up on the oppressive, stern, and joyless teaching of the church about the insignificance of man before a mysterious force which governs his fate arbitrarily and unaccountably, and that this teaching was affirmed as vividly and strongly as possible by all the conditions of social existence created by the senseless oppression of the Russian monarchy.

This teaching, affirming the impotence of man's reason and will, makes on his reason and will the greatest demands for deeds of virtue and, threatening him with eternal punishment in the fires of Gehenna, it could not and cannot be a stimulus of active energy directed toward the organization of an earthly life, toward the creation of happiness and joy in accordance with man's will and reason. Submerging man in the dark abyss of the realization of his own insignificance before God, this teaching found excellent illustrations of its formal logic in all the conditions of the socio-political life at the head of which stood the Tsar. This teaching, while disparaging man, not only tied up the energy, the initiative, and the independent activity of the people, but also penetrated deeply into the soul of the intelligentsia, pervaded Russian literature in its finest models, and covered our whole life with a veil of hope-lessness, quiet melancholy, and elegiac submissiveness to fate.

The intellectual ferment and the open struggle which our intelligentsia courageously and heroically carried on against the obsolete ways of living and thinking were prompted not by the allegedly humanitarian clerical and monarchist ideas, but, of course, in spite of them, by the instinct of self-preservation—a pagan instinct which created the Renaissance and has always served as a stimulus to the rebellion of man against his own, human conception of the invincibility of fate.

To continue this rebellion, intensifying and deepening it, is the sacred and heroic task of the intelligentsia. The revolution, the only one which is capable of freeing and ennobling man, must take place within him, and it will be accomplished only by cleansing him of the mold and dust of obsolete ideas.

Inasmuch as the people adopted certain ideas, they turned them into emotions that enslaved the freedom of their thought and their will. To overcome these emotions it is necessary to stimulate other, more positive emotions.

We are living in a catastrophic epoch, an epoch of heroism, and we must give the people spectacles, books, pictures, and music, which will develop in the masses the ability to feel the pathos of the struggle. Tragedy stimulates feeling in the strongest way; the pathos of tragedy tears man out of the filthy nets of life in the easiest way; and, finally, tragedy humanizes.

Contemplating a tragedy cannot but lift a sensitive observer above the chaos of the humdrum, the everyday; the exploits of the heroes of tragedy are an exceptional spectacle, a festive spectacle of man's great strength in a contest or battle against his fate.

———— • ————

Proceeding from these considerations—the sketchiness of which, I hope, does not obscure their clarity—I shall permit myself to say a few words about the practical experience of cultural-educational work which is now being carried on by various organizations and groups. I shall begin with this fact:

One of the workers' districts of Petrograd established a theater. The stage settings were done by a very gifted artist and portrayed muscular workers with rolled-up sleeves, factories and factory smokestacks—all this was done in cubist style.

The workers, looking at that work of art, resolutely stated:

"Take that away, we don't need it! What we need is the encouragement and development in us of a love of nature, of the fields and forests, of open spaces filled with the lively play of color and sun. Encourage in us a love of beauty, we don't need dreariness and everyday routine!"

That's exactly how it was said, and it was said by workers. In these words one hears clearly the legitimate and natural demand of the healthy person who seeks in art a contrast to that reality which wearies and torments his soul. He knows the repulsive everyday occurrences better than the artist, and if the artist is not a lyricist capable of illuminating the grey dusk of the worker's life with the tender and bright fire of his soul, if he is not a satirist with the power to portray the filthy hell of weekdays so that his picture, poem, or story will arouse a positive revulsion toward everyday life and an inherent urge to have a holiday, if he is incapable of revealing the heroic and significant in the usual and habitual—if the artist cannot give this—his art is of no use to the worker, the man who is accustomed to making the most delicate things, complex instruments, and powerful machines from formless masses of raw material. The worker is also an artist, for he gives a finished form to the formless.

Cubism and all the so-called "linear drawing" cannot please him or tell him anything new. It is quite likely that the new trends in painting have a future, but for the time being they are merely a kitchen of technique which can be of interest only to those of refined taste, to art critics and art historians. To show all this kitchen work to people craving perfect beauty is to give them Leo Tolstoy's *War and Peace* to read from his proofs with their hundreds of corrections.

Turning from painting to stage performances, I shall pose a seemingly paradoxical question: What is more useful for the social-esthetic education of the masses— Chekhov's *Uncle Vanya* or Rostand's *Cyrano de Bergerac?* Dickens's *The Cricket on the Hearth* or any play by Ostrovsky?[167]

I am for Rostand, Dickens, Shakespeare, the Greek tragedians, and the gay, witty comedies of the French theater. I am for this repertoire because, I dare to aver, I know the spiritual demands of the working masses. In them the awareness of class enmity and social distinctions is developed deeply enough; they want to see and understand the phenomena of universal brotherhood and unity; they already feel that awareness of the unity of emotions and thoughts is the basis of man's culture, the sign of the general human striving for joy and happiness, for the creation of a holiday on earth.

They want their souls to be touched by the very best of what has been created by man's feeling and thought; they want to admire man's genius, to understand and love it.

———— • ————

The poisonous fog of the workaday world, polluted by ceaseless fighting over a piece of bread, has been brightened and softened in all ages and among all peoples by the creativeness of science and art—only science and art ennoble our bestial way of life. And it is most timely and needful to introduce into our fantastically savage times all the highest achievements of creative minds in science and art, all that is precious in the world, all the treasures of its spirit, all that has the power to reeducate man, to raise him, the creator of facts, above facts.

Mankind has created a great deal of beauty; people create a mass of trash and filth daily, and under this pile of inevitable rubbish the beautiful disappears.

We must live so that the beautiful is always before our eyes—then it will be the stimulus of emotions, thoughts, and actions worthy of man.

But having put man into a pigsty, it is stupid to demand that he be an angel.

## UNTIMELY THOUGHTS

*Novaya Zhizn, No. 109 (324)*
*June 6 (May 24) 1918*

Observing the work of the revolutionaries of our time, you can clearly distinguish two types: one is, so to speak, the eternal revolutionary; the other is a revolutionary *pro tem,* for today.

The former, embodying the Promethian revolutionary principle, is the spiritual heir to the entire body of ideas which move mankind toward perfection, and these ideas are embodied not only in his mind but also in his emotions, even in the realm of his subconscious. He is the living, throbbing link in the endless chain of dynamic ideas, and in any social system he is forced, by the totality of his emotions and opinions, to remain dissatisfied all his life, for he knows and believes that mankind has the power to endlessly create something better out of something good.

He ardently loves his eternally young truth, but not so sensually and fanatically as to drive it with his fist into the hearts and heads of those who are enslaved by a dead truth of the past or who are incurably in love with the obsolete. To him people are an inexhaustible, living, nervous force, eternally creating new sensations, thoughts, ideas, things, and forms of life. He would like to enliven, to spiritualize all the brains in the world, as many as there are in the skulls of all the people on earth; but in pursuing this single and truly revolutionary goal of his, he is incapable of resorting to any method of coercing man other than in cases of unavoidable necessity and with a feeling of natural aversion to any act of coercion.

He firmly knows that, according to the true words of one of the outstanding Russian thinkers, "the horror of history and its greatest misfortune is that man has been cruelly insulted";[168] insulted by nature which, having created him, threw him into the wilderness of the world as a beast among beasts, providing him, for his development and perfection, with the same conditions as any other beast. He has been insulted by the gods whom he, in fear and joy before the forces of nature, created too hurriedly, clumsily, and too much "in his image, after his likeness"; he has been endlessly insulted by a cunning or strong neighbor and—bitterest of all—by himself, by his wavering between the ancient beast and the new man.

But the eternal revolutionary has no feeling of personal resentment toward people. He is always capable of rising above the personal and of overcoming in himself the petty, malicious desire to take vengeance on people for tortures and torments inflicted on him.

His ideal is man, the physically strong, handsome beast; but this physical beauty is in complete harmony with spiritual power and beauty. The human is the spiritual, that which is created by reason; from reason comes science, art, and a vaguely felt awareness by an ever larger number of people of the unity of their aims and interests. The eternal revolutionary strives with all the forces of his spirit to deepen and broaden this awareness so that it will embrace all mankind and, destroying everything that splits people into races, nations, and classes, will create in the world a single family of owner-workers capable of creating all the treasures and joys of life for themselves.

To the eternal revolutionary, changes for the better in the social conditions of life represent only a single rung in the endless ladder which leads mankind up to its proper level, and he does not forget that in this lies the meaning of the historical process in which he himself is one of countless necessary factors.

The eternal revolutionary is the leaven that keeps mankind's brains and nerves in a constant ferment; he is either a genius who, destroying truths established before him, creates new ones, or he is a modest man calmly sure of his strength which burns with a quiet, sometimes almost invisible fire, lighting the way to the future.

The revolutionary *pro tem,* for today, is a man who, with a morbid acuteness, feels social affronts and insults— the suffering inflicted by people. Embracing with his mind revolutionary ideas inspired by the time, he remains a conservative in the whole range of his feelings, a sad, often tragicomic spectacle of a man who came into the world just to distort, discredit, and reduce to the ridiculous, vulgar, and absurd the cultural, humanitarian, and altogether human content of revolutionary ideas.

First of all he feels sorry for himself, because he is not talented, not strong, because he was insulted even for the

fact that he once was in prison, in exile, once dragged out
the burdensome existence of an émigré. He is saturated,
like a sponge, with the feeling of revenge and wants to
repay a hundredfold those who offended him. The ideas
which he has embraced only with his mind but which have
never grown into his soul are in direct and irreconcilable
opposition to his actions; his methods of fighting the
enemy are the same as those the enemies used against him,
he has no room for other methods.

The temporarily rebellious slave of a god of punishment
and vengeance, he does not feel the beauty of the god of
mercy, forgiveness, and joy. Not sensing his organic link
with the world's past, he considers himself completely
liberated, but he is paralyzed internally by the heavy con-
servatism of animal instincts, and entangled in a dense
network of petty, vexing impressions above which he does
not have the strength to rise. His habits of thinking compel
him to search first of all, in life and in man, for the negative manifestations and features. At the bottom of his
heart he is full of contempt for man, for whom he has
suffered once or a hundred times, but who in turn suffers
too much to notice or appreciate the torments of others.
In striving to change the external forms of social existence
the revolutionary for today is not capable of filling the
new forms with new content, and brings into them the
same emotions against which he fought. If he—by miracle
or coercion—succeeded in creating a new way of life, he
would be the first to feel alien and lonely in the atmosphere of this way of life, for in essence he is not a socialist, not even a pre-socialist, but an individualist.

He treats people as an untalented scientist treats dogs and
frogs intended for cruel scientific experiments with the
difference, however, that even an untalented scientist, while
uselessly tormenting animals, does so in the interest of
man, whereas the revolutionary for today is far from being
consistently sincere in his experiments on people.

To him people are material, the less spiritualized the more suitable. If the degree of man's individual and social consciousness rises to the point of protest against purely external, formal revolutionism, the revolutionary for today unabashedly threatens protesters with punishment, just as many representatives of the above outlined type did and are doing now.

This is a cold fanatic, an ascetic. He emasculates the creative power of the revolutionary idea, and certainly he cannot be called the creator of the new history; it is not he who will be its ideal hero.

Perhaps it should be put down to his credit that, having awakened the ancient, cruel beast in the masses of humanity, he thus hastened the death of bestiality?

Cruelty tires you out and can finally provoke a natural aversion to itself, and in this aversion is its own destruction.

We, it seems, are beginning to develop in ourselves precisely this physiological aversion to everything that is bloody, cruel, and filthy; it is necessary that this aversion grow, that it become an idiosyncrasy of the majority.


## UNTIMELY THOUGHTS

*Novaya Zhizn, No. 113 (328),*
*June 11 (May 29), 1918*

People in hysterical moods write me ferocious letters—threaten to kill me.

This intention, I think, is not serious and is not so much criminal as illiterate. Killing proves nothing, except that the killer is stupid. Punishment by death does not make people better than they are. However many people are put to death, those remaining alive nonetheless follow the path

indicated by history—death is not strong enough to arrest
the development of historical forces.

Weren't there lots of people killed in our Russia, in all
the cities, in thousands of villages and hamlets, killed to cut
off the growth of revolutionary sentiments? But the revolution nonetheless matured into victory. And even now,
when they are killing no fewer than they did before, that
which is more intelligent and more robust will finally win
out, in spite of everything. Physical violence will always be
an incontestable proof of moral impotence—this has long
been known and it is time to understand it.

But to threaten a man with death for being what he
is—is illiterate and stupid.

———— • ————

They accuse me of "selling myself to the Jews." Also
stupid. I understand, of course, that in a country where
everybody has long been accustomed to bribing others and
selling himself, a man who defends a hopeless cause must
be considered corrupt. The psychology of the majority
demands that every man be discredited in one way or
another, that every one be stained. This is the specific
psychology of professional crooks—they cannot imagine a
man being honest because he wants to be that way, because such is the preference of his soul. But perhaps they
are envious: every one of them is ready to sell himself,
and not at a very high price—but some people cannot be
bought for any price. So they are angry: What's this! We
are placed in conditions compelling us to trade in our
conscience, but they, strange people, don't sell themselves.

And even if they themselves do not believe in the cor-
ruptness of these "strange people," they shout all the
same:

"He sold himself! They sold themselves!"

Oh you miserable people! You would be better to try to become honest people yourselves—there is something pleasing in that.

———— • ————

Also, they write me furious reproaches: I, allegedly, "hate people." This demands an explanation. I say frankly that those who speak grandiloquently of their love for the people have always aroused in me a feeling of distrust and suspicion. I ask myself, I ask them: Do they really love those peasants who, swilling vodka until they become savage, kick their pregnant wives in the stomach? Those peasants who, wasting millions of poods of grain in "moonshine," leave those who love them to perish from hunger? Those who bury tens of thousands of poods of grain in the ground and let it rot, but do not want to give it to the hungry? Those peasants who even bury each other alive, those who stage bloody mob trials in the streets, those who look on with glee when a man is beaten to death or drowned in the river? Those who sell stolen bread for ten rubles a pound?

I am sure that the loving citizens who reproach me for hating people do not, in their hearts, love these savage, selfish people just as I do not love them. But if I am mistaken and they nonetheless love the people as they are, please excuse me for the mistake, but I stand my ground: I do not love the people.

Moreover, I am sure that one should not love the people as they are; equally, one should not blame people for being what they are, and not something else. I think it will be better both for the people and their loving admirers if the latter selflessly give the people all their knowledge, all the wealth of their souls so that the people become humanized. And giving to the people all their best, they should not expect that their unselfish work will be appreciated and rewarded with the people's love—such things do not happen.

It is unimportant and of little interest how people treat us, but it is very important how we treat people—this is what we must understand!

## SPEECH AT THE MOSCOW PUBLIC MEETING OF THE SOCIETY "CULTURE AND FREEDOM"[169]

### *Novaya Zhizn, No. 126 (341), June 30 (17), 1918*

To prove the necessity of cultural-educational work is superfluous. This necessity is obvious—the dirty stones of our pavements and the eternal filth in people's hearts and minds both appeal eloquently for it. Now more clearly than ever before, we see how strongly the Russian people are infected with ignorance, to what a terrifying degree the interests of their own country are alien to them, what savages they are in the field of civic duty, and how childishly undeveloped is their sense of history, their understanding of their place in the historical process.

Speaking of the "Russian people," I certainly do not mean just the toiling masses of workers and peasants; no, I speak of the people as a whole, of all classes, for ignorance and lack of culture appertain to the entire Russian nation. From its millions of ignorant people, deprived of any idea of the value of life, there can be set apart only the few insignificant thousands of the so-called intelligentsia, that is, those who realize the significance of intellectuality in the historical process. These people, despite all their shortcomings, are Russia's finest creation in the

entire course of her ugly and difficult history. These
people truly were and still remain the heart and brain of
our country. Their shortcomings are explained by the
Russian soil, infertile for talents of an intellectual nature.
We all are talented as far as our emotions are concerned—we are talented in kindness, talented in cruelty,
talented in misfortune; there are not a few heroes among
us, but there are only a few strong and intelligent people
capable of courageously fulfilling their civic obligations,
heavy obligations in our Russian conditions. We love
heroes (if they are not opposed to us) but it is not clear to
us that heroism demands emotional exertion for an hour
or a day, while courage demands it for life.

In the conditions of Russian life, cultural work demands not heroism but rather courage, a sustained and
unflinching exertion of all the power of the soul. To sow
"the reasonable, the good, and the eternal"[170] in the
treacherous Russian swamps is a task of abnormal difficulty, and we already know that what we have sown of our
best blood, of the finest sap of our nerves, brings forth on
Russian plains poor, sad shoots. Nevertheless we must
sow, and this is the task of the intelligentsia, of that intelligentsia which is now forcibly torn away from life and
even declared an enemy of the people. However, the intelligentsia it is that must continue the work of spiritual
purification and regeneration of the country—work that
it began long ago—for we have no other intellectual force,
except the intelligentsia.

One may ask: "What about the proletariat, the foremost revolutionary class? And what about the peasantry?"

I don't think that one can seriously speak of the whole
mass of the proletariat as a cultural, intellectual force.
Perhaps this is convenient for polemics with the bourgeoisie, for intimidating them and for encouraging ourselves, but this is unnecessary here where, I think, there

are gathered people sincerely and deeply concerned about the country's future. The proletariat *en masse* is only a physical force, nothing more; the same is true of the peasantry. Our historically young intelligentsia of workers and peasants is another matter. This, of course, is a spiritually creative force, and as such it is now cut off from its own masses and is alone among them, just as our old, labor-camp intelligentsia is alone and cut off from all the toiling masses—a labor-camp intelligentsia not only because a part of them served terms in state labor camps, but because of all the conditions of their existence in Russia, because of their whole life and work.

It seems to me that the first appropriate step to take is to recognize the necessity of uniting the intellectual forces of the old experienced intelligentsia with those of the young intelligentsia of workers and peasants. The schema for all-Russian cultural-educational work appears to me along these lines:

First of all comes the organization of the whole intelligentsia that now feels and understands that it is impossible to educate the new man solely on political programs, on political propaganda; that the path of fomenting enmity and hatred leads people to utter brutalization and savagery; that immediate and intensive cultural work is needed for the country's regeneration; and that only this can free us from our enemies, both internal and external.

The concentration of our forces is the foremost task of the day and, in concentrating the country's intellectual forces, we should draw into the midst of the intellectual workers the whole reserve of the workers' and peasants' intelligentsia, all the workers and peasants who now struggle, powerlessly and alone, in an environment which is their own physically, but already alien spiritually, corrupted by the cynical demagoguery of sincere fanatics or disguised adventurers. These forces have an enormous significance as an iron link by which the old intelligentsia might be solidly united with the masses and given the opportunity of influencing them directly.

Concentrating forces, uniting them with the fresh forces of the workers' and peasants' intelligentsia, the cultural workers should be concerned with coordinating their own work—this is necessary for economizing energy, of which we do not have much, and this is necessary for eliminating duplication of effort.

Having covered the whole country with a network of cultural-educational societies, having gathered into them all the spiritual forces of the country, we shall kindle everywhere the bonfires which will give the country both light and heat, will help her recuperate and get up on her feet cheerful, strong, and capable of building and creating. The question is not of an external and mechanical unification of people who think differently, but rather of an internal and living blend of those who feel the same way. Thus and only thus can we come to real culture and freedom.

I foresee objections: "But what about politics?"

One should rise above politics, one should learn and know how to restrain one's political emotions. If one wishes to, one can do it. Politics is something similar to the lower physiological functions, with the unpleasant difference that political functions are unavoidably carried out in public.

Politics, whoever indulges in it, is always repulsive, for it is inevitably accompanied by lies, slander, and violence. And since this is the truth, everyone must know it, and this knowledge in its turn must make one realize the advantages of cultural work over the political.

A more serious obstacle to cultural work is the noticeable decline in the intelligentsia's vitality, a decline caused by hunger and disenchantment, an apathy which oppresses the intelligentsia more and more.

One should fight hunger by developing mutual aid

among individuals who work with their brains; and as for this "disenchantment" with the people, with socialism, with Russia—I don't think I can say anything on this subject.

Of course, it would have been better not to succumb to the enchantment in the past, for there has never been anything enchanting in the Russian people at all; but if one has been carried away and then disenchanted—it cannot be helped. Enchantment is a matter of faith; disenchantment is a retribution for blind faith. Knowledge helps well against disenchantment, and this is the only thing one can recommend to the disenchanted. I, personally, all my life and in all my feelings, thoughts, and deeds, have taken man as my point of departure, being permanently and unshakeably convinced that only man exists, that all the rest is his opinion and action.

And in these days, frightening for all, for the whole country created by a great many generations who brought us up to be what we are; in these days of madness, horror, and the triumph of stupidity and vulgarity, I remember one thing: all this comes from man, all this is done by him.

. . .

He it is too who created everything beautiful on earth— all its poetry, all the magnificent feats of courage and honor, all the joys and festivities of life, all its charm, all its comical and great things, its beautiful dreams and wonderful sciences; he created his own daring mind and unbending will to pursue happiness.

And he, man, who always through all the days of tragedy, suffering, and torment, stubbornly believes in the victory of new good principles over the old and evil ones— he, man, all-invincible, has brought us together here for a friendly, human talk.

So let us go to man who has sinned filthily and much, but who atones for his filth and sins by the greatest, unbearable sufferings.

Can we create an atmosphere in which man can breathe more easily?

We can and must.

## TO THE EDITORS OF *PRAVDA, NORTHERN COMMUNE,* AND OTHERS

*Novaya Zhizn, No. 127 (342), July 2 (June 19), 1918*

You are interested in the question: "Where does *Novaya Zhizn* get its money?"[171]

*Novaya Zhizn* was organized by me with money borrowed from E. K. Grubbe[172] in the amount of 275 thousand rubles, 50 thousand of which have already been paid to the creditor. I could have paid the remaining sum long ago had I known where E. K. Grubbe lives.

In addition to this money, there was invested in the newspaper a part of the honorarium that I received from *Niva* (The Cornfield) for the publication of my books. All this money was turned over by me to A. N. Tikhonov, the actual publisher of *Novaya Zhizn.*

I see nothing to the discredit of the newspaper in the loan taken by me for the purpose of organizing it, and regard the accusations of venality brought against it as polemical malice.

But, for your information, I will say that hundreds of thousands of rubles, spent for the cause of the Russian Social-Democratic party, passed through my hands in the period from 1901 to 1917; in this sum my personal earnings are counted in tens of thousands, and all the rest was drawn out of the pockets of the "bourgeoisie." *Iskra* (The Spark) was published with Savva Morozov's money,[173] and he, of course, did not lend but donated it. I could name a good dozen respectable people, "bourgeois," who

materially helped the growth of the Social-Democratic
party. V. I. Lenin and other old party workers know this
very well.[174]

In the case of *Novaya Zhizn,* there are no "donations,"
there is only my loan. Your slanderous and dirty attacks
on it disgrace not *Novaya Zhizn,* but you.

# NOTES

1. A Tartar Khan whose army was crushed by the Russians in the bloody battle on Kulikovo field in 1380. The expression "rout of Mamay" became proverbial in Russian, meaning 1.) a bitter battle or 2.) chaos.

2. Probably a reference to the line in Goethe's *Faust:* "Im Anfang war die Tat!" (In the Beginning was the Deed!). As an admirer of action, Gorky was fond of this expression and quoted it in slightly varying versions in his writings.

3. These were armed groups of common people formed in 1905 by the police and monarchists to fight the revolution. Later this term was applied to all reactionary and nationalistic organizations, such as "The Union of the Russian People" (1905-1917) which published the newspaper *Russkoe Znamya* (The Russian Banner). The Union was involved in Jewish pogroms and assassinations of liberal politicians.

4. Aleksey Alekseevich Brusilov (1853-1926), commander of south-western armies since spring of 1916 and Supreme Commander-in-Chief in June and July 1917. Later served in the Red Army.

5. Three men were reported killed and six wounded in a clash on the Nevsky Avenue between workers, demon-

strating against the Provisional Government, and soldiers. See "Strelba na Nevskom," *Novaya Zhizn,* April 22 (May 5), 1917. On the same day the newspaper *Rech* (Speech) accused Gorky, as the *Novaya Zhizn* editor, of allowing the publication of incorrect reports and of glossing over the fact that there were also demonstrations in support of the Provisional Government. Gorky was reminded of his appeal to speak the truth made in "Untimely Thoughts" of April 21 (May 4). See N. Rudin, "Otkrytoe pismo M. Gorkomu," *Rech,* April 22 (May 5), 1917.

*Rech* (1906-1917) was the mouthpiece of the Constitutional-Democratic party, whose members were usually referred to as Cadets. Founded in 1905, this party advocated the establishment of a truly democratic and constitutional form of government and the necessity of agrarian reforms in favor of the peasants. The Cadets rejected revolutionary violence as a means for the attainment of their goals. The core of the Cadet party consisted of Russia's intellectual elite.

6. "Restraint" (*samoogranichenie*) is used here to mean political moderation dictated by circumstances. In *Luch,* socialist Gorky would have had to cooperate with some moderate liberals such as the prominent historian Pavel Gavrilovich Vinogradov (1854-1925), who lectured for some time at Oxford and was knighted by the King of England, and the economist Mikhail Vladimirovich Bernatsky, who later became Minister of Finance in the Provisional Government. *Luch* was expected to come out early in 1917 with Bernatsky as chief editor and Gorky in charge of its literary section.

Gorky might have brought out the question of "restraint" because *Rech* wondered how he could work together with Vinogradov, a strong advocate of an Anglo-Russian rapprochement, if *Novaya Zhizn* considered Britain's victory no more desirable than Germany's. See "Pechat," *Rech,* April 20 (May 3), 1917. In this review of the press, *Rech* also discussed the political program of *Novaya Zhizn,* commented on some vagueness in it, and welcomed Gorky's insistence on cultural work, quoting his familiar statement: "By no means should we think that the revolution has spiritually cured or enriched Russia" ("Revolution and Culture," *Novaya Zhizn,* April 18 (May 1), 1917).

In a short while, *Rech* returned to the problem of "restraint" with the assertion that Professor Vinogradov was willing to work with Gorky when the latter deemed it necessary to "restrain" himself. But this was no longer possible, especially since German newspapers reprinted from *Novaya Zhizn* its anti-British statements and advertised them under such headings as "The Independent Position of Maxim Gorky" or "The Opinion of Maxim Gorky." See "'Novaya Zhizn,'" *Rech,* May 16 (29), 1917.

7. Refers to the Constitutional-Democratic party. This designation was first used in 1909 by its founder and leader, historian Pavel Nikolaevich Milyukov (1859-1943), to stress that the Cadets were not *in* opposition to the Tsar, that at this time a constitutional monarchy was acceptable to them. In 1905 they were for a republic. From March to mid-May 1917 Milyukov was Foreign Minister of the Provisional Government.

8. This appeal was addressed to the "native country and the whole civilized world" by Russian writers, artists, and actors. It blamed Germany for atrocities and destruction of culture and reproached her scientists, poets, and public figures for furthering the unjust cause. See "Ot pisateley, khudozhnikov i artistov," *Zhurnalist,* No. 13-14, Novem-

ber 1914, pp. 1-2 or *Russkie Vedomosti,* September 28, 1914.

Ivanov-Razumnik maintained that the words and deeds of those who signed the appeal were at variance. They talked of their passionate desire to take away weapons out of Germany's barbaric hands but would not try to do it personally, instead they incited others to go to war. See "Voyna i 'spravedlivost,' " *Delo Naroda,* April 21 (May 4), 1917. Lenin too chided Gorky for singing "cheap chauvinistic protests that can mislead politically unversed workers." See "Avtoru 'Pesni o Sokole,' " *Sotsial-Demokrat,* December 5, 1914.

Ivanov-Razumnik (pseudonym of Razumnik Vasilievich Ivanov, 1878-1946), a literary scholar and politician, was connected with Socialist-Revolutionaries (S.R.'s). This party came into being in 1902 as an offspring of Russian Populism. Its ultimate goal was socialism. The S.R.'s did not deny the leading political role of the urban proletariat, but regarded the peasantry as the main revolutionary force. The party had a special "Battle Organization" entrusted with terrorist action against Tsarist officials. Among the prominent S.R.'s were their leader Viktor Mikhaylovich Chernov (1876-1952) and the last Premier of the Provisional Government, Aleksandr Kerensky. *Delo Naroda* (1917-1919) was an S.R. political and literary daily.

The strongest socialist rival of the S.R.'s was the Russian Social-Democratic Workers' party (S.D.'s) formed in 1898 on the basis of revolutionary Marxism. In 1903 it split into two factions: the Bolsheviks and Mensheviks, headed by Lenin and Martov respectively. The Bolsheviks advocated a tightly organized party with a nucleus consisting of professional revolutionaries. They insisted on a strict selection of members so that revolutionary ideals would not be contaminated by reform-minded liberals who might find their way into the party. In the initial, "bour-geois" stage of the coming revolution the Bolsheviks favored an alliance with the peasants, while the Men-sheviks, distrustful of the peasantry's urge for ownership, preferred to cooperate with the liberal bourgeoisie.

9. Tsarina Aleksandra Fedorovna who was Princess Alix von Hessen before her marriage to the future Nicholas II in 1894.

10. Grigory Rasputin whose last name might well have been derived from *rasputny* meaning "licentious," "dis-solute." Another possibility is that it came from *rasputie,* a crossing of roads. Rasputin was known for his lewdness before and during his association with the imperial fam-ily.

11. Anna Vyrubova, Lady-in-Waiting in the personal suite of the Empress, was close to the imperial family and served as an intermediary between it and Rasputin, whom she greatly admired. In September 1917 she was ordered to leave Russia. See "Vysylka za granitsu A. A. Vyru-bovoy i dr.," *Rech,* August 25 (September 7), 1917.

12. In this case a secondary school predominantly or ex-clusively for upper-class girls.

13. Evno Azef (1869-1918) is by far the most notorious of them all. A leader and theorist of the Socialist-Revolu-tionary party, in charge of its terrorist "Battle Organiza-tion" responsible for assassinations of the highest offi-cials, he was, at the same time, an agent of the Tsarist police, betraying to it plans, meetings, publishing houses, and members of his party, including his fellow workers from the "Battle Organization." After his final exposure in

1908 the party sentenced him to death, but he managed to escape abroad. Azef's career is the subject of a novel by Roman Gul called *General B. O.* in English and *Azef* in Russian.

Mikhail Ivanovich Gurovich (Gurevich, 1859-1914) was a police official associated with a journal of "legal" Marxists.

14. See V. Iretsky, "Ne to," *Rech,* April 30 (May 13), 1917. Iretsky (pseudonym of Viktor Yakovlevich Glikman, 1882-1936) wrote that the revolution of 1917 was not inspired by romanticism, unselfishness, and sacrifice, but by cool, logical calculation, and acquisitive greed.

15. The existence of the first three heroes, who saved the lives of the Russian Tsars, may be attributed to patriotic legends. Most Russian historians, however, think that the peasant Ivan Susanin, the hero of Mikhail Glinka's opera *A Life for the Tsar,* was a real person. The World War I exploits of the Don Cossack Kuzma Kryuchkov are regarded by some as greatly exaggerated. Mikhail Sholokhov, for example, strips Kryuchkov of heroic veneer in his novel *And Quiet Flows the Don.* In the Civil War Kryuchkov fought in the ranks of the White Cossacks and was killed in 1919.

16. Two famous revolutionaries. Andrey Ivanovich Zhelyabov (1851-1881), one of the leaders of the revolutionary party *Narodnaya volya* (The People's Will), a selfless and heroic idealist. He was executed for organizing the assassination of Alexander II. The impressive arrest and exile record of Ekaterina Konstantinovna Breshko-Breshkovskaya (1844-1934) goes back to 1874. Nick-named "grandmother" by revolutionaries, she was one of

the founders and leaders of the Socialist-Revolutionary party and strongly anti-Bolshevik.

17. To this *Rech* retorted that just to bow was not enough. Gorky should fulfill what the peasant demands and fight the real danger instead of issuing extremist slogans which stir up all sorts of scum. The *Rech* advice sprang from its opinion that *Novaya Zhizn* was engaged in a wild hunt for the counterrevolutionary bourgeoisie, without noticing the real enemy of the revolution behind its own back. *Rech* also reproduced nearly all of the peasant's letter to support its earlier claim that the revolution lacked romanticism. See I (?). G., "Kontr-revolyutsiya," *Rech,* May 7 (20), 1917.

18. Probably a reference to acts of violence against the German population at the outbreak of World War I.

19. Most likely Gorky has in mind the Jewish pogroms in Kishinev (1903), Kiev (1905), Odessa (1905), and Belostok (1906), the cruel suppression of revolutionary movements in Odessa and Tiflis (1905), and the four-day massacre of the Armenians by the Turks in Baku (1905).

20. At this point *Rech* reminded Gorky of having been the only newspaper which shouted this warning in July 1914 and which was shut down for doing so. *Rech* expressed its satisfaction with the fact that Gorky realized the gravity of the situation and it quoted a few excerpts from his article. See "Pechat," *Rech,* May 10 (23), 1917.

21. Petr Arkadievich Stolypin, Chairman of the Council of Ministers from 1906 to 1911, a conservative statesman known for his unconstitutional treatment of the Duma,

harsh measures against the revolutionaries, and the well-meant plan to help the peasants of overpopulated areas by resettling them in Siberia. In 1911 Stolypin was assassinated by a Socialist-Revolutionary who was also a police agent.

22. V. Iretsky commented: "The Bolshevik Gorky discovered apparently with horror that culture is in danger." "Dusha bolit," *Rech*, May 11 (24), 1917. Iretsky bracketed Gorky and the Bolsheviks together because they both were socialists and sharply critical of the bourgeoisie. Iretsky was only too glad to point out that Gorky finally noticed those who would tear up "for leggings the banner of Zhelyabov and Breshkovskaya."

23. A line from the poem *Duma* (Meditation, 1839) by Mikhail Lermontov, expressing the poet's judgment of his generation.

24. This may refer to the heading "Anarchy" under which *Rech* published regular reports on murders, lynchings, robberies, destruction, and so on. Other newspapers were also filled with information on the growing violence and lawlessness.

25. The article "Two Souls" appeared in the December 1915 issue of *Letopis*. In it Gorky drew a sharp contrast between the East and the West. In the East he saw a contemplative attitude toward life and a passive acceptance of the existing surroundings. In the West the people were active and changed life in accordance with their will. The West viewed man as the highest purpose of nature; in the East, man had neither significance nor value. In the West there was freedom and equality; Eastern society was based on slavery. As a nation between the East and the

West, the Russians have two souls. One is inherited from the nomadic Mongols. It is the soul of a dreamer, mystic, idler, and believer in fate. The other is the soul of a Slav. It can flare up beautifully and brightly. But it cannot burn for a long time. It succumbs to the poison of its Eastern counterpart. The Russians have acquired the basic characteristics of the Eastern psychology. The Muscovite state was despotic, Asiatic. The Russian nobility was cruel to the slaves and slavish to the rulers. Oblomovism, i.e., laziness, inertia, escapism, are typical of all classes of the Russian people. Russian democracy should be aware of its weak will, passivity, anarchism, its urge for intoxication and dreaming—the failings bequeathed to it by Asia. And it should be equally aware of what it has received from Europe, "ever active, untiring in work, believing only in the power of reason, research, and science."

The answer to the critics of "Two Souls" Gorky gave in the form of "Letters to the Reader," *Letopis,* No. 3, March 1916, pp. 171-177. He defended the ideas of "Two Souls," stressing the need for general education and the resurgence of will power, as opposed to mysticism, shallow optimism, and indulgence in useless talk. Among the principal targets of his criticism were Russian provincial stagnation, dreamy and sleepy existence, and lack of initiative and of talented people. He also assailed immorality and thievery, more shameless and more widespread than in Europe.

Both "Two Souls" and "Letters to the Reader" formed a kind of journalistic manifesto. The views contained in them were repeatedly expressed in "Untimely Thoughts," occasionally in identical images. Moreover, both articles appeared side by side in a 1918 collection. See M. Gorky, *Stati 1905-1916 gg.,* 2nd ed., "Parus," Petrograd, 1918, pp. 174-195.

Gorky's new mention of "Two Souls" provoked a

prompt reply from *Rech*. It contended that Gorky himself possessed two souls, the Eastern being the stronger at that particular time. This was, allegedly, manifested in Gorky's political maximalism, his belief in the immediate establishment of a new system, disregard for an organized state and tradition, and lack of restraint and equilibrium. Gorky was believed to experience a tragic duality. He exercised restraint under the monarchy but not in the republic. He planned to work with the moderate liberal Vinogradov but ended up working with the radical socialist Sukhanov. He had money for *Luch* but gave it to the Bolshevik *Novaya Zhizn*.

The last contention was rejected by Gorky as a slander. See I. Clemens, "Dve dushi," *Rech*, May 25 (June 7), 1917, and Gorky's letter to the *Rech* editors, *Novaya Zhizn*, May 27 (June 9), 1917.

26. "Defeatism" is a policy aimed at the defeat of one's own country. During World War I it was pursued by the Bolsheviks in order to bring about a socialist revolution in Russia and, possibly, in the whole world. Therefore the Bolsheviks called "defensists" and considered traitors those socialists who advocated fighting for their native lands. *Rech* challenged Gorky's statements on anarchy and defeatism in its review of the press of May 19 (June 1), 1917.

27. Plekhanov, the father of Russian Marxism, criticized in *Our Disagreements* (1885) the Populists' reliance on the peasantry and called for the formation of a workers' party. Socialist revolution, he argued, would be prepared by the development of the forces of production and by their organization, which would be accomplished by capitalism. The author of *Critical Notes on the Question of the Economic Development of Russia* (1894) also stressed

the inevitability of a capitalist stage in Russia's historical evolution. In conclusion he appealed to the Russians to admit their lack of culture and take lessons from capitalism. The book was received as a manifesto of a new social movement. Petr Berngardovich Struve (1870-1944), a thinker and economist, began his public career as a "legal" Marxist, but left the Social-Democrats to become a leader of the liberal intelligentsia and then a prominent figure in the Constitutional-Democratic party.

28. This is an appeal in the name of "The Free Association" in the formation of which Gorky took an active part, serving as a member of its Organizing Committee.

29. The newspaper of the group "Unity" composed of right-wing Social-Democrats under the leadership of Plekhanov. Four of its issues were published in 1914 and the rest in 1917. Suppressed by the Bolsheviks in December of that year, it continued to appear for a short while as *Nashe Edinstvo* (Our Unity).

30. During such a strike the workers go to their jobs but either do not work or perform their duties very slowly. These methods were first used on Italian railroads.

31. Advertised in the conservative newspaper *Novoe Vremya,* June 7 (20), 1917.

32. The largest market in Petersburg, with some eight hundred stalls and lively flea markets where it was a good idea to keep one's hands on one's pockets.

33. "Mona Lisa" was stolen in 1911 by Vincenzo Perugia, an Italian painter who had previously worked in the Louvre putting glass over pictures. When the museum was

closed for cleaning he entered it in a workman's smock and, since he was known to the guards, he left unhindered with the painting under his blouse. In 1913 the picture was recovered.

34. From Nikolay Nekrasov's poem *Rytsar na chas* (A Knight for an Hour, 1863).

35. One of the prosperous sections of Petersburg. By 1910 about twenty percent of the city's nobility, sixteen percent of its citizens of privileged status, and twelve percent of its merchants lived there.

36. *Zhorzh Zand. Ee zhizn i proizvedeniya* (George Sand. Her Life and Works), vol. I, Saint Petersburg, 1899 and vol. II, Petrograd, 1916. Vladimir Karenin is a pseudonym of Varvara Komarova (1862-1942).

37. Or "People's Palaces," cultural and recreational centers for broad segments of the population established in Britain in the second half of the nineteenth century and, later, in a number of European countries. The "People's Houses" featured libraries, lecture halls, employment offices, savings departments, inexpensive restaurants, theaters, gymnasiums. They organized evening courses, excursions, concerts, chess tournaments, and other types of cultural activities and entertainments. In the early 1900's several large "People's Houses" were opened in Russian cities. In the rural districts an important part in their organization was played by Zemstvo workers.

38. A somewhat derogatory diminutive for the newspaper *Birzhevye Vedomosti* (The Bourse Gazette, 1880-1917) which had no definite political course of its own but tried to swim with popular currents.

39. This appeared in the liberal *Rech* of June 27 (July 10), 1917, and on the same day an account similar to the preceding one was published in the conservative *Novoe Vremya* (New Times). Asnin, a former criminal, was killed when he and the sailor Zheleznyakov (see note 101) tried to resist arrest at General Durnovo's country house which the anarchists turned into their nest.

40. A slightly altered quotation from Konstantin Aksakov's (1817-1860) poem "The Free Word." It should be: "the miracle of God's miracles" (*chudo iz bozhikh chudes*).

41. Gorky has in mind the demonstrations of soldiers and workers carrying the Bolshevik slogan, "All Power to the Soviets." The demonstrations caused confusion and bloodshed. They began spontaneously on July 3 (16) and later the Bolsheviks took charge of them.

42. A paraphrase of two lines from the Russian revolutionary song known as "The Workers' Marseillaise," an imitation of its French counterpart. It was first published in 1875 as "A New Song" by its author P. L. Lavrov. Proclaimed the national anthem after the February Revolution, it was replaced by "The International" after the October Revolution.

43. A strong denunciation of war was made by Gorky in his article "An Honest Book," *Novaya Zhizn*, August 10 (23), 1917. The article was not translated for this collection because almost all of it consists of extensive quotations from Sir Philip Gibbs's book *The Soul of the War* (1915).

44. A member of the Octobrist party. This party grew out of the "Union of October 17th" founded by conservative

reformers to cooperate with the government in the imple-
mentation of measures proclaimed in the Tsar's Manifesto
of October 17 (30), 1905, which granted basic civil rights
to Russians and made the country a constitutional monarchy of sorts. With time the Octobrist party became more
conservative and nationalistic. They were in the majority
in the Third Duma (1907-1912) and, to a large extent,
supported Stolypin.

45. Smug complacency, excessive sweetness, day-dreaming;
derived from the last name of the landowner Manilov in
Gogol's *Dead Souls*.

46. Picturesque town south of Petersburg; residence of
imperial family. Renamed Detskoe Selo after the October
Revolution and Pushkin in 1937.

47. Former Tsarina, wife of the abdicated Nicholas II.

48. A hint at the reputed intimacy between the Tsarina
and Grigory (Grishka) Rasputin.

49. In the original this is an episode told to Baudouin de
Courtenay by his friend (in the first-person singular). See
"Svoeobraznaya 'krugovaya poruka,' " *Shchit,* 2nd ed. en-
larged, Moscow, 1916, p. 143. *Shchit* was put out by
"The Russian Society for the Study of Jewish Life" of
which Gorky was a founder. The editors of *Shchit* were
L. Andreev, Gorky, and F. Sologub. Professor Ivan Aleksandrovich Baudouin de Courtenay (1845-1929) was a
distinguished linguist.

50. David Yakovlevich Ayzman (1869-1922), primarily
a short-story writer.

51. *Rech,* for example, spoke of *Novaya Zhizn* and Gorky, as its editor, in the press reviews of July 21 (August 3), July 22, 23, 26, 27, August 2 (15) and 3. *Novaya Zhizn* came under fire for showing more interest in the International than in the native country and for its allegedly sympathetic attitude toward Germany. On one occasion *Rech* expressed its indignation over "the treacherous behavior of Maxim Gorky's newspaper." *Rech* also criticized *Novaya Zhizn* for bad taste in writing and tone, predicting that Gorky would come out with his usual repentence.

52. This assertion was rejected as "unconvincing" by Petr Ryss in his article "Belletristicheskaya publitsistika," *Rech,* August 5 (18), 1917. Ryss also brought out Gorky's familiar statement about his admiration for and dislike of the people of strict consistency ("On Polemics"). To Ryss, Gorky was a typical impulsive and moody artist, and a poor journalist and politician. In the opinion of Ryss, the old regime had to be subjected to the sharpest criticism, directed toward overthrowing it. The revolution, on the contrary, was busy building new forms of life and demanded discipline, for political creativity cannot tolerate recklessness.

For additional details on *Luch* and "restraint" see "On Polemics" and note 6.

53. Quoted from "Petrograd, 3 avgusta," *Rech,* August 3 (16), 1917. *Rech* maintained that the socialist press irresponsibly blamed the bourgeoisie for delaying the elections to the Constituent Assembly. Such accusations, according to *Rech,* aroused savage passions and incited socialists to bloody violence in local elections. An example of such violence can be found in "Egorievskie ubiystva," *ibid.*

54. This may refer to the so-called "Progressive Bloc" formed in the Fourth Duma (August 1915) on the Cadets' initiative. The majority parties in it were the Octobrists and the Cadets. In the interests of winning the war, the Bloc demanded the establishment of firm and efficient rule and the abolition of political and social restrictions for workers, peasants, and national minorities. It is also possible that Gorky thought of the Cadets' and Octobrists' joint vote on a number of issues in the Third Duma (1907-1912).

Beginning with their Second Congress (1906), the Constitutional-Democrats also called themselves the "Party of People's Freedom." For the appellation "His Majesty's Opposition" see note 7.

55. Or rather "Stolypin's necktie." Fedor Izmaylovich Rodichev (1854-1933), a prominent Cadet, condemned with these words the government's treatment of revolutionaries in his speech to the Third Duma in November 1907. Though he made an immediate apology to Prime Minister Stolypin, he was expelled from the Duma for fifteen meetings.

56. The title bears an obvious resemblance to "I cannot Be Silent!" the heading under which Tolstoy published his famous protest against executions in 1908.

57. To this article Stalin replied with a mocking rebuff. The future dictator put Gorky among the company of "terrified neurasthenics from *Novaya Zhizn*" who were "deserting the ranks of the revolution." The revolution, Stalin warned, consigned to oblivion many celebrities for refusing to learn from it. This happened to Plekhanov and Breshkovskaya. If Gorky was envious of their laurels, he may as well follow them into the "museum of antiquities."

"The revolution is not disposed either to pity or to bury its dead," Stalin concluded. See his unsigned article " 'Okruzhili mya teltsy mnozi tuchny' " ("Strong Bulls of Bashan Have Beset Me Round"), *Rabochy Put,* November 2 (October 20), 1917. *Rabochy Put* (The Workers' Road) was one of *Pravda's* names in 1917 used to escape political persecution after the events of July 4th (17th).

Two days after Stalin's attack, *Rabochy Put* complained that Gorky depicted the Petrograd workers and soldiers with exactly the same colors that were applied by the bourgeoisie to depict the rebellious proletariat in 1848 and in the days of the Paris Commune, in 1871. See "Vchera i segodnya," *Rabochy Put,* November 4 (October 22), 1917.

The *Novaya Zhizn* issue with "One Must Not Be Silent!" carried also the statement of a leading Bolshevik, Lev Kamenev, to the effect that he and Zinoviev opposed an immediate Bolshevik uprising, considering it premature. Lenin viewed this statement as outright treason and Stalin made full use of it nineteen years later in the first of the notorious Moscow show trials which sent Zinoviev and Kamenev to their death.

On October 19 (November 1) *Novaya Zhizn* published a statement by Trotsky, which could hardly allay the fears of its editors. Trotsky denied that an open action was scheduled, but "when the Petrograd Soviet of Workers' and Soldiers' Deputies finds it necessary to go ahead with this action, all of the working class, all of the revolutionary garrison will join its revolutionary banners."

The decision to resort to an armed uprising was taken by the Bolsheviks' Central Committee on October 10 (23), 1917. They were the only socialist or revolutionary party that resolved not to wait for the convocation of the freely elected Constitiuent Assembly, knowing that they would be a hopeless minority in it. They did not even have

the majority in the Soviets whose mouthpiece, *Izvestiya*
(*The News*) *of the Soviets of Workers' and Soldiers' Deputies,* took a sharply critical attitude toward the imminent
uprising calling it, as the title of its editorial of October 25
(November 7) clearly states, "The Mad Adventure." The
success of the uprising did not make *Izvestiya* change its
mind. Its editorial of October 26 (November 8) charac-
terized the Bolshevik victory as "not a transfer of power
to the Soviets, but the seizure of power by one party—the
Bolsheviks." To *Izvestiya* this meant the wrecking of the
Constituent Assembly—"the greatest conquest of the revolution"—and the consequent threat of a civil war.

58. M. I. Tereshchenko (1888-1958), a beet-sugar mil-
lionaire, Minister of Finance and then Foreign Minister in
the Provisional Government. A. I. Konovalov (1875-
1948), a textile manufacturer, Minister of Trade and Industry in the Provisional Government, and a leader of the
"Progressists," a party of the liberal bourgeoisie which
stood between the Cadets and Octobrists. M. V. Bernatsky is identified in note 6.

59. Probably an encounter at Pulkovo between the Cossacks of General Petr Krasnov and Bolshevik forces soon
after the October upheaval. The Cossacks were brought in
by Aleksandr Kerensky, Prime Minister of the deposed
Provisional Government.

60. The destruction caused by the Bolshevik troops during the fight for the city against the cadets of the military
schools. It is difficult to ascertain whether Nikolay Bukharin, a Bolshevik leader, had Gorky in mind when he
answered the charges of destruction in Moscow and other
cities brought against the Bolsheviks by various newspapers. Gorky's accusation was published on the same day
as Bukharin's reply. Bukharin, however, mentioned *No-*

*vaya Zhizn* several times. By reporting the alleged Bolshevik outrages, he said, *Novaya Zhizn* and other newspapers intended to raise a turmoil in the revolutionary
army and "facilitate the victory of the counterrevolutionary bourgeoisie." It was a shame to read *Novaya Zhizn,* he
felt. See "Rech Bukharina," *Pravda,* November 20 (7),
1917. An earlier attack on *Novaya Zhizn* for spreading
alarm and confusion by publishing contradictory reports
was made by a certain M. Markovsky in his letter "To
*Novaya Zhizn* Readers," *Pravda,* November 15 (2),
1917.

The Bolsheviks denied as a slander all reports concerning destruction and outrages caused by them. See, for example, Babushkin, "V revolyutsionnye dni," *Pravda,* November 20 (7), 1917; anon., "Ne verte klevetnikam,"
*ibid.,* November 23 (10), 1917; and Neytralny, "Eshche
o Moskovskikh sobytiyakh (27 okt.-2 noyabrya 1917
g.)," *ibid.,* November 29 (16), 1917.

61. A number of the Rightist, Cadet, and Menshevik
newspapers were suppressed immediately after the October Revolution, even before the publishing of the People's
Commissars' decree of October 27 (November 9), 1917,
forbidding the existence of an openly anti-Bolshevik press.
Since then the suppression or fining of newspapers had
become a normal procedure. In Trotsky's opinion, people
like Gorky and Korolenko protested against the Bolshevik
treatment of the press because they were "wholly under
influence of the petty and banal prejudices of the Philistine
milieu." See "O svobode pechati (Iz rechi Trotskogo v
manezhe Grenaderskogo polka 27 noyabrya)," *Pravda,*
December 13 (November 30), 1917.

62. V. K. Pleve (Plehve, 1846-1904), Minister of the
Interior from 1902 to 1904, an instigator of the war
against Japan and the ruthless suppressor of liberal and

revolutionary movements. Assassinated by the Socialist-Revolutionaries.

63. Sergey Gennadievich Nechaev (1847-1882), an anarchist and conspirator, one of the most sinister figures of the Russian revolutionary underground. Ambitious, unscrupulous, and single-minded, he considered moral everything that furthered the revolutionary cause. He resorted to lies, slander, bluff, theft, murder. His revolutionary work was carried out primarily among college students. The last decade of his life he spent in the Peter and Paul Fortress. He stoically endured all its hardships and wrote letters in his own blood to fellow revolutionaries with whom he managed to communicate, thanks to his tremendous influence on the prison guards. To a considerable extent his ideas and methods are reflected in the revolutionary characters of Dostoevsky's *The Possessed*.

Mikhail Aleksandrovich Bakunin (1814-1876), theorist and leader of anarchism, fomented revolution throughout Europe and dreamed of creating an international federation of states named "The Union of World Revolution Against the Union of All Reactions." In 1869, in cooperation with Nechaev, he composed the *Revolutionary Catechism*, the central thesis of which was that the end justifies the means, that a revolutionary must direct all his thoughts and energy to one aim: merciless destruction.

Brigandage was to Bakunin and Nechaev the only true revolutionary force in Russia. They extolled it as the most honored way of Russian life and called for elemental peasant uprisings like those of Razin (1670-1671) and Pugachev (1773-1775).

It was this appeal to the dark and destructive forces of the masses on which, in Gorky's opinion, the Bolshevik political strategy was based, and he repeatedly condemned it. Vyacheslav Polonsky (1886-1932), literary critic and

authority on Bakunin, also drew a similar historical parallel when he wrote that there were "not a few flowers of
evil brightly blossoming in our days and growing out of
the soil of the very same Nechaev's conviction that for a
good end all means are right." See his "Nechaev i sovre-
mennost," *Novaya Zhizn,* May 22 (9), 1918. Bakunin's
life and philosophy (and partly those of Nechaev) are
described in Professor E. H. Carr's book *Mikhail Bakunin,* New York, Vintage Books, 1961.

64. Thus were called the second and third cabinets of the
Provisional Government made up of both socialists and
non-socialists. The first cabinet (March-May 1917) was
composed almost entirely of the conservatives and Cadets.

65. A reply to this article appeared in *Pravda* of November 22 (9), 1917, in the form of a letter, "We and They
(To M. Gorky)," signed Iv. Loginov, a worker. I. S.
Loginov, a minor proletarian poet and a frequent contrib-
utor to *Pravda,* wanted to know to what democracy Gorky
addressed himself—was it to such people as the writer
Kuprin, in whose words the workers' democracy was
merely "a mob sated with human blood, a corrupt city
scum," or the poet Balmont who entitled one of his poems
"To General L. G. Kornilov" and spoke in it of the lawlessness, crookedness, and oppression generated by the
new regime? Instead of becoming indignant at such abominations by his fellow writers, Gorky becomes indignant at
the crimes and abominations committed, allegedly, by
Lenin and his associates, who were indeed "the genuine
workers' democracy."

A general answer to the criticism of the Bolsheviks in
*Novaya Zhizn* was given by *Pravda* of November 28 (15),
1917, in V. Bystryansky's article "About the Proletariat
and the 'Demagogues.'"

66. This assertion prompted "An Open Letter to M. Gorky" signed by three non-commissioned officers and printed in *Pravda* of November 25 (12), 1917. The noncoms, wondering whether Gorky was naïve or lied on purpose, demanded from him an answer to the question: "Who is dishonoring the Russian revolution more—comrades Lenin and Trotsky, or you, comrade Gorky?"

A. V. Kartashev, Professor of Religion and Cadet, was Procurator of the Holy Synod in the Provisional Government. Bernatsky and Konovalov were identified in notes 6 and 58 respectively.

67. As Alexander Kaun has pointed out, Gorky might have meant here such politicians as Zinoviev, Kamenev, and Lunacharsky who at various times had theoretical or tactical disagreements with Lenin. See Kaun, *Maxim Gorky and His Russia*, New York, Jonathan Cape and Harrison Smith, 1931, p. 472.

68. This statement, plus the opening phrases of the preceding and the second paragraphs of this article, plus definitions of the Bolsheviks as "blind fanatics and dishonest adventures" and "conspirators and anarchists of Nechaev's type" (from "To the Democracy") were all quoted right after the title of Ilya Ionov's article "Kak mozhno iz-za dereviev ne videt lesa" (How One May Not See the Wood for the Trees), *Pravda* (evening ed.), December 8 (November 25), 1917. Ilya Ionov (pseudonym of Ilya Ionovich Bernshteyn, 1887–1942), a proletarian poet, asserted that Gorky wrote about the Bolsheviks and their leaders virtually in the same way as had the bourgeoisie and Black Hundreds. "A writer to whom broad proletarian masses listened for many years has joined the chorus of those who set themselves the aim of slandering the workers' movement," observed the disappointed poet

(later to occupy important positions in the Soviet state publishing apparatus).

69. A reference to the Russian habit of chewing the seeds of sunflower, pumpkin, and watermelon, which is, in this instance, used as a symbol of intellectual and social indifference.

70. Probably a reference to the letter of T. Tkachenko, a factory mechanic, published in *Pravda* of November 23 (10), 1917. Tkachenko "saw with horror" that Gorky, who claimed to have lived for the people twenty-five years, "was leaving us." Instead of congratulating yesterday's slaves on a great victory, Gorky felt compassion for arrested ministers, mourned the passing of the golden era of the bourgeois press, and composed frightening articles against the common people's government. Tkachenko concluded: "Thank you, Maxim Gorky and various other 'fighters for the people,' for removing your masks at the right time. The people will pronounce their judgment upon you." For Gorky's remark concerning his devotion to the people see note 73.

71. Quoted with the omission of the words: "of marvelous stories by A. N. Tolstoy" (between "a nobleman" and "says").

72. *Rech* was suppressed by a resolution of the Petrograd Revolutionary War Committee on October 26 (November 8), but continued to appear until August 1918 under various titles such as *Nasha Rech* (Our Speech), *Vek* (Age), *Nash Vek* (Our Age). The ink was hardly dry on Gorky's pen when the Council of People's Commissars ordered the suppression of nine newspapers for publishing, without changes or editorial comment, the defunct Provisional

Government's appeal to the people and its decree scheduling the meeting of the Constituent Assembly for November 28 (December 11), 1917, which did not suit the Bolsheviks. See "Zakrytie gazet," *Pravda,* December 2 (November 19), 1917.

73. Gorky's defense of Burtsev is especially remarkable in view of the fact that only four months before a bitter polemic flared up between the two men. It was caused by Burtsev's announcement that the *Novaya Zhizn* editor helped the Germans and Bolsheviks demoralize Russia by taking the "defeatist" position. Gorky called his accuser a "pitiable man," demanded the retraction of his "vile slander," and stressed his own service to his country and people for twenty-five years. For details see Burtsev's articles "Ili my, ili nemtsy i te, kto s nimi," *Russkaya Volya,* July 7 (20), 1917, "Ne zashchishchayte M. Gorkogo!" *Novoe Vremya,* July 9 (22), 1917, "V. L. Burtsev o Lenine i M. Gorkom," *Russkaya Volya,* July 29 (August 11), 1917, and Gorky's "Burtsevu," *Novaya Zhizn,* July 9 (22) and 12 (25), 1917.

Burtsev, whose views were close to those of the Socialist-Revolutionaries, was arrested and taken to the Peter and Paul Fortress on the night of October 26 (November 8), 1917, and his newspaper *Nashe Obshchee Delo* (Our Common Cause) was closed. See "Arest Burtseva," *Pravda,* November 9 (October 27), 1917. Gorky called Burtsev "cesspool cleaner of the political parties" in connection with his reputation of uncovering the double agents. It was he who finally unmasked Azef. Unfortunately, he was too zealous at times, and, as a consequence, some innocent people suffered.

74. The source of this and preceding quotations could not be found. Possibly, it was an article by the proletarian

poet Ilya Ionov published in the unavailable part of *Pravda* of November 28 (15), 1917. This supposition is based on Ionov's emphatic reference to the "bright festival" in his *Pravda* article (already noted) of December 8 (November 25, 1917). In it he reproached Gorky for not seeing the wood for the trees. Gorky, he explained, turned his attention to such unavoidable and secondary things as the thievery in Ermolova's dressing room or the poor performance of the typesetters, but he failed to notice the event of tremendous importance, the fact that the workers and soldiers put an end to the slaughter and brought nearer the peace negotiations. "And this is what I call that bright festival on the threshold of which we are standing," Ionov solemnly declared.

Three days earlier another proletarian poet, Leonty Kotomka, bemoaned Gorky's abandonment of the "madness of the brave" and still could not quite believe in the possibility of the metamorphosis: "Can it really be that from a stormy petrel you've turned into a loon for which there is no 'joy of battle?' How sad, how infinitely sad!" Gorky came to be called the "stormy petrel" after the appearance of his famous revolutionary poem in prose, "The Song of the Stormy Petrel" (1901).

More direct language was used by the soldiers of a Siberian engineering unit in a letter to *Pravda's* editors. After rebuking *Novaya Zhizn* for slandering and belying the people, the soldiers stated: "The mask has now been removed, and we hold up to shame the treacherous behavior of the *Novaya Zhizn* people." See *Pravda*, December 20 (7), 1917, and Kotomka's letter to Gorky, *ibid.*, December 5 (November 22), 1917.

75. Literally, "zoological anarchism." "Zoological" was a favorite epithet of Gorky's when he spoke of the animal manifestations of human nature. *Pravda* writers reacted

with particular bitterness to "animal anarchism." To them
it was a great struggle of the people led by the Bolsheviks.
Gorky's failure to see the real revolution meant that he
was no longer its "stormy petrel," but "an outright traitor
to it." See Intelligent iz naroda (An Intellectual of the
people), "Sotsialnaya revolyutsiya i M. Gorky," *Pravda,*
January 20 (7), 1918, and also V. Polyansky, "V putakh
starogo mira (Po povodu 'Nesvoevremennykh mysley' M.
Gorkogo v 'Novoy Zhizni')," *Pravda,* December 23 (10),
1917. The article by the "Intellectual of the people" (I. S.
Blank), dated December 26, 1917, is *Pravda's* longest and
most comprehensive criticism of Gorky, dealing with his
*Novaya Zhizn* articles from December 6 (19) to December 24, 1917 (January 6, 1918).

76. Derived from the last name of the Don Cossack,
Emelyan Pugachev, leader of the impetuous peasant rising
in 1773-1775. The normally restrained Pushkin, describ-
ing it in *The Captain's Daughter,* exclaimed: "God save us
from seeing a Russian revolt, senseless and merciless!"

77. Countess S. V. Panina, Assistant Minister of Education in the Provisional Government, was arrested on November 28 (December 11), 1917, for refusing to sur-
render to the Bolsheviks 93,000 rubles of public money.
She firmly stood by her conviction that the money could
be handed in only to a freely elected Constituent Assembly. She was sentenced to be held in prison until she sur-
rendered the money to the Bolshevik authorities. During
the trial she enjoyed tremendous public support and was
released ten days later when a committee paid the 93,000
rubles.

Her "People's House" in Ligovka (Petersburg),
founded in 1903 with her own money, was the most famous and popular of its kind. In addition to a variety of

NOTES                                                    271

cultural and recreational facilities, it offered legal aid.
Gorky was one of its governors. The Countess's "People's
House" served also as a place for political gatherings of
Petersburg workers, and in 1906 Lenin, who was at that
time underground, made a speech there, an event captured
in a painting of P. Zhilin, a Soviet artist.

For his defense of Panina, Gorky was attacked by V.
Polyansky, who asserted that Panina took money to "fight
the people" ("V putakh starogo mira," *Pravda*, December
23 (10) 1917). Some details on Panina's case may be
found in Kn. Pavel Dmitr. Dolgorukov, *Velikaya razrukha*, Madrid, Rafael Taravilla Paul, 1964, and in "Sud
nad gr. S. V. Paninoy," *Nash Vek*, December 12 (25)
1917.

78. Town in central Russia, northeast of Ivanovo-
Voznesensk (now Ivanovo). Konovalov is identified in
note 58.

79. Ieronim Ieronimovich Yasinsky (1850-1931), of
noble birth, changed his political affiliations several times.
He was a radical, then a reactionary, then after the October Revolution he joined the Bolshevik party. Anatoly
Vasilievich Lunacharsky (1875-1933), politician and
writer, was the People's Commissar of Education.

80. This caused an agitated reaction in V. Polyansky.
There was no reason for Gorky, he argued, to write in
praise of the Cadets' effectiveness or to complain about the
plans to throw them out of the Constituent Assembly. It is
a class struggle and the Cadets try to strangle the Russian
revolution by means of civil war, treason, sabotage, con-
spiracies, and provocations. And Gorky defends these
people as honorable! See "V putakh starogo mira,"
*Pravda*, December 23 (10) 1917.

81. A river in the central part of Petersburg.

82. Nikolay Gavrilovich Chernyshevsky (1828-1889), radical thinker, socialist, writer, and literary critic. Believed in the peasant commune as foundation of Russian socialism and exerted strong spiritual influence on Russian Populism. Spent almost twenty years in Siberian exile. Aleksandr Nikolaevich Radishchev (1749-1802), writer, author of *A Journey from Petersburg to Moscow* (1790) which presents a gloomy picture of the slavery of the peasants and justifies violence for the sake of their liberation. Regarded as a rebel, he was sentenced to death. The sentence was commuted to ten years of exile, on returning from which he committed suicide.

83. Smolny Institute in Petersburg, seat of the Bolshevik government, formerly the most exclusive school for daughers of the nobility founded by Catherine the Great in 1764.

84. *Pravda* asserted that the wine riots were organized by the "counterrevolutionary Kaledintes-Cadets" as a new means of undermining the government of workers and peasants. See "Ot Petrogradskogo Soveta Rab. i Sold. Dep. Ko vsemu naseleniyu Petrograda," *Pravda,* December 18 (5), 1917. The term Kaledinites, in Bolshevik parlance, meant the anti-Bolshevik forces gathered in southern Russia under the leadership or protection of General Aleksey Maksimovich Kaledin (1861-1918), Ataman of all the Don Cossacks.

85. Towns chosen to typify provincial Russia. The former is in the Ukraine, the latter in central Russia, north of Kostroma. *Pravda* disagreed with Gorky by saying that the Soviet authorities were accused of crudeness by former

highly placed functionaries who disliked being under a revolutionary regime. Does Gorky know how much workers' blood would have been shed by the bourgeoisie had the October Revolution been defeated? Gorky should not teach people but learn from them; he has become a "whimpering Philistine" (*khnykayushchy obyvatel*). See anon., "Raskisshy Gorky," *Pravda,* December 22 (9), 1917.

86. The "Intellectual of the people" cited this sentence, among others, to illustrate that Gorky betrayed the revolution. See "Sotsialnaya revolyutsiya i M. Gorky," *Pravda,* January 20 (7), 1918. Vladimir Kirillov, a leading proletarian poet, objected to Gorky's "terrified yelling" about the cruelty of the working class and the animal (*zoologicheskie*) instincts of the crowd. To Kirillov no revolution was so merciful to the vanquished enemy as the October Revolution. See "Svoevremennye mysli," *Gryadushchee,* No. 1, 1918, p. 11, as quoted in *Letopis zhizni i tvorchestva A. M. Gorkogo,* vol. III, Moscow, Akademiya nauk SSSR, 1959, p. 66.

87. Most probably a reference to V. Burtsev's accusations. See note 73.

88. The daily *Russkoe Znamya* edited by the head of "The Union of the Russian People," A. I. Dubrovin, was published from 1905 to 1917. See also note 3.

89. To this the "Intellectual of the people" replied that the Bolsheviks and Left Socialist-Revolutionaries were translating into reality the political and economic aspirations of the majority of the workers and peasants. Of course, the entire peasant population of Russia cannot be turned immediately into socialists, but the social revolu-

tion, which Gorky considers premature, should be the first and vital step in this direction. Gorky's ideas of the peasants' and workers' political backwardness are reactionary. Everyone who loves Russia with fear and torment, as Gorky says he does, should welcome the speediest advent of social upheaval. See "Sotsialnaya revolyutsiya i M. Gorky," *Pravda,* January 20 (7), 1918.

90. Prince Pavel Dmitrievich Dolgorukov (1866-1927), a leading Cadet, arrested without any apparent reason and then detained as an "enemy of the people" on the basis of the People's Commissars' decree of November 28 (December 11), 1917, which put this ominous label on the entire Cadet party and called for the immediate arrest and trial of its leaders. An émigré since 1920, Dolgorukov twice went incognito to Soviet Russia, was finally caught there, and executed with nineteen other men in retaliation for the assassination, in Warsaw, of Soviet diplomat Voykov. In his recently published memoirs one finds an interesting account of his arrest and detention in the Peter and Paul Fortress together with Bernatsky, Tereshchenko, and other politicians. See *Velikaya razrukha,* Madrid, 1964.

91. A river in the central section of Petersburg.

92. This could be an allusion to Gorky whose last name means "bitter" in Russian. *Pravda* of January 13, 1918 (December 31, 1917) published a poem by Demyan Bedny entitled "The Bitter Truth." It was dedicated to writers like Gorky and Korolenko who, in Bedny's words, "recoiled from the people."

93. Irakly Tsereteli (1881 or 1882-1959), a prominent Menshevik, member of the Second Duma (1907) and Minister of Post and Telegraph in the first coalition cabi-

net (May-August 1917) of the Provisional Government. Gorky's opinion of him was instantly questioned by *Pravda*'s allegations that Tsereteli betrayed democracy and was "a little swindler" rather than an "absolutely honest man." *Pravda* also noted the continued appearance of "Untimely Thoughts," saying that they were "stale" and "would have been bitter if they had not been simply ridiculous." See "Obzor pechati," *Pravda*, January 6, 1918 (December 24, 1917). This issue of *Pravda* carried the article "Svyataya burzhuaziya i Gorky" signed Aleksey Ga—r. Its author wondered why Gorky kept accusing the masses of lack of culture and of cruelty and paid no attention to bourgeois actions aimed at the bloody suppression of workers. A similar accusation of political blindness and partiality was made against Gorky by L. Sosnovsky in "Znatnye inostrantsy (O pisatelyakh iz 'Novoy Zhizni')," *Pravda*, January 16 (3), 1918.

94. This assertion provoked ironic comments in "Obzor pechati," *Pravda*, January 6, 1918 (December 24, 1917).

95. The last two paragraphs were quoted approvingly by the "Intellectual of the people" who hopefully saw in them the sign that Gorky could not have betrayed the social revolution forever. See "Sotsialnaya revolyutsiya i M. Gorky," *Pravda*, January 20 (7), 1918.

96. This occurred at several points in Petersburg, notably in front of the Winter Palace where the crowds hoped to meet the Tsar. The event, known as "Bloody Sunday," was described by Gorky in his story "The Ninth of January" published abroad in 1907.

97. *Pravda* accounts of the demonstrations are given in its issues of January 17 (4), 19 (6), 20 (7), and 22 (9),

1918. The Constituent Assembly met in the Tauride Palace, formerly the seat of the Duma.

98. Actually, out of 703 deputies there were 168 Bolsheviks allied with 39 Left Socialist-Revolutionaries. Nonetheless the Bolsheviks were in a hopeless minority opposed by 380 regular S.R.'s, 18 Mensheviks, 17 Cadets and Rightists, and all the rest. Out of the total number of votes cast throughout Russia the Bolsheviks received only one fourth, the Socialist-Revolutionaries twice as much. To retain their power, the Bolsheviks dispersed the Constituent Assembly and prevented its further meetings by resorting to armed force. Important factors contributing to the Bolshevik success were that they won more votes in Petrograd than any other party and that they had troops under their command.

99. Physician and economist Shingarev (1869-1918), Minister of Finance in the first coalition cabinet of the Provisional Government and a deputy to the Constituent Assembly, was arrested during the search of Countess Panina's house and kept in prison in accordance with the decree which branded the members of the Cadet party as "enemies of the people" and ordered the arrest and trial of their leaders. Because of poor health he was transferred from the Peter and Paul Fortress to a hospital where he was lynched by sailors and soldiers. Lynched together with him was the Cadet Fedor Fedorovich Kokoshkin (1871-1918), Professor of Law, State Controller in the second coalition cabinet of the Provisional Government, and a Constituent Assembly deputy. Kokoshkin was arrested simultaneously with Shingarev, arraigned on identical charges, and transferred to the hospital for similar reasons. Their arrest, detention, and murder are described in I. O., "Kak eto bylo . . . (Dnevnik A. I. Shingareva),"

*Nash Vek,* May 3 (April 20), 1918; L. Kin, "Delo ob ubiystve A. I. Shingareva i F. F. Kokoshkina," *ibid.,* June 18 (5), 1918; and in the book of their fellow prisoner, Prince Pavel Dolgorukov, *Velikaya razrukha,* Madrid, 1964.

100. Apparently out of modesty Gorky omitted the actual concluding words from the "Intellectual's" article: "Gorky is too dear to our social revolution so we cannot believe that he will not soon take, in the ranks of its ideological leaders, the place which has long belonged to him as the stormy petrel of the world-wide social revolution." See Intelligent iz naroda, "Sotsialnaya revolyutsiya i M. Gorky," *Pravda,* January 20 (7), 1918.

101. Probably Anatoly Zheleznyakov, a former anarchist (see note 39), who was in charge of the Bolshevik detachment guarding the Tauride Palace where the Constituent Assembly met on January 5 (18), 1918. In accordance with the Bolshevik will, he ordered the Assembly members to disperse saying that "the guard was tired." In 1919 he was killed in action against the Whites.

102. In their utterances, Lenin and other Bolsheviks requested a prompt and thorough investigation of the case. See *Pravda,* January 21 (8), 1918 (evening ed.), and January 22 (9), 1918. In fact, things were different and the People's Commissar of Justice, Petr Stuchka, admitted that the investigation "for a long time made no progress whatsoever." See *Nash Vek,* March 22 (9), 1918. Much later five men who played secondary roles in the murder were indicted. See *Nash Vek,* June 18 (5), 1918.

103. Literally, "into the language of our native country's aspens" (*na yazyk rodnykh osin*). This expression comes

from I. S. Turgenev's epigram (1884) against a translator
of Shakespeare, N. Ketcher, whose renderings were too
close to the original. It is used to indicate a crude translation into one's mother tongue.

104. Probably a reference to the behavior of Russian
troops that entered Northern Persia in the course of
World War I and stayed there for some time after the
October Revolution.

105. Probably the monument to Pushkin erected in 1880.

106. This statement was cited as indicative of Gorky's
sitting on the fence, his inability to side either with those
committing outrages in the name of social revolution or
with the intelligentsia in whose opinion the Bolsheviks
were not consolidating but liquidating the conquests of the
revolution. See D. Filosofov, "Poluburzhuy" (A Semi-
Bourgeois), *Nash Vek*, January 25 (February 7), 1918.
Literary critic and religious thinker Dmitry Vladimirovich
Filosofov (1872-1940) had long been an ideological opponent of Gorky with whose art and philosophy he dealt
in a number of his pre-revolutionary articles.

107. Last Sunday before Lent.

108. The 1913 trial of Mendel Beylis (Beiliss), a Jew,
organized for political reasons in Kiev. Beylis, charged
with the ritual murder of a Christian boy, was acquitted.
The details can be found in Maurice Samuel's *Blood Accusations*, Philadelphia, The Jewish Publication Society of
America, 1966.

109. A reference to the massacre of striking workers in
the Lena goldfields (Siberia) in 1912.

110. The economists Grigory Borisovich Iollos (1859-1907) and Mikhail Yakovlevich Gertsenshteyn, or Herzenstein (1859-1906), were representatives of the Cadets in the First Duma. Gertsenshteyn, an opponent of the government's agrarian policy, was murdered by members of the reactionary "Union of the Russian People"—Larichkin, Polovnev, Yuskevich, and others, whereas the assassination of Iollos this "Union" entrusted to a factory worker who was deliberately misinformed about the political identity of his victim.

111. See notes 99 and 102.

112. Six students and an unidentified man were shot on March 2. Prior to the execution the students, accused of plotting against the regime, were imprisoned in the cellar of the Smolny Institute, seat of the Bolshevik government. Three of the executed were brothers and French citizens, just about to leave for France to join the army. The execution called forth numerous protests. For details see "Po povodu rasstrelov," *Nash Vek*, March 9 (February 24), 1918, several reports in March issues of this newspaper, and "K kazni semi," *Novaya Zhizn*, March 14 (1), 1918.

113. Probably atrocities committed by pro-Bolshevik sailors while establishing Bolshevik rule in the Crimea, where until the end of 1917 the Soviets were dominated by the Socialist-Revolutionaries and Mensheviks. The Bolsheviks had also to overcome the resistance of the native Tartars.

114. To this assertion *Izvestiya* retorted: "Yes, conscience is dead, but not only where Gorky thinks. Let him look at himself in a mirror." See anon., " 'Sovest izdokhla,' " *Izvestiya*, March 23 (10), 1918.

115. Quoted from "Chto poseyali, to nado i zhat (Otklik na Gorkovskuyu 'sovest')," *Krasnaya Gazeta,* March 19, (6), 1918. This short article is an answer to the preceding issue of "Untimely Thoughts." *Krasnaya Gazeta* was published by the Petrograd Soviet of Workers' and Soldiers' Deputies.

116. Dmitry Vasilievich Grigorovich (1822-1900) gave a sympathetic portrayal of peasants in his stories and novels.

117. This and the preceding passages were apparently quoted by Gorky, with his own italics, from "Rech Lenina," *Novaya Zhizn,* March 17 (4), 1918. As printed in *Novaya Zhizn* both excerpts give every reason to believe that they are parts of Lenin's speech reproduced verbatim (the second excerpt is even put in quotation marks). The speech in question is the so-called "Closing Speech" of March 15, 1918, delivered at the Fourth Extraordinary All-Russian Congress of Soviets which met in Moscow to ratify the peace treaty of Brest-Litovsk concluded between the Bolsheviks and Germany. Neither of the two passages appears in *Pravda* of March 19, 1918, where the "Closing Speech" is supposedly printed in full, or in the 2nd, 3rd, and 4th Soviet editions of Lenin's works, or in the latest, 5th edition, designated as *A Complete Collection of Works.* In all these editions the "Closing Speech" is reprinted from *Pravda,* with some slight alterations of a political nature. Thus, either *Novaya Zhizn* quoted Lenin incorrectly or the Bolsheviks decided to keep quiet about certain parts of his speech. Lenin's report to the Congress on March 14 contained some passages similar to those cited by Gorky. In one place Lenin defended the abandonment of Finland and the Ukraine by arguing that if one of two friends walking at night is at-

tacked by ten people, his companion cannot be called traitor for running away. This viewpoint apparently causes
some embarrassment to the propagators of official Communist ethics, so the editors of the *Complete Collection of
Works* commented that Lenin's words were probably
taken down inaccurately and they should mean just the
opposite: the deserting friend is a traitor. See V. I. Lenin,
*Polnoe sobranie sochineny,* 5th ed., Moscow, Gos. izd.
politicheskoy literatury, vol. 36 (1963), p. 106. No other
edition of Lenin's works has such a comment and it is
clear from the context that his words were taken down
correctly.

118. This could be a reference to an article by K. Samoylova, "Maksim Gorky o sovremennom momente,"
*Pravda* (Petrograd), March 17 (4), 1918. Mme. Samoylova argued against Gorky's view of the Russians expressed in "Untimely Thoughts" of March 16 (3) and
stated that, "having broken away from the popular
masses, he spits on the people." She also took Gorky to
task for saying that the Soviet regime did not dare to enlist
the help of all the intellectual forces of Russian democracy. To her this was a justification for the intelligentsia's
refusal to work with the Bolsheviks.

Two weeks later, on March 29 (16), *Izvestiya* published a brief article by G. Ustinov entitled "50 Years" in
connection with the fiftieth anniversary of Gorky's birth.
Ustinov mentioned favorably Gorky's revolutionary role
in the past but emphasized that Gorky "had now gone
away from the people into another camp" and "is no
longer with us."

119. The proclamation dated March 18 may be found in
*Nash Vek* of March 22 (9), 1918, under the general
heading "Official Reports." The title of the proclamation

in *Nash Vek* differs from that given by Gorky by being more complete. It is clear from this version of the title that the proclamation was made not by the representatives of the entire Red navy but a coast-guard unit. Gorky apparently used another source.

120. *Krasa i gordost revolyutsii* or, in another version, *slava i gordost revolyutsii* (glory and pride of the revolution)—designation of the sailors. Trotsky is said to have called thus the Kronstadt sailors in his appeal to them to release V. M. Chernov, Minister of Agriculture in the Provisional Government. Chernov was arrested by them during the disturbances of July 4 (17), 1917. See I. G. Tsereteli, *Vospominaniya o fevralskoy revolyutsii,* vol. II, Paris, Mouton and Co., 1963, p. 307.

121. In *Pravda* somewhat differently: "For each of our heads—a hundred of yours." See its editorial "Beregites!" (Watch Out!) in the evening edition of January 15 (2), 1918. The threat was prompted by somebody's shooting the day before at the car in which Lenin was riding. He was unharmed. In saying that the body of Lenin's automobile was punctured with a penknife, Gorky might have wanted to stress the abnormal brutality of the Bolshevik threat.

122. See note 113.

123. Massacres of striking workers at the Zlatoust Cannon Works (Southern Ural) in 1903, and in the Lena goldfields (Siberia) in 1912.

124. A reference to the heavy casualties inflicted on the crew of the mutinous cruiser *Ochakov* by the loyal Tsarist navy in a bitter sea battle outside Sebastopol in 1905. The

*Ochakov* mutiny is the subject of Boris Pasternak's lengthy poem *Leytenant Shmidt* (Lieutenant Schmidt, 1927), named after the executed leader of the rebellious seamen.

125. Probably taken from Nikolay Nekrasov's poem *Zabytaya derevnya* (A Forgotten Village, 1856):
*Vot priedet barin—barin nas rassudit* (Just wait till master comes—master will settle our disputes).

126. Platon Karataev, a peasant character in *War and Peace*. Meek, forgiving, wise, and religious, he represents, in Tolstoy's opinion, the true virtues of the Russian peasantry.

127. This work consists of stories from village life written in 1882. On everal occasions Gorky praised Uspensky's realistic portrayal of peasants, especially of the irresistible power of the soil over them.

128. The complete title is *Our Crime (Not a Nightmare But a True Story). From Contemporary People's Life.* The book appeared in 1909 and went through several editions raising lively controversies. The author stated in the preface that the Russian people had become drunken, angry, savage, unable and unwilling to work. For all this he put the blame on Russian educated society that isolated itself from the common people. Rodionov claimed to have presented an unembellished picture of life. The novel abounds in descriptions of drunkenness, cruelty, ignorance, lewdness. The central event is the senseless murder of a peasant for which the culprits received a very light sentence. Rodionov clearly suggests that leniency of the courts contributed to crimes.
Gorky was particularly indignant about a dialogue in

which the peasants were said to be much worse than brutes and beasts. He also thought that Rodionov expressed through one of his characters his own approval of the hanging of peasants. See Gorky's article "About Self-Taught Writers" (1911). The critic L. Gurevich, however, found Rodionov's work true to life but weak artistically. She disagreed with the writer Korney Chukovsky who called the novel "the most repulsive, the most exciting, the most talented of contemporary books." See Lyubov Gurevich, *Literatura i estetika. Kriticheskie opyty i etyudy,* Moscow, "Russkaya Mysl," 1912, pp. 133-140.

129. Razin and Pugachev, Don Cossacks, leaders of peasants' and Cossacks' risings in 1670-1671 and 1773-1775 respectively. Razin, a favorite figure of Russian folk poetry, is the hero of the popular song "Stenka Razin" written by the poet Dmitry Sadovnikov (1847-1883).

130. The riots of the 1830's and 1840's caused by the peasants' refusal to plant potatoes and by an epidemic of cholera. Cholera riots spread also to the cities and military settlements.

131. An untranslatable pun based on the popular pronunciation of the word *otchestvo* (patronymic) as *otechestvo* (fatherland). Addressing a man by his first name and patronymic implies respect for him, especially among the peasants who usually call one another by their first names only.

132. In this article Cadet A. S. Izgoev (pseudonym of Aleksandr Solomonovich Lande, 1872-1935) maintained that the tragedy and guilt of the Russian intelligentsia consisted in its persistent and abstract preaching of socialism without taking any positive action, while at the same time

undermining the foundations of the Russian state. Now, when socialism is being put into practice by the Bolsheviks, Russia is threatened with destruction. Izgoev rejects socialism as alien to the Russian people and state and advocates a return to the principles of private ownership with certain restrictions of big business. See "Tragediya i vina," *Nash Vek,* April 5 (March 23), 1918.

133. Two Cadet dailies.

134. In Ivan Krylov's fable "The Fly and Horses" (1808) the fly claimed that it helped the horses to pull an overloaded carriage up a hill by flying around and buzzing.

135. See note 7.

136. Gorky may have in mind "'Svoevremennye mysli'" ("Timely Thoughts"), *Pravda,* March 30 (17) and April 4 (March 22), 1918. This article, with the obvious allusion to Gorky in its title, was signed G. L—ov. Though G. L—ov stoutly defends the political maturity of the peasants, he does not mention Gorky by name and does not use the words "scornful spitting." He, speaks, however, in strong terms of those who do nothing to help the people with their knowledge and skill but who hate the new regime of workers and gloat over the difficulties experienced by the people. This may lead to an assumption that Gorky took G. L—ov for Gorlov and quoted him inaccurately, possibly confusing him with someone else or with Mme. Samoylova, who asserted that Gorky "spits on the people" (*Pravda,* Petrograd, March 17 (4), 1918). Bearing in mind Gorky's excellent memory, one may also assume that there is an article by a Gorlov published in one of the unavailable *Pravda* issues from March 24 to March 29.

137. Grigory Zinoviev (1883-1936), Chairman of the Soviet of Commissars of the Petrograd Workers' Commune, that is, party and city boss. One of the reasons why Gorky left Soviet Russia in 1921 was Zinoviev's hostility toward him, expressed in such actions as the search of his apartment. See V. Khodasevich, "Gorky," *Sovremennye Zapiski,* No. 70, 1940, p. 137. This and an earlier article of Khodasevich's, "Gorky (Vospominaniya)," *ibid.,* No. 63, 1937, represent an insightful portrait of Gorky drawn by a Russian émigré poet who knew Gorky very well personally and who was asked by Gorky to write about him after his death.

138. From Aleksandr Pushkin's *A Voyage to Arzrum* (1836), ch. 2, where the author regrets that outstanding people disappear in Russia without leaving any trace because "we are lazy and incurious."

139. Gorky was the moving spirit behind the formation of this society and it came into existence in March 1918 under the name "Culture and Freedom. Educational Society in Commemoration of the 27th of February, 1917," with Gorky as its chairman. The reference to the 27th of February (March 12, the February Revolution and the fall of the autocracy) in the name of the society is indicative of its members' attitude toward the October Revolution. In addition to Gorky, the Organizing Committee of the society included such figures of the revolutionary and social-democratic movement as Plekhanov, Vera Figner, and Vera Zasulich.

Among the first steps taken by "Culture and Freedom" was the establishment of "people's libraries," to which Gorky donated over eight hundred volumes from his own collection, and the organization of food supplies for people with intellectual occupations. The society set up its own publishing house, and it was here that the collection *Un-*

*timely Thoughts,* consisting of forty-eight reprinted articles with the same heading, was published in 1918, a fact
about which the Soviet scholars and bibliographers of
Gorky say not a word.

140. In the original: "yako obri ikh zhe nest ni plemeni,
ni roda." This is a slightly modified expression taken from
the old Russian *Primary Chronicle* (about 1100) where it
referred to the sudden and spectacular downfall of the
mighty Avars who dominated certain Western Slavic tribes
from the second half of the sixth century to the end of the
eighth.

141. Ivan Krylov's fable "The Pig under the Oak Tree"
(1825), in which the ungrateful pig digs up the roots of
the tree after stuffing himself with its acorns.

142. N. A. Rubakin, V. P. Vakhterov, and A. M. Kalmykova were writers and educators who greatly contributed to the enlightenment of the common people.

143. Books and periodicals issued by this house covered
various fields of knowledge and were intended primarily
for the popular masses. One of the "Intermediary's"
founders and collaborators was Leo Tolstoy. Many of his
works were written for and published by the "Intermediary."

144. "For his work in the fatherland's printing and publishing industry S. [Sytin] received a personal pension
from the Soviet Government," we learn from *The Great
Soviet Encyclopedia,* 2nd ed., vol. 41, 1956, p. 417.

145. Quoted from "Skverny anekdot," *Nash Vek,* May 3
(April 20), 1918. "Sovdeps" is an abbreviation of Soviets
of Deputies. The abbreviation can be found in official Bol-

shevik pronouncements, but it was widely used in a derogatory sense by the opponents of the Bolsheviks in reference to their regime or to Soviet Russia, called also Sovdepiya in such cases.

Filosofov's article was most likely prompted by "Untimely Thoughts" of May 1, 1918, in which Gorky appealed for the intelligentsia's unification on a non-party basis, and by the fact that Gorky discussed with Lunacharsky, People's Commissar of Education, the work of "The Free Association for the Development and Dissemination of the Positive Sciences." Filosofov objected to the intelligentsia's cooperation with the Bolshevik regime because the members of the intelligentsia were denied freedom and were treated in accordance with their political reliability, as in Tsarist times.

146. Either Gorky's modesty or his unwillingness to hear an enemy praise him is responsible for an omission here. In the original: "Gorky is a great figure. He appears and acts before the public."

147. Somewhat different and more sarcastic is the original: "Gorky's plan to convert the Academy of Sciences and the Free Association of Sciences into a Shanyavsky 'people's university' is very noble."

The Moscow People's University named after Alfons Leonovich Shanyavsky was organized in 1905-1908 in accordance with the provisions of his will. It was a unique school. No diplomas were needed for admission. Examinations were optional. Students were of all ages and backgrounds. The main goal was to link learning as closely as possible with the life of society. The faculty was as good as in other universities. Distinguished scholars who were expelled from other schools for political reasons could teach at Shanyavsky University. Though the University was not officially accredited, its graduates were readily employed by private firms. Details on Shanyavsky University can be found in A. A. Kizevetter (Kiesewetter), *Na rubezhe dvukh stolety* (*Vospominaniya 1881-1914*), Prague, Orbis, 1929, pp. 470-495.

148. A reference to the criticism of the Cadets in "Untimely Thoughts" of April 7 (March 25), 1918.

149. The last three paragraphs beginning with ". . . socialist democracy has no enemy angrier . . ." were reprinted in *Nash Vek* and *Russkie Vedomosti* (Russian News), a Cadet daily. *Nash Vek* compared Gorky's hounding of the Cadets with that conducted in Tsarist days by the Black Hundreds. Gorky, as this newspaper saw it, wanted to demonstrate his loyalty to the revolution and to point out to the authorities the threat of the counterrevolutionary people's enemies. See "Pechat," *Nash Vek*, May 11 (April 28), 1918. The next day *Nash Vek* was discontinued. Soon thereafter *Russkie Vedomosti*, in scorning Gorky's attack as a "journalistic denunciation," stated that it could not be either asserted or denied that Gorky helped to suppress *Nash Vek*. See anon., "Vrachu, istselisya sam," *Nash Vek*, June 18 (5), 1918. *Nash Vek* resumed publication of June 15, 1918, but was permanently suppressed in less than two months.

150. A large number of Moscow and Petrograd newspapers were suppressed or fined between May 10 and 14. Among the discontinued dailies were *Nash Vek* (Our Age) and *Sovremennoe Slovo* (The Modern Word) of the Constitutional-Democrats, *Zemlya i Volya* (Land and Freedom) of the Socialist-Revolutionaries, and *Novy Luch* (The New Ray) of the Mensheviks. In Petrograd, all evening newspapers were closed except for the Bolshe-

vik *Vechernyaya Pravda* (Evening Pravda) and *Krasnaya Gazeta* (The Red Gazette). Some newspapers were suppressed for "slanderous" reports on the worsening of Soviet-German relations; others, for bringing to light the "counterrevolutionary" acts of the workers who protested against the executions of their comrades by the Bolsheviks, and demanded the abolition of existing food agencies, the reelection of the Soviets, the inclusion of non-Bolshevik socialists in the government, and the convocation of the Constituent Assembly.

*Novaya Zhizn* reacted vigorously to the Bolshevik treatment of the press. Two articles condemning it were published next to Gorky's: "The Triumph of Stupidity" by Raf. Grigoriev and "A Dreadful Danger" by B. Avilov.

151. N. N. Glebov (Putilovsky), "Pod kulturu" (Upward to Culture), *Novaya Zhizn,* May 15 (2), 1918. The main thesis of this article was the necessity of creating a "United Workers' Party" on a class basis. Disagreeing with Gorky's view of the intelligentsia as the leading force in the dissemination of culture ("Untimely Thoughts" of May 1 (April 18), 1918), Glebov put the stress on the workers' independent desire "to rise upward to culture from below."

152. "Saryn na kichku!"—the old command of the Volga robbers to the bargees after seizing a boat.

153. P. V. Shumakher, a minor poet, contributed to *Iskra* (The Spark), a Russian Marxist newspaper published abroad from 1900 to 1905. Lenin, Plekhanov, and Martov were on its editorial board. Over fifty of Lenin's articles were published in *Iskra* before he left it in 1903, when the Mensheviks took charge of it.

154. S. Gusev-Orenburgsky or G. Grebenshchikov?

155. Igor Severyanin (pseudonym of Igor Vasilievich Lotarev, 1887-1941), leader of Russian "Ego-Futurists," enjoyed great popularity shortly before World War II. Marked by mannerism, his poetry expressed the materialistic aspirations of the urban population. Gorky considered Severyanin gifted, but with no touch of greatness.

156. Zinaida Gippius? (Woman poet.)

157. Tambov and Kaluga, two typical provincial capitals in central Russia.

158. See note 32.

159. In August 1900 a joint force of Japanese, Russians, British, Americans, and French marched on Peking to relieve their legations beseiged by the rebellious Boxers. The city was seized and thoroughly looted, particularly by the Russians.

160. During the Boxer uprising, Russia occupied Manchuria, went back on her promise to evacuate it, and attempted to gain control over Korea. A group of adventurers persuaded Nicholas II to pursue this aggressive policy which led to a disastrous war with Japan in 1904-1905.

161. Immediately after seizing power, the Bolsheviks forbade the newspapers to publish private advertisements and notices by the decree "On the Institution of a State Monopoly in Announcements" drafted by Lunacharsky and signed by Lenin. See L. M. Farber, *Sovetskaya literatura pervykh let revolyutsii (1917-1920 gg.)*, Moscow, "Vysshaya shkola," 1966, p. 10.

162. The image of the triumphant pig is taken from a
dramatic dialogue between the Pig and the Truth in M. E.
Saltykov-Shchedrin's collection of satirical writings entitled *Za rubezhom* (Abroad, 1881). The Pig, which
mocks and tortures the Truth, symbolizes a smug, vulgar,
and cruel reactionary.

163. From Nikolay Nekrasov's poem "To the Sowers"
(1877) dedicated to the disseminators of truth and
knowledge among the people.

164. It is not quite clear whether Gorky referred here to
*Pravda* or *Petrogradskaya Pravda*. Many issues of the latter are not available outside the Soviet Union. Material
considered important could have been published in both
newspapers. In any event Gorky might have had the following articles in mind: V. B., "Izgoev o bolshevikakh"
(Izgoev about the Bolsheviks), *Petrogradskaya Pravda,*
May 4 (April 21), 1918, and Klara Zetkin, "Za bolshevikov" (For the Bolsheviks), *Pravda,* May 12 (April 29),
May 14 (1), 15 (2), 17 (4), 18 (5), 1918. Zetkin's
article was prefaced by Zinoviev. He spoke of Zetkin as a
former Menshevik sympathizer who identified herself with
the Bolsheviks after the October Revolution.

V. B. quoted approvingly Izgoev's assertions from his
article "O zaslugakh bolshevikov" (About the Bolsheviks'
Merits), *Russkaya Mysl,* No. 1-2 1918, to the effect that
the Bolsheviks were implementing socialism in the only
possible way and acting in accordance with their beliefs.
In doing so they were more honest than the Socialist-
Revolutionaries and Mensheviks who proclaimed socialist
slogans but carried out the program of reforms advocated
by the Constitutional-Democrats. V. B. rejected, of
course, Izgoev's idea of the anti-national and anti-cultural
nature of socialism, as well as his contention that Russia

rendered a great service to other countries by showing what the introduction of socialism really means. Klara Zetkin praised the Bolshevik daring and vigor in translating into life the basic precepts of socialism, and she defended the Bolsheviks against the criticism of foreign socialists. Toward the end of her article she expressed a profound conviction that "the day will come when *history will proclaim the Lenins and Trotskys the heirs of the revolutionary spirit of Marx.*"

165. This is probably in an issue of *Petrogradskaya Pravda* that is unavailable.

166. V. Volodarsky (1891-1918), People's Commissar of Press and Propaganda for the Petrograd Commune. Notorious for the persecution of newspapers. Assassinated by Socialist-Revolutionaries.

167. Aleksandr Nikolaevich Ostrovsky (1823-1886), a prolific playwright who influenced greatly the development of Russian drama. Known for his firm grasp of the detail of everyday life and for his vivid portrayal of the merchant milieu.

168. Statements similar to this and subsequent assertions can be found in N. K. Mikhaylovsky's treatise "Darwin's Theory and Social Science" (1870). Gorky, however, might have referred to another "thinker."

169. The speech was given on June 25 (12), 1918. On the society "Culture and Freedom" see note 139.

170. See note 163.

171. This question was asked in the following *Pravda* articles: A. Alekseev, "Pust raskroyut karty" (Let Them Show Their Hand), June 26 (13), 1918; anon., "Na soderzhanii u bankira" (In the Banker's Pay), June 28 (15), 1918; and an untitled item by B. Volin, an important functionary of the Bolshevik press, *ibid*. They accused *Novaya Zhizn* of selling itself to the imperialists, industrialists, landowners, bankers, and bourgeoisie. The anonymous article on the first page might well have been the expression of the *Pravda* editors' opinion. It was particularly vituperative and abusive. The editors of "Gorky's newspaper" were compared to prostitutes: "The modest girls from *Novaya Zhizn* have such a weakness for the highly profitable caresses of fat bankers."

This was a direct continuation of the vilification of *Novaya Zhizn* begun on June 13, 1918, by *Petrograd Pravda*. This organ of the Central and Petrograd Committees of the Bolshevik party was enraged by a *Novaya Zhizn* report on Admiral Kolchak's movement in Siberia. As *Petrograd Pravda* saw it, *Novaya Zhizn* was siding with Kolchak and blaming the Bolsheviks for starting a war with Siberia. A violent diatribe entitled "Podlaya gazeta" (A Base Newspaper) charged *Novaya Zhizn* with being in reality "not only a house publication of the Black-Hundred party of the Right S.R.'s but also of Putilov's band of bankers. . . . All its reports are placed at the service of the counterrevolution." Next to this obviously editorial blast was printed the article "Dva stana" (Two Camps) by N. Kuzmin. It drew a parallel between the *Novaya Zhizn* demands for the Constituent Assembly and Kolchak's intention to convoke it. This was an absolutely unjustified comparison, for the *Novaya Zhizn* columnist was emphatically against receiving the Constituent Assembly from "the hands of military conspirators." See Raf. Grigoriev, "Voyna s Sibiryu" (War with Siberia), *Novaya Zhizn,* June 12 (May 30), 1918.

*Pravda's* onslaughts on *Novaya Zhizn* were made by big guns. The editorial board of *Petrograd Pravda* featured Zinoviev and N. Kuzmin who was soon to take the place of the assassinated Volodarsky as the Commissar of Press and Propaganda in Petrograd. It is not surprising that immediately after Grigoriev's article *Novaya Zhizn* was suppressed. But it managed to resume publication in a couple of days, and its first new issue carried an indignant comment on its suppressors: "Nothing else could have been expected from a regime which is afraid of daylight and publicity, is cowardly and undemocratic, violates elementary civic rights, persecutes workers, and sends punitive expeditions against peasants" (" 'Novaya Zhizn,' " *Novaya Zhizn,* June 16 (3), 1918).

A month later Lenin decided to do away with *Novaya Zhizn.* On July 16, late in the afternoon, a representative of the Commissariat of the Press of the Petrograd Commune entered the editorial office of *Novaya Zhizn* with the order for its suppression. Gorky's attempts to revive it proved futile.

172. Banker and secretary-treasurer of "The Free Association for the Development and Dissemination of the Positive Sciences" (see p. 43).

173. Savva Timofeevich Morozov (1862-1905), a wealthy textile manufacturer, patron of the arts and of revolutionaries. He gave 24,000 rubles annually to the Social-Democratic *Iskra* (The Spark) of which Lenin was a founder and editor. Morozov hid revolutionaries and their literature; committed suicide from fear that he was losing his mind. Gorky was Morozov's friend and left interesting reminiscences of him in his letters to the writer Sergey Grigoriev (*Literaturnoe nasledstvo,* vol. 70, p. 130), in the article "L. B. Krasin. Iz vospominany," *Izvestiya,* December 19, 1926, and in a sketch written in

1922 and published posthumously in *Oktyabr,* No. 6,
1941.

# INDEX

Academy of Sciences, 169, 171, 179, 180
Aleksandra Fedorovna, empress, 20, 79
Americans, 53–54, 57
anarchism, 71, 96, 115, 200; Bolsheviks and, 85–87, 132
anarchy: monarchy encouraged, 34–35; rhetoric about, 40, 43; Russians inclined toward, 41–42, 173; Bolsheviks foment, 132, 134
anti-semitism, 10, 34, 52, 60–62, 63, 80–81, 143, 219–24, 234
army, collapse of, 195–99
art: and the human spirit, 8–9, 36, 227–29; devalued in Russia, 53–54, 100; uniqueness of Russian, 204–5. *See also* culture
artists, 9, 23–24
Ayzman, David, 80
Azef, Evno, 29

Bakunin, Mikhail, 85
Belinsky, Vissarion, 144
Bernatsky, Mikhail, 18, 85, 87, 93, 108
Beylis, Mendel, 143
Black Hundreds, 10, 104, 167
Bloody Sunday, 123, 152
Bolsheviks: Gorky's relations with, vii–x; hostile to freedom, 51, 85–87, 114; utopianism of, 93, 94, 99, 106, 115–16, 122, 149; experimenting on Russia and the proletariat, 88–89, 106–7, 122, 128, 140, 211; demagoguery of, 83, 107, 146, 148, 168; arouse people's dark instincts, 96, 115–16, 132, 134, 146, 148, 168; and the working class, 63, 85–87, 89, 128, 132, 144, 146, 168; crudeness of, 102, 110; egoism of, 142; like old regime, 131, 182; opposition to, 176; positive aspects of, 210–11. *See also* Lenin

bourgeoisie, 33, 165
Breshkovskaya, Ekaterina, 33
brotherhood, 8, 11–12, 48, 77, 117–118
Bruno, Giordano, 181
Bunin, Ivan, 154
bureaucrats, 79
Burtsev, V. L., 92

Cadets (Constitutional-Democratic Party; Party of the People's Freedom), 79, 82–83, 98, 103–4, 163–65, 246n5. See also *Rech*
censorship, 92, 182–83
Chekhov, Anton, 154, 177, 228
Chernyshevsky, Nikolai, xvi, 101, 144
children, 39–40, 45, 58–59, 69, 100, 109
Christ, 61, 77, 118, 208
constituent assembly, 124
Constitutional-Democratic party. See Cadets
criticism, 51, 146–48, 179
culture: meaning of, 35, 55, 184–188, 199–203; need for, 6–8, 35–36, 40, 47, 74, 94–95, 100–101, 164, 200–203; and knowledge as power, 5–6, 24, 64, 171; and the mass press, 20–22, 50–52, 55, 57, 70; and values, 36, 40; popular desires for, 65, 69; as goal of the revolution, 55, 65; and the war, 76; and peasants, 100, 201–3; and the proletariat, 59, 99, 237–39. *See also* art, intelligentsia, science

defeatism, 41
defensists, 113
democracy, 51–52, 86, 92–93, 142, 164–65, 183
Dolgoruky (Dolgorukov), Prince Pavel, 108